DOUBLE HARNESS

Double Harness

An autobiography by

ROBIN TANNER

TEACHER AND ETCHER

IMPACT BOOKS

First published in Great Britain 1987
by Impact Books, 112 Bolingbroke Grove, London SW11 1DA

This edition first published in Great Britain 1990
by Impact Books, 112 Bolingbroke Grove, London SW11 1DA

Phototypeset by Sunrise Setting, Torquay, Devon
Printed in Great Britain by The Bath Press, Avon

ISBN 0 245–60136–8

© Robin Tanner 1987

ACKNOWLEDGEMENTS

I should like to thank the Ashmolean Museum and my friend Paul Drury for their kind
permission to reproduce Paul's portrait drawing (frontispiece). I should also like to thank
Denis Thorpe of *The Guardian* for allowing his photographs to be used on pp. vi, 204
and 210. I am deeply grateful to my publisher, Jean-Luc Barbanneau and to the
designer, Peter Cartwright, for their sensitive handling of the material of this book and
the immense care they have expended on its production.
ROBIN TANNER

For Heather and Dietrich
and my countless friends

ILLUSTRATIONS BY ROBIN TANNER

All men whatever be their condition who have
done anything of merit, or which verily has some
semblance of merit, if so be they are men of truth and
good repute, should write the tale of their life with
their own hand. Yet it were best they should not
set out on so fine an enterprise till they have
passed their fortieth year.
Here my life's struggling story I make plain
to thank God or Nature who has still tended
the soul he gave me.

from *The Memoirs of Benvenuto Cellini* (1500–1571)

1

Those white designs which children drive. HENRY VAUGHAN

I was born on Easter Sunday in 1904, the third of six children, and – as my mother often reminded me – by far the heaviest to bear: 'You spoilt my waist for ever,' she would say with a warm laugh which showed that she didn't really mind.

She had known life like a character out of Hardy in the green village of Kington Langley in North-West Wiltshire where she was born. Her mother was only sixteen years older than she, though her father was fifty-three and a widower. He was a timber merchant who lived in the moated remnant of the manor, and although he recognised my mother as his own, and put golden sovereigns into her hands from time to time, he never married my grandmother. She lived to bear thirteen more children, and my mother naturally took a great part in bringing up the family.

My father too had a Hardyish start in life, for his mother was the daughter of strict Baptist parents who 'made a public example' of her and sent her to the workhouse to bear her illegitimate son.

He grew to be a sound craftsman in wood, and he and my mother loved each other till death. But unlike hers his imagination failed to ripen; he tended to be negative, leaning always on my mother's positive judgment and never matching her astounding vitality. But he led a harmless, blameless life. He would contemplate his four various sons and his two dissimilar daughters with a wondering look. Me especially he tended to disown; my left-handedness always bothered him, and my early craving to draw and paint alarmed him and made him wonder if I should ever be able to earn my own living.

My mother was the centre, the source, the inspiration, the whole cause of our childhood. This great Saskia of a woman was, I suppose, a 'natural', tied neither to class nor to convention – unlike her husband, harmful and full of blame!– dangerously independent in her thinking and her actions, with an

[1]

unquenchable longing to learn all she had lost by having to leave school at the age of ten to become a housemaid; and with a genius for contriving to manage her large household in such a liberal way that we never realised we were poor. We lived a few miles from her birthplace, in a small and inconvenient terrace house. Yet, with an income of never more than a hundred and fifty pounds a year she clothed and fed us well, and we never knew ugliness or squalor. She was an artist. Whenever one of us wanted something badly, she would say, 'Well, let us make it.' Here my father's good material standards were an influence, and using our hands deftly and well was a common experience for us all. Each one became a good craftsman.

Sometimes in the early evening, exhausted by the long day's labours, my mother would fall asleep in her chair. It was then that we used to invade and manhandle her. We would plait the stray tendrils of hair around her neck that refused to be contained in the general bun and tie each one with a bow of ribbon. We would unbutton her and I would trace with my finger the curious zigzag turquoise-coloured vein on her left breast which I had often seen. And once I pulled out from her stays the blade of ash wood which my father had shaped for her for extra support and which she called 'my Bone', and reversing the Genesis story I enacted God creating Adam out of Eve's rib, to the awed consternation of my audience.

I loved an audience. In order to win a breathing space my mother sent us to a Primitive Methodist Sunday School, and it was here that from the age of two – dressed in a sailor suit, with my curls carefully rolled and placed – I readily recited poems at anniversaries and other special occasions. 'Look straight ahead at the clock,' my mother warned, 'and don't dare to smile at anyone in the congregation.' I obeyed. They stood me on a chair so that I could be seen, loudly declaiming appalling moral doggerel chosen by my teacher and trite narrative verses from *Mother Siegel's Syrup Book*. The more verses the better, I thought. The choicest was called *A Mother's Reverie*, which I was instructed to pronounce 'Revéery'! It was guaranteed to bring tears to the eyes of my audience. Sometimes local preachers would take me on their pony-trap journeys to outlying village chapels where I was caused to bring variety to the evening services by my performance. I lapped up praise, ate the ripe apples I was given, and accepted the strange Edwardian situation with smug pleasure.

[2]

Robin Tanner (centre) with two brothers, 1908

But my most consuming joy as a young child was to take from a bookcase in our best room a page from a large illustrated Bible that was issued in fortnightly parts from about 1900, and from which the engraved plates had fallen apart, and use its wide margins and the plain backs of the plates for drawing upon.

I drew women with outrageous hats. I was enchanted by the wide straw brims of 1910 and 1911, turned up at the back to hold a mass of flowers from which issued ribbon streamers, or mounded round the crown with bunches of cherries (disappointingly stuffed with cotton wool as I discovered), purple and green grapes, cornflowers, wild moondaisies, bearded wheat, and many-petalled silk roses. I drew them in endless variety, their extravagances streaming down the outer margin and winding round the lower edge of the page. Also I drew faces with fanciful beards, curled and decked out with flowers. Any plant was a miracle and mystery to me. Any leaf or thorn or twisting stalk or complicated calyx held me. Daily throughout one summer I visited a plant of fumitory which my father had missed when weeding his potatoes: each time I knelt to see its feathery grey leaves and lightly poised purple flowers with dark tips I thought I had never seen anything so rare and extraordinary. It was a sad day when it was burned with the potato haulms at the end of the season.

I had no use for mechanical toys; and railway trains, bicycles, carts and horses, and those rare newfangled vehicles called motor-cars all passed me by. I never drew them. Nor should I be able to draw them today if I tried. I cannot remember clearly what my own car looks like, nor even the construction of my beloved etching press. I suppose I have always been so obsessed with certain natural forms that I have never felt I have seen enough of them, while others I have not really seen at all and they are still outside my narrow range.

The shapes of letters and the pattern of paragraphs upon a printed page were immediately magical to me. A book was a most marvellous invention. To make letter forms and write and to construct a crude book was heaven to me. I liked order. I liked to be clean. I remember clearly a time before I went to school — and I attended before my third birthday — when after our midday meal was cleared away I would say to my mother, 'Now let us dress', and I cherished the hour before tea when she was perhaps able to sit and mend or darn or sew, wearing her best blouse and her only gold brooch.

At my infant school in 1907 we were caused to sit crowded on long backless forms and to unravel small squares of perfectly good tweed (which must have been tailors' samples of suitings), place the threads together in a bunch, tie them in the middle, and spread them out to make a woollen ball. But why? I have never discovered the fate of all those ill-shapen grey and navy blue balls.

In 1908 I was promoted to brushwork, which was an advanced enterprise for that time. We were taught to paint in blobs. A soft brush fully charged with water-colour was brought slowly down to the paper so that it left a petal or leaf shape behind. One hot July afternoon, following our teacher step by step, we painted on grey card a three-petalled snowdrop with a leaf on either side, and we framed it with macramé twine, 'to take home at Christmas', she said, but we never did.

In 1909 I was declared clever. I could write neatly, so I was never chided for using my left hand; I liked to read and recite, and although I hated them I got my 'T-U-sums' right. So I 'jumped' a class, and now performed, in addition to brushwork, a strange destructive ritual called 'Handwork'. We took nice squares of bright paper, and folded and cut and pasted them to make tiny boxes, baskets, and dog kennels, all of which our teacher threw away at the end of the lesson. I thought it a pitiable waste but said nothing. I was a very 'good' boy, she declared to any visitor. Indeed, she used to sit and cuddle me unduly. Strands of her hair tickled me so that I shrank from her advances. She made me a monitor because I could be trusted, she said, and I took my honoured seat at the back of the class.

I was soon however to commit my first crime. It was the monitor's privilege to distribute materials before a lesson and sometimes even to bring plants or other things needed. I brought a fine shiny lump of coal for an object lesson, a branch of horse chestnut with sharp sticky buds for nature study, and on a sleepy autumn afternoon in 1910 I brought sprays of bluish-mauve Michaelmas daisy for brushwork. His Majesty's Inspector was to visit our school. He had announced his coming, and we children were glad. He was a friendly person, who wore black clothes and arrived from the station in a fly. Last time he came he had asked me what I wanted to be when I grew up, and I had said, 'I want to do what you do.'

I arrived at school early and my teacher told me to strip the flowers and place a sprig for every child. This seemed a pity to me: the tall branched sprays were so handsome, and the little oddments I laid along the desks had wilted by the time the registers had been called. Moreover, our teacher made no reference to them at all. It was a nice feeling squeezing out dabs of Sap Green – the colour of evil pond water – and blue – the colour of cold hands – into china dishes and placing a brush beside each as for a meal. Our teacher gave out sheets of paper of intimidating whiteness and we began to paint. She pinned hers to the blackboard and demonstrated each step. First we were caused to paint a Sap Green stalk down the middle of the page with leaves of single blobs on either side. Then I carried a jam jar of water down the aisles and everyone vigorously washed their brushes. Then with the sickly blue paint our teacher showed how to arrange petal-blobs to form the flower: the first to the North, then one to the South, now one to the East and one to the West, and now the difficult job of squeezing four more into N–W, S–W, S–E and N–E, and lo! there was our Michaelmas daisy. Sadly, we disregarded its mounded gold centre with the curled pistils and bright stamens I love so much.

There was such an acreage of paper still untouched that without a thought I painted another daisy, and another and another and a whole fat bunch of them; I painted a Sap Green vase for them, which I decorated with bands of blue. I stood my vase in a window, and painted draped curtains spotted blue and tied with blue bows, and coming down the garden path beyond I painted a green-habited postman bearing a blue letter in his hand. I was flushed with excitement. A frame seemed right for my picture, so I used the remains of my own and my neighbour's ration to paint one. It was splendid. I didn't know where I was: I had lost my teacher and the classroom and forgotten all my monitorial duties – until HMI entered. Our teacher ordered us to hold up our work for him to admire, saying she was sure that mine would be the best. 'But whatever has happened?' she asked in astonishment. 'Bring it for me to see', and I bore my precious picture as though I were bearing a masterpiece.

I only remember my tears and the note 'Governess' gave me to take to my parents after I had stood in my corner with my face to the wall till the end of the day. But I loved the inspector, who told me I had been very naughty but did 'a capital picture'.

I was chastened, though I never understood my wrong-doing; and just before I left Standard 1 for 'The Big School', I committed a second and what 'Governess' called a far more serious crime, also in the cause of art.

The school was a sordid and noisome building, with primitive lavatories across the desolate playground. With no roof over our heads we boys stood against a tarred wall with a runnel at its foot that was usually blocked with leaves and other debris. But when this wall was dry I found its dark grey surface a perfect one on which, by cunning manipulation, to spray swirling patterns. I would ask to 'leave the room' at about half past two, by which time I calculated the wall would be restored to its dry matt texture, and it was then that I practised this very personal pattern making.

My fellow monitor was a girl who was the first of my many childhood sweethearts. What I adored most about her was her long shiny black boots which were laced right up to her knees. Sometimes one would come undone, and she would let me do it up, taking the laces carefully crisscross over the little studs and tying a perfect bow below the knee. Once I made her a wire ring threaded with blue beads, and she gave me a fleecy leaf of lamb's ear (*Stachys lanata*) from her garden. Now it occurred to me that I could do for her what she could not do for me, and I invited her to ask to 'leave the room' one afternoon when I did and I would give her a performance. It was a huge success. But alas! in a fickle mood next day she split on me. 'Governess' charged me with a most grievous and disgusting offence, and once more I was made to take a note home to my mother. She read it with a wicked smile, slapped my bottom playfully, and said, 'Well; it isn't fair. You've never given *me* a performance!' And no more was said.

I was now six, and by some oversight I had not been christened, though my younger brother had been 'done', as we said. But now, as we had a baby sister, my mother – who really set little store by such ceremonies – was persuaded to remedy the omission. So on a Thursday afternoon in autumn all three of us went to Mothers' Meeting, held in the schoolroom of the Primitive Methodist Chapel. After several rousing hymns, and a prayer which I did not understand but which seemed to be scolding God for not sending us enough rain, the minister christened my three-months-old sister, who wept bitterly. He was a kindly man, with a head so bald and polished as to look quite unreal and rather frightening – the more so because of a large knob on the very top. When my turn came I walked boldly up to the table that held the basin of christening water and held out my left hand to shake hands with him. But he asked me to put out the right hand instead, and shook it vigorously. I instinctively wiped off the wet cross he made on my forehead, so he drew a second one, and when the operation was over he smilingly asked me a question: 'Now you are a clever boy. Tell me this. A farmer had twenty-six sheep, and one died. How many were left?' 'Twenty-five,' I said promptly. 'Wrong! Nineteen', he said, 'they were twenty sick sheep! not twenty-six. But I think you'll be Prime Minister one day.' Then we had tea and cakes, and several mothers patted my curls and said what a stout boy I was – which seemed to me a gross and insulting word.

All the Edwardian summers are sunny, hot and dry in my memory, and 1911 blazes with eternal sunshine in a white-hot sky. I see the swampy waste below a railway embankment, rich with bulrushes and purple loosestrife and that rare and stately buttercup a yard high with strange knife-edged leaves – the greater spearwort – and under the railway a damp and awesome arch with ferns and mosses in the stonework.

It was here that I would lead my hapless willing band of friends, all my own age, in an orderly crocodile through the long grass and rushes, and sit them in a row along a stone ledge just wide enough but too high for some of them to lodge in comfort. Then I gave each a paper on which I had drawn an undressed lay figure – a sort of nude hermaphrodite – ready to be clothed. I distributed crayons, and my class dressed the figures with them. I would give no help, though I criticised freely; and when the pictures were finished we ranged them along the ledge and admired them all – the frilled and sprigged gowns, the top hats, the elegant furs and muffs with claws and tails dangling from them, the long wedding train of lace and flowers.

Then came the prize-giving. I gave a prize to all, but some were better than others. There were lids of boot polish tins which I had lined with paper and laid with formal patterns of petals, leaves, berries, and seeds. There was the bottle of scent I had made. The bottle had held eucalpytus oil, and the ingredients of my scent – the orange peel, the chopped leaves of rosemary

[8]

and lad's love, and flowers of lavender – were not powerful enough to combat its lingering nauseous odour. Little books I had made in plenty by folding sheets of various wrapping papers octavo and stitching through three holes. There was a dress for a doll, which I had cut out magyar fashion because this relieved me of the intricate business of fitting in the sleeves. There were an empty picture frame of card which I had decorated in gold paint, skeleton leaves of holly I had collected, and shapely pebbles I had rescued from the gravel heaps placed along the lane to be used when it was icy.

I do not recall how these excursions ended. Perhaps there was disorder, though I do not think so. I was a stern disciplinarian, and my willing captives never mutinied. The hours were long, the arch was cool, the swampy waste was hot, and I was in my heaven and all was right with the world.

Playing games gave me no great satisfaction. I was never skilful with a ball: I always thought it an over-rated object. And competitions had little hold on me, though if I had to play a game or compete I usually fared rather well. I spent my time differently.

My father hung wallpaper with great skill, and I enjoyed the easy, masterly way in which he cut off the plain inch-wide margin of the roll. I captured this and made what we called a 'scroll' of it. At regular intervals I drew kings and queens, chimney-sweeps, gardeners, engine-drivers, postmen, tramps, and lords and ladies, and invited my cronies to have a pull, keeping their eyes shut the while. Wherever they happened to stop showed them either what they would grow up to be or whom they would marry. Why this should have given endless pleasure it is hard now to see, but we never tired of having pulls.

Nor did the offerings of 'a pin to see the peepshow' cease until I had too many to know what to do with them. My best peepshow lay pressed under glass, and I would bear it slowly on the palm of my hand, draped with my best handkerchief. The elaborate design radiated geometrically from a centre of silver paper: scraps of embossed Christmas cards and the silk cords they were tied with, shapes cut from stiff blue sugar bags, thorns, coiled tendrils of white bryony, winged seeds of sycamore, and the separated seeds of traveller's joy – the wild clematis, each with its own curled feather.

I think I must have been eight, just after I had entered the 'Big School', when I was 'converted'. We still attended Sunday School, and on a wild winter afternoon, when the cold chapel was filled with smoke from the inadequate stove, we were addressed by someone called an Evangelist. I thought that was his surname, and a very nice one too! He ranted and pleaded and implored us in a sobbing voice: 'Will no-one give his heart to Jesus? Will no-one come to the Mercy Seat and be saved?' Once we had done so, he assured us, and we were truly converted, we should be changed utterly, unrecognisably: we should be born again. It was all very distressing, for no-one answered the call. So again he besought us, in a voice of great anguish, 'Will no-one, not any one of you little ones, give his heart to Jesus? Will no-one come to the Mercy Seat?' Some people were weeping. It was too much: I could bear it no longer. I came up to Mr. Evangelist, and he made me kneel in front of a long wooden form which I took to be The Mercy Seat. Two other boys followed; then one of the older girls, so four of us were saved by the end of the day. We remained behind and were each given a bun, and then we went home. And I felt dismayed next morning to find myself quite unchanged, with the customary round of Monday before me as though nothing had happened.

In the 'Big School', once a week, we made dreary outline drawings with mercilessly hard unyielding pencils, of whatever objects were easily available and could be hung flat upon the blackboard: a coal hammer, a walking stick, a closed umbrella, and – most advanced of all – a reaphook or sickle, though as a rare treat we were allowed to bring what we had learnt to call 'specimens', which we drew in outline and tinted with water-colour. You stuck your dogrose or buttercup in a hole in a wooden block made for the purpose and did your best before the poor thing drooped and withered. I found it a callous and disheartening business.

Several times a week we suffered hand-writing lessons when we copied the immaculate copperplate example which our teacher wrote upon the blackboard. We were now promoted to pens. The word 'Bleak' was printed on the nibs, and no name could have described these evil little spikes more accurately. With the lightest pressure on the page they would break, and we used them for making paper darts. I do not know how I contrived to get away with neither using a 'Bleak' pen nor copying the writing on the blackboard. Perhaps my left-handedness saved me, for my teacher tended to abandon me to my own devices since what I produced was neat – and neatness was all. I used a 'Waverley' nib, which had a stiff, turned-up end instead of a pliable point, and I wrote a hand that grew out of what I daily saw and loved in books. At home I copied page after page of Roman type, which I specially loved in its italic form: these shapes were positively my friends, and I knew them intimately. But it still remains a mystery to me that I was never stopped from going my own way.

Only in the matter of ink did I fail. It was my duty as 'Ink Monitor' to arrive at school very early on Monday mornings to make the week's supply. In the cold dark cloakroom I would make this anaemic brew by tipping a packet of grey powder labelled 'Best blue-black for schools' into a pretty copper can like a miniature watering-can with a spout so narrow that it often became blocked, and filling the can with water and stirring with a stick. Then I went the rounds, filling the china inkwells to the brim. Many were choked with screws of blotting-paper or scraps of chalk dyed a cadaverous grey, for they were all left uncovered like some neglected cruet, and the dust of ages settled upon them.

How I longed for ink that was a full, rich, fruity black like the letters in our illustrated Bible at home! It occurred to me one Monday that if I emptied a double quantity of powder into my can I might achieve this, but all I produced was a dreadful soup which clogged the pens and brought me trouble.

The sole event of these years at school that moved me so that it is still vivid in my memory was a bulb show, when we all brought hyacinths and narcissi we had nurtured through the winter – for the most part in cupped vases of water sold for the purpose, in which you could see the waving trail of roots coiling itself to squeeze into too small a space. The prussian blue and violet iridescent scales on the fat hyacinth bulbs were as great a delight to me as the flowers. I was allowed to arrange the entries, tier upon tier, on an erection of wooden forms, and to letter the cards, 'First Prize', 'Second Prize', and 'Highly Commended', though I was scolded for drawing patterned borders round them. The day after the show our headmaster's wife died. We had never seen her, but he decided to place the flowering bulbs in their vases all round her coffin, and we were made to file past in solemn procession. And ever since I have been appalled by the scent of hyacinths, which means the scent of death to me.

This eccentric and non-conforming headmaster grew more so in his loneliness as a widower, burying himself in extravagant but short-lived enthusiasms. One was scouting, which was to take up many of our afternoons. There were countless badge-earning tests, which I loved and excelled at. Blindfolded, I had to recognise six leaves by their shapes and textures, and six by their scent only. I learnt to tie beautiful if mostly useless knots. I gathered together 'useful things for an emergency in the desert': those were the instructions. I arranged them in an old biscuit tin with a lid which I painted orange because that was the colour of my patrol. There were home-made books for many purposes. One contained basic recipes, such as for making bread out of gathered ears of corn and concocting an unlikely remedy for burns. I drew maps, and I made diagrams for making tents. There was a ginger beer bottle with its green glass marble, and there was a collection of various cloths for unspecified purposes, which I had crudely hemmed and carefully folded. This tin load earned me full marks, but I do not know what happened to it. When I left in 1915 for a secondary school I left my childhood behind. I left a world behind too, for the old ways ended with the onslaught of war, and life would ever after be spoken of as pre-war and post-war. The slow, quiet tempo was never to return. All was changed, utterly and irrevocably, for better or for worse – and mostly, alas! for worse.

2

The first Light which shined in my Infancy
in its Primitive and Innocent Clarity was totally
Ecclypsed: insomuch that I was fain to learn all again.
If you ask me how it was Ecclypsed? Truly by the Customs
and manners of Men, which like Contrary Winds blew it
out: by an innumerable company of other Objects,
rude vulgar and Worthless Things that like so
many loads of Earth and Dung did over
whelm and Bury it . . . By the Evil
Influence of a Bad Education that
did not foster and cherish it.

THOMAS TRAHERNE
(*The Third Century*, Paragraph 7)

Six years in an indifferent school at a bad time for the human race might
have left my fellows and me more scarred than they did. But the young have
astounding resilience. They inhabit an inner world which adults cannot
enter or meddle with. Not even world-shaking disasters can destroy their
spirit: they find new zest and hope when their elders despair. Their worries
and the bitter anguish they suffer are mercifully brief: they are quick to
recover and quick to forgive. And if home is a safe anchorage and a place
where love is they can face whatever unreality, waste, or stupidity they must
contend with outside it.

So when I look back and try to see that eleven-year-old boy, so confident
and capable and eager, and that passionate youth of seventeen, filled with
positive ideas and consumed with burning interests, I find them both essentially happy. The years between – the sordid time of filthy jingoistic war, and
the mean uneasy aftermath – had curtailed childhood, narrowed experience, and cramped development, yet they had not killed desire nor stifled
the will to do, to make, to originate and create.

Few of those who taught us were qualified whether by training or attitude

[13]

to do so. Both they and we were bullied by a brash headmaster. He dismissed a member of staff for some human misdemeanour publicly and with much ado in front of us all at morning assembly, and he made a horrible public performance of beating a boy who was an attractive character but had done some petty wrong. He exploited us ruthlessly. We were his puppets in a Grand March on prize day, when we sang *Land of hope and glory* and *God save the King* in unison in the open air. I joined in neither, though I liked the tune of the former. I was ashamed of this land of hope and glory; nor had I any reason for wanting God to save, particularly, the King. My four uncles in Flanders needed saving as much as he. My mother vehemently condemned all war, knowing instinctively that it could never be right. She was not disposed to hate the German people, whom she had never seen, and call the rest her 'allies', and I suppose I was greatly influenced by her. When we were marched from school to what was called the Picture Palace to see a disgraceful propaganda film called *The Battle of the Somme* I knew without doubt where I stood.

The headmaster made me spend many hours making large diagrammatical drawings of the pitcher plant and sundew and other strange plants for lectures he gave to a local naturalists' society. There was never a word of thanks. In six years he never once said one friendly word to me. His senior mistress employed me to make programmes for frequent whist drives which she organised. I must confess I enjoyed designing them, especially when I was able to do the work while I should have been doing algebra or chemistry. She too gave local lectures. The topics ranged from Longfellow to Landor and the tercentenary of Shakespeare, for all of which she needed dramatic interludes. My early prowess at declaiming and acting was called on once more. She had a nice habit of rewarding us with books for our various services. She encouraged everyone to build up a personal library, and I still cherish volumes – mainly from Dent's Everyman series – which she inscribed.

Some of these I read aloud in bed to my younger brother: *David Copperfield, The Cloister and the Hearth, Silas Marner* and *Under the Greenwood Tree*. He was the perfect listener, and his emotional response was always so ready that I tended to exploit it, causing him to weep freely or rage with anger at what I read. He was the most lovable member of our family. Like my mother, he

[14]

was a natural artist; he lived his short life outside the conventions of class or creed, always working with his hands, delighting in his remarkable physical prowess, giving no thought for the morrow, and leaving no enemies behind him.

The headmaster met my disinclination to waste evenings and Saturdays at organised games by writing to my parents to say that unless I mended my ways he would recommend the Education Authority to withdraw my scholarship. My mother replied, inviting him to do so, saying that to kick a piece of leather about a field was not the reason for my being at school. She heard no more.

He caused me to enter the annual county arts and crafts competition. I remember how he ran out on to the playing field where the upper forms happened to be at the time, waving the silver cup I had won for his school. I repeated the performance in three successive years, and the unlovely object on its imitation ebony stand was captured by him for keeps and placed on the mantlepiece of his study.

But in this unstable world there was for me a haven in the art room, where a meek and sensitive woman, dedicated to her work, encouraged me to go further than making a design for a fire screen, based on the meadow cranesbill – which had been my required work for the county arts and crafts competition. She set me to draw the great plaster cast of a classical Greek nude athlete. She encouraged everyone, and was herself sustained by the few who responded to her delicate ways. She soon left to teach elsewhere for a while and then entered a nunnery. But before she left us she introduced us to the elements of English ecclesiastical architecture which opened up an amazing new world to me. For, every few miles in North-West Wiltshire, there stands an ancient church with something fine and memorable about it, and this was for me the beginning of a lifetime's exploration and drawing.

My constant companions were second-hand nineteenth-century editions of Parker's *Introduction to Gothic Architecture* and his *Concise Glossary*, and I cherish both today. Their bevelled purple boards have faded to a nicer brownish red; the gold titles and stamped devices are as bright as ever; the cold, accurate, melancholy engravings still evoke for me the strange smell of old churches and the atmosphere of the past. But my bible was Clement Shorter's *Highways and Byways in Buckinghamshire*, which had been first

[15]

published when I was six. I had never seen that county and have never read the text. But the incomparable pen drawings by Frederick Landseer Griggs were to me a marvellous revelation: they changed my sight; I pored over them day and night; they seemed to say all there was to say about the pastoral England of my boyhood.

At last I had become, in a measure, unassailable; I contrived to live my own life at school while conforming sufficiently to avoid trouble. Almost daily the words were bellowed at us, 'Toe the line and play the game!' I did neither. Yet my last year at school was a happy one.

There were only seven of us left to make a sixth form in September 1920 – three boys and four girls. Our base was an unused biology laboratory leading to the masters' staff room. We all brought sandwiches for lunch which we ate grouped round the blackboard, where I entertained the company. I have no gift for caricature, yet the comic drawings I made each day – mostly of members of staff and the lurid happenings of their and our lives – were relished with noisy laughter, and sometimes I was persuaded to leave a particularly pointed cartoon on the blackboard for masters to see as they made for their staff room. One of them lodged with the chairman of the school governors, who was also the mayor, and reported that I had ridiculed this important personage in a drawing of our prize-giving. Actually the mayor was a man whom I admired for his adoration of Morris and Ruskin, but his goatee beard and sharply pointed features were too enticing not to draw. He reprimanded me in person for taking such liberties, which I'm afraid I often took again.

There were delicious days and nights spent in my mother's old home, the cottage where my grandmother lived till she died at the end of the war and was still lived in by two of her daughters. I would leave school on Friday evening with an ecstatic sense of release. The roads and lanes then were of white limestone, muddy in winter and dusty in summer. Today we entirely miss that telling contrast of tone between dark green hedgerows and creamy-white stone: our modern tarred roads have robbed us of that peculiar beauty. Even the road leading from the market town was white and rutted, and soon it was darkened overhead by tremendous elms that took it into deep country.

My way lay by narrow paths through three lush meadows, whose wooden gates and stiles were perfect pieces of country workmanship. The typical oak field gate had a splendidly shaped harr and finely chamfered rails held together by wooden dowels. It was light and graceful, swinging easily and closing softly with its lissom ashwood blade. The stile was commonly a 'squeeze-belly', the two curved posts and the step between pared down with chamfered waggon-work like the gate; and neither gate nor stile was ever painted but left to weather. I loved to draw them in minutest detail, with all the opulent bosky foliage and flowers about them. It was Birket Foster country, all primroses and may.

Then came the wood called Birds' Marsh, and the strong smell of its damp acid soil and foxes. Here in autumn there were frightening fungi under the oaks and beeches. In winter it was never lifeless, and in spring it was a glory of anemones, moschatel, wood sorrel, ferns, and bluebells. All through the summer it was submerged in heavy green, looming and dark and wet even in the driest weather. Meeting the startling light as I left it and came out on to the hillside under the great chestnuts was always a shock.

It was here at this gateway that my father when a boy had seen what he called 'a ghost funeral', passing beneath the chestnuts into the dark wood. It was late evening, and he was frightened at the unwonted sight. He stood aside to let the nebulous procession pass, and, trembling, watched it fade into the trees. This matter-of-fact man never tired of describing the strange experience to us, and we in re-telling it loved adding details of our own.

Now on the opposite hill I could see my grandmother's cottage in The Barton, three fields away. These stone houses with thatched or stone-tiled roofs and mullioned windows were a Wiltshire version of Cotswold: something less perfect perhaps: Cotswold with a rough, earthy difference. Indeed, the whole countryside was like that. Here, close to the Gloucestershire border, was splendid building stone, but in deep rich dairy country that was West of England rather than West Midland. Sheep were rare. It was said that there were more cows than people in my grandmother's village. Grass grew head-high, and the hayfields were gardens of cherished flowers – spotted and pyramidal orchids and the melancholy thistle, moondaisies, sorrel and wagwants (as we called the quaking grass) always growing together, and down below them the dwarf and creeping plants – frog orchis, ground ivy and self-heal, tormentil, eyebright and creeping Jenny. Every hedge and steep hedge-bank harboured huge clumps of hartstongue and male ferns and woodland plants. It was a land flowing with milk and honey. The song thrush was still the mavis and the wood pigeon the quist. There were the misty lights of glow-worms along the grass verges. Oil lamps lit up the cottages and greater houses. Boys played quoits on the common, the children in the village school wrote on slates. And the silence over it all was of a quality that has now gone from the world.

The cottage in The Barton seemed wonderfully complete to me within its walled garden. On one side was the deep clear pond that cows and moorhens and the blacksmith shared, and on another the open green common scored by a white road and tracks to the houses grouped about it. At the front was a broad cobbled way used by people coming to post letters or buy stamps, for the cottage was also the village Post Office. The best room was reserved for this modest enterprise. The counter was a table draped in a green plush cloth with tassels, and the various official papers and packets were ranged along the mantelpiece with vases of dried quaking-grass and family photographs. My mother had bought the post box with 'V.R.' on it set below the window when she was a servant girl, with money she saved from her meagre wages. That old stone window, framed in clipped ivy, was good to draw. Sheets of stamps and bundles of postal-orders sat among plants and the family bible on its broad sill. The lace curtains were never drawn far back, so that their patterns of impossible flowers showed clear against the darkness within. I do not know how it was done but with every wash they were dyed a deep golden ochre, and the parchment-like blind, that was always drawn a few inches, was edged with lace of the same strong dye. Honeysuckle and a Gloire de Dijon rose climbed up to the mossy stone tiles, and I remember that a garden of houseleek and stonecrop thrived on the great hood over the Post Office doorway. I drew its finely carved brackets and the heavy iron knocker shaped like a coil of knotted rope. A well was set in the flagged courtyard, and I drew the horse-shoe-shaped wall around it with its vast flat slab in front where you bent over to lower your crook and bucket deep into the icy water. In a dark ferny place behind it a gnarled toad lived an undisturbed life, and a tame jackdaw would come to the well-head to be stroked. The windows at the back of the house looked over tiny mounded meadows sloping away to the South, and from the attic where I

[18]

A gate 'harr', with burdock growing near.

An oak gate and staple catch,
with great mullein growing near.

[19]

slept I loved to try to draw the whole haphazard patchwork of field and hedgerow, lane and coppice, the dark clubbed wood on the opposite hill, and the far line of the Downs.

My dear companion was my aunt – my grandmother's youngest child, whom my mother had actually suckled as a baby when her own mother was too ill to nurse her. She was only some five years older than I, and was my ideal of what a country girl should be, with fair freckled skin and flaming hair, and an absorption in the life of the village, its common, meadows, lanes and woods, as deep as my own. The postman would bring all the letters for the village at a very early hour in the morning, and it was her job to deliver most of them; so she knew every footpath and stile and woodland track in the parish; she tramped the old cobbled bridle ways to remote farms and cottages, and called at the half-dozen large and handsome houses within the village. This is how she came to know where the plumpest mushrooms would appear in wet September and where the finest hazel nuts and blackberries grew. She and I would gather mushrooms at five in the morning and cook them for breakfast. We would fill gallipots with filberts and bury them in the garden until Christmas-time.

Autumn was a slow and gradual season. The elms were still green by mid-November, their overhanging veils darkening the white limestone lanes. Then on some pale sunny morning all was suddenly transformed; the great trees were now heavy with ochreous gold, row after row of rich yellow receding into the blue distance. There was no motion anywhere: each enormous tree stood tranced and transfigured in a brooding world of chrome and white and blue, until at last a wet wind from the West released a gentle flutter of yellow leaves, patterning the rutted white mud, and by evening completely covering it. Yet not before December were the lofty fan-traceried tops etched bare and black against the sky, the fallen leaves all withered and brown, and the wide landscape drained of brilliant colour.

On Monday morning I would start early to school, stopping to pick plump newborn mushrooms which I peeled and ate raw, or helping myself to the best blackberries and hazel nuts as I passed the heavy bushes. And in the wood I would stand and wonder at the awesome army of fungi among the dead leaves: the scarlet-capped fly agaric, and once its innocent-looking relative, the still more deadly death cap, and – most appalling of all in its reality – the stinkhorn, so perfectly named *Phallus impudicus*. I took one once in its egg-like stage and drew it on successive days, watching the breaking of the skin and the uprising of the phallus, soon to disintegrate with a foetid stench that flies loved. I would arrive at school glowing, hot, and so absorbed in my real life that it did not greatly disturb me that our course was now narrowed down to five 'matriculation subjects' and that I could no longer draw or paint.

There was but little education: only a long succession of textbook lessons in this or that, quite without plan and with no relation to life. But I began to read Hardy, Jefferies, and W.H. Hudson, and I made countless sentimental drawings of an exaggeratedly picturesque kind of setting suns and elm-shaded lanes. Poetry was a solace, and I would go about murmuring some marvellous line of Tennyson's. I dreamed of the Pre-Raphaelites and began to make execrable Beardsley-esque illustrations for romantic poems; and I fell in love.

We were most innocent and circumspect, yet we resorted to elaborate concealment and subterfuge. A duty we shared as prefects each day was to take a register of absentees from form to form. When I handed her the book she knew there would be inside it some tender expressions of admiration or perhaps a plan to meet, and when it was my turn to have the book I would look for her gentle and guarded reply. She came to school by train, for our homes were five miles apart, and we magnified the vast separating distance. Sometimes we met in a lane midway between, where we would perhaps read a poem or two from the schoolbooks we religiously carried, stand at a gate or wander into a favourite hazel copse where I would say the affected melancholy things all seventeen year-olds say. The great butterfly orchis and white helleborine grew here for us alone to see, we thought. Next day we told no-one, and the secret ritual of the register of absentees continued.

The summer of 1921 was hot and long, and the fields were white with drought: no cloud appeared in the sky for several months. And at last our schooldays were over, and we parted. Heather was nine months older than I and went to London university, while I became a humble student-teacher in a local school, then called in a derogatory way 'elementary'. I could not see then that this was to be the resumption of that real life I had lived as an infant, that here was my salvation.

[21]

3

The Taste and Tincture of another Education.
THOMAS TRAHERNE

It was with an exhilarating feeling of freedom and expectancy that in the autumn of 1921 I entered a world with no rebel reputation trailing behind me and where my days had a purpose and a plan. On Mondays the twelve student-teachers scattered about Wiltshire converged on the town of Trowbridge some miles from my home and met in an awkward building called, I remember, The Tabernacle; and here we continued our education – or, in my case, began it. For we spent the day sunning in the brilliance and wit, the ingenuity and humanity of the most inspiring teacher I had known – Agnes Grist. She remains for me the greatest teacher of my life.

She would arrive after her long train journey from Salisbury Training College where she was then 'Mistress of Method', weighed down with books and plants and her lunch packed in a country basket. I suppose she looked an odd, eccentric woman in her man's shirt and tie, her leather belt and serviceable tweed skirt and brogues, but such a vitality and sense of wonder and joie de vivre irradiated her that I found her beautiful. We began the day with English. Her handling of *Coriolanus* and *Richard II* made those plays my favourites for ever. Browning, too, and the sonorous prose of Ruskin (which she often caused me to read aloud to the company) she made vital and necessary to us. She made even such remote studies as Logic and the Administration of Justice both understandable and reasonable. When she discovered the Pasque flower, corn marigold, and the beautiful Adonis or pheasant's eye on the downland we were as excited as she, and I drew and painted them with the care I would lavish on some rare and delicate fragment of medieval carving.

Each term we embarked on some ambitious and independent work of our own choosing. Through the autumn and winter I painted a series of sunsets. All were deplorably vulgar, but she was generous about them. In spring I

[22]

described and drew – in what I misguidedly imagined to be Griggsian detail – eight village churches, binding my work into a stout volume which I labelled sentimentally *Old Faces*. She took the title seriously and genuinely enjoyed what I had done. I think she knew that I had poured out my very lifeblood on the paper for her. Certainly I had put my whole heart and what skill I had into pen drawings of fonts, pillars, and window tracery, carved ball-flowers and foliage, the great tombs of crusaders and wool merchants, and all the lesser but most intimate and endearing features of those silent grey stone places. Her knowledge of Gothic architecture was vast and her memory stupendous, so I never escaped with a wrong fact or a superficial description. Preparing the book had meant countless visits to the churches, which I usually made on foot, and often my younger sister accompanied me. She had a keen eye and the power to record what she saw, and I employed her, so to speak, to draw what I had not time for. She would sit long in some cold transept, absorbed in the complications of a capital of stiff-leaved foliage or a carved bird or animal, and when we returned home I would use her work as information for the finished drawings for my book.

In the final term I studied both black and white bryony and the bulbous and meadow buttercups, making line-and-wash drawings of them and taking special pleasure in arranging my annotations in formal lettering on the tall pages as in a herbal. I found it all life-enhancing and life-giving. It was good to feel certain of approval and encouragement. Criticism was pungent and uncompromising, but always informed by a gentle wit and sensitive understanding. We talked and talked: I blossomed and shone and grew, and I worked as never before. The stimulus and refreshment which these Mondays brought throughout the year, their sense of urgency and their intense reality after my grey secondary school days amounted to a major upheaval. I shall never forget them. I would read Browning's dramatic monologues to my mother over the wash tub, and would rant and rave over Ruskin's balanced prose, for this answered my own social and political wonderings and seemed to reach out to a better world than the confused post-war present.

For the rest of the week I lived a life that was singularly different yet equally engrossing. The school where I watched others teach and tried my hand at the craft myself was for children from barely three to fourteen years old, and the entire community was ruled and dominated by quite the most forceful and distinguished teacher in the area. He was tall and spare, with a handsome head and a severe bearing. He had been trained in the old school of disciplinarians, and he demanded absolute obedience from children and complete conformity to his exacting methods and standards from his seven assistants. He was widely read, a penetrating local historian, an able musician, and a good gardener and naturalist; and in a somewhat oblique way as though he was ashamed of it he showed great faith in the arts. I knew instantly that he liked me, and I liked him; and quickly he let me loose on his own precious Standard VII, the cream of his school, now in their last year. My four fellow students and I were required to give several set pieces called 'criticism lessons' each week, when the headmaster and students together sat in judgment on the victim and each wrote at length about the performance. I have to confess that, still enjoying an audience and anxious to please, I enjoyed these ordeals.

Alas! only boys were allowed to draw and paint, while the girls hemmed and seamed in another room. The older boys had been thoroughly initiated into the mysteries of perspective. Churns had often been borrowed from a dairy near by for the teaching of ellipses, and the local ironmonger lent various objects that doubtfully demonstrated that receding parallel lines tend to meet on the eye level. A wheelbarrow was chosen for a special lesson of mine, for drawing this – as the headmaster pointed out – would involve both ellipses and parallel lines, and so would test the boys' whole grasp of perspective!

It was a handsome wheelbarrow, handmade of elm and beautifully shaped. I took the liberty of removing the green baize sheet that cloaked the piano, and placed the wheelbarrow upon its lawn in the middle of the room. Then I ranged gardening tools and a bushel basket about it, and my fellow students and the headmaster took their places, opened their notebooks, and I began to teach. I told the boys to see a picture in which the wheelbarrow was the central interest only. The gardener himself might be there. Was the wheelbarrow standing under a laden apple tree, or perhaps among vegetables at harvest time? And what about the distance? The gardener's cottage, a church on the hill? or just a garden full of flowers? I saw rather more than surprise on the headmaster's face, but there was an unwritten law that no-one could interrupt a 'criticism lesson' and he kept his peace. The boys worked silently, in deep concentration. To my amazement they all grasped the notion, and I was startled at their easy attack on the human figure and the distant landscape, for they had never before had such an experience. I remembered the disaster of my Michaelmas daisies in 1910, but here was only a triumph. This august and greatly respected and formal headmaster, notorious for his rigidity, was positively excited at the boys' work, and even, to my delight, said what a pity it was that there was no time that day to *paint* the pictures, promising that we should do this next day!

I wish I could see those finished paintings of half a century ago. I remember vividly that above all they were composed with an innate feeling for design that astonished me. They were in no sense naturalistic but were organised decorations. The wheelbarrow was no longer an exercise in perspective but the central motif of a picture. I little realised at the time that, in a fumbling and tentative way, these wonderful bucolic boys were making history. Professor Cizek had not yet come to England to show the tender, decorative paintings of his Viennese children, and Child Art – as it came to be known – had not yet been born.

Sometimes I spent a day with the 'Babies' class', the under-fives, where I was encouraged to tell them stories and to draw and paint for them, though it never dawned on their teacher that these active little creatures would themselves draw and paint if they were but given the chance. It would have been wonderful to see them, as I already knew from contriving secretly to let two or three of the more adventurous dip into my paint. But their day had not yet come: they had to be content with little more than I had had at their age. They made the most of discouraging balls of sullied plasticine and broken bits of crayon, and they attempted something called 'paper work' with scissors that were never intended to cut. It seems strange to me now that nowhere in this school, which in some ways was well ahead of its time, did children use their hands with materials creatively. The girls' needlework was as formal as arithmetic, and what was known as 'cardboard modelling' for the boys *was* arithmetic, with a little geometry thrown in. They made oblong trays of white card which became soiled long before the end, and they bound the edges with gummed, coloured tape, and were invariably defeated when they tried to make a mitre at each corner. The height of

[25]

achievement was a hexagonal tray, but I never saw one of these completed. No-one ever asked the purpose of this strange occupation, and the unseemly objects it produced were of course never put to use. I could have shown these boys how to make simple, useful books at far less cost. But I was still a student, and I knew my place.

While I relished the present I thought of the future. I needed help in choosing a college. I drew a blank from my secondary school, for neither the headmaster nor the senior mistress had any knowledge of art schools or training colleges, and I was no longer their responsibility. It was my Monday teacher who furnished me with names and addresses of possible colleges, and I read their prospectuses critically and made my decision without any difficulty. I sent a long letter of application in my very best script to Goldsmiths', a college of London University that shared a building with a school of art and a vast adult education centre, all of the same name. I shall never forget the surprise of the warm, humane, and welcoming reply, for there was no interview. The letter ended with: 'We like your drawings and we like your handwriting. We hope you will be very happy here.'

So, with uncertainty over, I became totally engrossed in learning and teaching, drawing and painting, and the year rushed to a close and I ended my student-teachership in July. I was paid twenty-seven pounds for the year – though girls received only twenty-one. This was but a minute contribution to my upkeep, and I knew that my parents would soon have to make further sacrifice since my grant for college would be inadequate. It was sobering too to learn that there was already a fear of unemployment among teachers and that only the best students leaving college would obtain posts. These were stern and serious reasons for doing well.

Sometimes through the long summer holiday we two met in our lane, where the wayfaring tree was already berried and the traveller's joy was seeding. Heather would tell me about London, which I had seen for only a day; and she talked with fervour about the Anglo-Saxon texts she was studying at King's College and read me lines from them. I showed her my *Old Faces* and the illustrated notes of lessons I had given. We ate oatmeal biscuits she had made and Beauty of Bath apples from her garden. The soapwort flowers beside the gate and the scabious and silvering calyx-heads of knapweed meant for us the coming of autumn and our loss of this green peace. But we lived for the day, and the day was halcyon and kind: we seemed to take rain and wind as the trees and cows did. I remember only that all was well. 'Everything was at rest, free and immortal.'

4

I was Entertained like an Angel.

THOMAS TRAHERNE

I felt ill when I reached Paddington on my way to college and was prostrate when I arrived at Charing Cross at noon. A disreputable looking character who was sitting in the waiting room saw that I was sick and laid me out on a seat, put my raincoat over me, and waited with my luggage beside me until I was able to continue my journey some hours later. He asked for nothing, though was pleased with what little I gave him. The ride on the open top of a 48 bus from New Cross revived me. I followed my instructions to walk across Blackheath to the park gate in the high wall and made my way past the twisted, blackened chestnut trees across the orderly gardens around the Greenwich Observatory to the gate in the opposite wall that was to be my exit and entrance for two years. The warden of Clyde House across the road was immaculate like a surgeon, and his young wife was like a nervous nurse in training. In my sparse and graceless cubicle where everything possible was painted in that unhappy colour we call green bice – the disastrous result of mixing too much white with a cold blue-green – I was nevertheless at home at once. It seems now that I straightway made friends with everyone. The different accents of my fellow students fascinated me, and for the first time in my life I met a Jew, an Irishman, an Indian, and four Welshmen.

There were several artists among the students, whose easy warm companionship meant much to me. They liked to see my paintings and enjoyed listening to my talk about Wiltshire, and we would share the black-currant jam and thickly fruited cake that my mother used to send me.

There was a great comforting cherry tree in the garden that was turning yellow and orange. The hooting of barges down on the river was unfamiliar and strange. Our food was meagre and my purse was shallow, but I was very happy.

The strangely dual life of learning about children and how to teach them

[28]

and of learning fresh things myself seemed exactly to fulfil the longing I had always had to be both teacher and artist. Intuitively I knew this balance was right for me – absurdly didactic child that I had been – and I never questioned it. I could not have said then, nor could I say now, which has held me more – the desire to give shape to my love of a few square miles of English countryside or to teach and help others to teach. For me there was no contradiction. And although at the time such notions as 'education through art' had not been born I do not think it was surprising that an eighteen-year-old then should have dreamed vaguely of that emphasis. There were astonishingly brave pioneers – mainly women – on the college staff who were convinced that young children had far greater potentialities than so-called education had ever recognised, and that a far broader, richer, freer life for boys and girls would bring undreamed-of advance; and I listened eagerly to them and read and talked and thought, and of course came a cropper when I attempted on my first teaching practice to take these ideas into a grim prison of a school.

The two women who taught art had been brought up in a ladylike school of water-colour painting, though they too had independent minds, and they encouraged experiment as long as there was sound drawing. 'Sound drawing' was their watchword. I must confess I often longed to escape through the partition that divided us from the school of art, where I had seen miraculous etchings being produced and drawings and paintings from life that filled me with awe.

But often on Saturdays I supped at the fount. Twopence would take me to the Tate, the National Gallery, or the Victoria and Albert Museum, and those were my three temples. Sometimes Heather and I would meet, first in a café over rolls and butter and one cake divided between us, and then in the print room at the V. and A., or among the Pre-Raphaelites at the Tate or the Italian primitives in Trafalgar Square. And when we were turned out at closing time we walked in the cold windy park or down the Embankment, talking of Middle English and child psychology and Rembrandt's etchings, and of our lanes and woods at home; and we made our plans for meeting during the next holiday.

North-West Wiltshire was never far from my thoughts and yearnings. Friends took me to their homes in Kent and Sussex, Hertfordshire and East

Anglia – beautiful places, all of them; but a fatal flaw, a strange bias and limitation – perhaps it was homesickness – inhibited me and somehow prevented me from wanting to draw seriously there. Not for me the open downland or the wide horizons of the East: I craved for my small enclosed landscape, ancient, deep and sheltered, and rich with foliage and ferns. Always my sight was fixed on the hedgerows of home, the great cruciform barns and the conical topped ricks standing on staddle-stones, and the old footpaths over fields of flowers. There was more to say in that small parcel of land that a long life would allow; and although I pleased my tutors with water-colours of London roof-tops and street markets and the fine prospect of the Thames from the heights of the park, they knew and I think sympathised with my nostalgia and let me compose picture after picture from studies I had made at home.

There were good evenings when a music student devoted to the sonatas of Beethoven would leave them and to please me would play music that spoke to my condition – Delius, Vaughan Williams, and Butterworth. And sometimes after our plain unvarying supper the warden would beckon me to descend the stairs to his elegant flat. He would show me his astounding workshop. He loved wood, and he hoarded a great assortment which he almost feared to use because it was so perfect. His tools were ranged in gleaming order and everything was surgically clean. As a privilege and honour I was allowed to letter minute labels for his many tiny boxes and drawers. I loved him for his perfectionism, and responded to his fastidious ways with his materials. He had been appallingly battered during the war, and I'm afraid he was not happy. He would pour Benedictine very delicately into two frail engraved glasses for us, and as we sipped it he would put his arm round me and ask if I would become his adopted son. The sorrows of the human race concerned him deeply, and he did all manner of good works in the East End, where he sometimes took me to show me what life was really like, as he said.

During my second year in London I became positively addicted to visiting the V. and A. print room to pore over the intimate domestic etchings of Van Ostade and the pastoral prints of Potter and Van de Velde. The 17th-century Dutchmen were as obsessed with their own surroundings as I felt all men should be. But it was the work of Griggs at the spring exhibition of the

Royal Society of Painter-Etchers that damaged me permanently, so to speak. I cannot now remember which haunting Gothic plate it was that so affected me; could it have been an early state of the carefully named *Anglia Perdita*? or the strange deserted *Palace Farm*? or the dreaming gables and arches of *Linn Bridge* or *Potters' Bow*? Now I only recollect knowing that here was my man. The Catholic overtones and the chaste Gothic severity were not for me, nor the grandeur of scale and the sad emptiness and sense of loss, but the marvellous realisation of stone and water, foliage and sky, and the intense feeling for Cotswold England bowled me over. For here was the full flowering of that genius that had moved me as a boy through the early pen drawings of Buckinghamshire. I was uplifted and excited now as by some great event, and for days I could think of nothing else. Strangely, as it seems now, there was no-one at college with whom I could share the event. To paint was the thing: 'black and white', the overall description for everything else, was considered a lesser accomplishment. So I painted happily as a member of the group, and worked at my designs in pen or bistre in my cramped cubicle. Leaving college in July, where I had been so spoiled and kindly treated, was not the break I had feared, for in September I was to teach in a school in Greenwich, only a mile or so away, and on four evenings a week I should be a student in Goldsmiths' school of art.

I returned after the long holiday to the bedsitting-room I had found not far from my college hall, bringing with me a folio of drawings of the interior of a great tithe barn and of a farmyard with a simple church beside it. And my head was full of ideas for my work with children.

The intimidating three-storeyed school building with a slimy stream beyond its harsh playground was a very poor place for children. When three hundred boys from seven to eleven years old lined up on that first foggy morning and climbed the stone stairs to the top, and I found myself with sixty-one of the youngest – wedged tightly into a galleried classroom with walls of shiny privet green and cow colour – I was greatly dismayed. But the headmaster was an essentially good, perceptive, optimistic and loving person who abhorred corporal punishment and whom boys and masters equally liked. He somehow helped us all to minimise our problems, and these young boys showed quite extraordinary resource and humour in making the best of shocking conditions. The poorest of them came to school

[31]

in anonymous garments, sewn up for the winter, and not all had stockings and a few were without shoes. Their hair was dull and lifeless, and their grubby little hands were usually cold. At midday some would go to a rough eating house opposite the school where for a penny they ate a doughnut and some pickles as their dinner. On the second day one fell and broke an arm, and I carried the rickety little creature in my arms to his home at the top of a tenement building near Deptford Broadway, where his dehumanised mother met us, screaming with rage at me, as though I was the culprit. In 1924 there was much unemployment, and fathers loitered about the mean streets. There was little self-respect except in the Jewish families; twenty of my boys were Jews, and however poor they were cared for by devoted parents. The contrast was striking.

My job was to teach everything. I spent all day and every day with my own class. By December diphtheria had killed three of my children for whom I had great affection, and three others had been removed to hospital for prolonged treatment. But how to cope with the fifty-five left? It was hard even to see them all at once! Many could neither read nor write, and I had to find my own ways of teaching them. As was inevitable, I suppose, I stumbled upon most of the methods and devices teachers commonly use, one or other of which appeared to meet the needs of most, and I was rather proud of our progress. I tried to lighten both their load and mine by telling them stories of a serial kind which I made up more or less as I told them, about life in the country with animals and birds. The country, of course, was my home, and talking about it was both a comfort and an escape for me. After a weekend in Wiltshire I would bring back nuts and berries and feathers and wild flowers, which delighted them. I must have conveyed the impression that Wiltshire was heaven, for one frail child asked, 'Is God up in Wiltshire?', and small wonder!

There were few materials with which to draw, and no-one in the school ever painted; but we soon began to improvise. We drew with our pens more often than we wrote with them, and we did our best with greasy unsatisfactory crayons. Then one day in the stock cupboard I discovered a forgotten hoard of 'Greyhound' pastels, each stick wrapped in its paper label, which the headmaster said I could use as I liked. What we needed was paint – not the timid water-colour of my schooldays but something with

Robin Tanner, 1924

more substance and power. So I set a group of eight-year-olds to peel these nice pastels and grind them down to powder with pestles and mortars which the headmaster himself produced from an unknown source. This we mixed with weak size – an enjoyable business – and so produced a serviceable body colour.

I rescued huge sheets of rather brittle, coarse-grained, flecked and oaty packing paper whenever new consignments of materials were delivered to the school, and the boys and I cut them into convenient pieces and painted them with common whitewash which I bought for a penny or two. On these pristine panels we painted – only a few children at a time, alas, with so little space to move in: two used my blackboard and easel, and four painted with their paper flat upon the floor. Meanwhile the rest resignedly engaged in less demanding pursuits, patiently waiting for their own great day. I remember brightly suggesting what to paint, but I think my ideas were never accepted. Every boy knew exactly what he wanted in his picture – perhaps Greenwich pier from which you could sail up to Westminster, or the great observatory on the hill, or Deptford High Street market on Saturday night. I marvel now at the mirth and surprise and evident satisfaction of the headmaster when he came into my room, as he invariably did, to see the results of this unheard-of activity. He always made me feel safe. I knew he would protect me from the philistines if need be. He delighted in the flushed happiness and the prowess of these Dickensian, urchin-looking little boys, and he would give me a wrenching handshake, which was his best reward.

He once let me take a small group to the Tate Gallery while he looked after the rest. A tram slurred slowly and nauseatingly as far as Vauxhall, and we walked the remainder of the journey. I learnt a lot from watching these thin-legged children, who surprised me by devouring Turner and dismissing most of the portraits.

There were walks to their beloved river to watch the tugs they were always drawing, and on one of these outings they asked if they could bathe, knowing I should say no. But I said they could surely *imagine* themselves paddling and sporting in the water, and when I went on to suggest that a group might like to make a picture of this tomorrow they jumped at the idea. Above my classroom was a disused store with empty walls lit by a skylight, and it was upon one of these that they painted their first mural. It was a large and spirited design of naked boys up to all sorts of antics, splashing and bobbing up and down, with brown boats sailing by and the far bank brought very near. It interested the headmaster so much that he showed it with some pride to a young LCC inspector on his first visit to the school, but he shunned it with shocked disapproval, pointing out to me that the perspective of the river was wrong, anyhow, and that the proportions of the bathing boys were incorrect, and that obviously these children were not ready for the human figure yet. Quietly, and with one of his painful handshakes, the headmaster said to me afterwards, 'And d'you think *he* is, poor chap?'

At twenty my energy was boundless, and after an exacting day at school I would walk through the depressing streets to the art school for a session of

[34]

three hours. On one or sometimes two evenings I drew from the nude under that fine artist and great teacher, Clive Gardiner, and spent the other nights in the etching room. The teacher here was Stanley Anderson, an outstanding engraver and etcher who had a consummate mastery of his craft. He was a spare, cool, taciturn person, so admirably disciplined himself that he countenanced only the highest standards from others in his workshop. There were marks of a hard life upon him, and he gave away but little of himself. He manifestly loved the Midi and constantly condemned London weather. I guessed his political views were Left, but once when I attempted a political conversation with him, showing clearly where I stood, he closed it down with a frown. I hardly think he had any interest in his students as people. He once told me I was foolish to teach: that was all. I never heard him give praise, though he never failed to show approval of sound workmanship. I found him uninspiring, and I cannot say I greatly admired his own work, but to this day I feel immensely grateful for his meticulously careful and patient teaching. No detail of the craft passed him by, and he shared his knowledge with us as a medieval craftsman might have done with his apprentices. He would move silently among us in his indigo smock, his fine strong hands always at work. Step by step each one of us followed his directions, and there was no escape. I remember how he kept me grinding ink for proving my first plate for a full half-hour. I had mixed Heavy and Light French Black and Frankfort Black and a pinch of Indian Red together with burnt linseed oil upon the stone, gathered all together into a dusty paste with a palette knife as he directed, and then wielded the marble muller to and fro until the ink seemed beautifully smooth; but he found an unground speck or two, which he warned me would scratch the copper. He was not satisfied until I had continued grinding and he had tested the result once more and at last found the shiny black mass 'about right', he said.

Before the session ended the blue-green acids were returned to the great bottles and the white porcelain dishes washed; the work benches were cleared, the pressure of the press loosened and the blankets lifted over the rollers. Each night we had to leave the room in perfect order for the next day. How often in winter as I left the acrid, penetrating smell of the Dutch bath, I was met outside by an even more appalling stench of a thick stifling ginger-coloured wall of fog, and was scarcely able to see the lights of my 48 bus! How warily it crawled through the muffled streets and up the unseen hill and over the blind heath to the terminus! whence I fingered my way along railings and past wet laurels to the last house in the Old Dover Road where I lived. But on fine nights I rode on the upper deck, choosing where I would sit at this late hour when there were few passengers; and if it rained I unrolled the tarpaulin shield that was provided, fastening it round my neck like a baby's bib. I loved the windy journey across Blackheath, the speed of which was unpredictable, for either the bus raced to the terminus because it was late or dawdled because it was too early. I got to know two of the conductors well, and we had long broken conversations that were never finished, about the different jobs we did, and sometimes they asked to see my drawings.

I set out for school early each morning, and unless I had much to carry or the weather was bad I walked. The good houses bordering the heath belonged to a stable, affluent world of nursemaids and tended gardens, but as I descended the hill towards my school I entered a seedy world of poverty and decay, of pawnshops and cheap stores, the ghoulish establishments of undertakers, doubtful cafés and worse. Usually a few straggling children came to meet me, and begged to be allowed to carry the books or rolls of pictures or plants I had brought for the day. A few of these boys I remember well. Some were without shoes and always seemed cold; they would ask to put their little blue hands up my sleeves to warm them. But they were eager and happy, and we spent good days together in that crowded, galleried classroom. Quite unlike the other boys were the Coles twins, Harry and Teddie, who lived above a bank in Deptford Broadway. Harry was biddable and quiescent, with perfect manners. Teddie was alert, with an independent and enquiring intellect, and he daily called on all my resources. His mental energy and his grasp of human situations astonished me; I think he was the most engaging and stimulating boy I ever taught.

Some forty years later I received a letter from him. He was now an Anglican monk, of the Community of The Resurrection in Johannesburg, doing humane work among poor black people. He had happened to read a review of my work in *The Listener* and somehow found my address. When he came home on leave he spent a memorable weekend with us. It was good to find that all his gifts and resources were being called upon in the dangerous work he had chosen to do.

Etcher by night and teacher by day seemed to suit me well, and had there been the chance I hardly think I would have ordered my life differently. For me, the one activity complemented the other: both loves were satisfied.

The winter of 1924 held two dissimilar events for me which proved unforgettable. The first was that matchless work of art, Sybil Thorndike's Saint Joan, which I went to see twenty times, so that at home I was able to enact Shaw's entire play for my family, imitating the voices as I read every part. One day the warden of my college hall, whom I sometimes visited, gave me a ticket for a superb seat, and Shaw himself crept in, wearing carpet slippers, and sat beside me. During the intervals we talked like friends. Who was the greater, I wondered, he or this Saint Joan? He certainly thought the latter.

Then, at college I had been greatly moved by a pamphlet by Francesca Wilson called *The Child as Artist: some conversations with Professor Cizek*, and had longed to see the woodcuts and coloured drawings which children from eleven to fifteen years old had made in his class under his powerful influence at the Vienna School of Arts and Crafts. At last I did; and I immediately recognised their grave, un-English, fairy-tale idiom as something genuine and indigenous to these Austrian children – so utterly unlike the rough Cockney pictures of my little boys. If only the two classes could meet, I thought! And what would this astonishing prophet, whose faith in young children was so profound, cause them to produce? Seeing these beautiful decorations – some made as early as 1919 – strengthened the belief, to which my own pupils were leading me, that for a child a drawing or painting is always a design. My boys invariably began with a frame, as they called it, for their pictures, and the design was artlessly organised to fit it and fill it. They never drew in a vacuum: everything had its boundary and was itself a whole. I now realise, of course, that even when, some years later, the work of Cizek's boys and girls became well known in England teachers generally were little affected or influenced, and the lessons we could have learnt from that gentle pioneer went largely unheeded. I told my class about these children in Vienna, and showed them reproductions of their very decorative, almost 'Art Nouveau' work, but I must admit they were far less excited by them than I. What I found so inspiriting was the knowledge that, scattered about Europe, there were already pockets of enlightened experiment where, often in conditions as unfavourable as ours, children were beginning to come into their own.

I worked so hard each day to try to bring some grace and beauty into these impoverished lives I was coming to know so well that the art school became a most necessary haven and release. The first plate I etched was a poor thing – obvious, trite, and derivative. My teacher thought the studies I had made of a fine tithe barn at home were 'reasonably competent', and it was from them that I composed my working drawing in ink with sepia washes. But it turned out to be an unhappy hybrid between Clausen and Blampied – a travesty of both – and painfully unsure of itself. I was ashamed. I am glad I cannot recollect preparing the plate or needling or biting it, or even the ceremonial pulling of the first proof. I only knew that from the start I felt it was not mine, though through it I at least learnt the feel of a needle on copper and was humbled by my mistakes. Not until nearly two years later, after much travail, did I really begin to find my way.

Alington in Wiltshire was a theme that was very dear to me, and I poured into it all my homesickness and love for the grey stone farms and white lanes of home. Although I used the drawings I had made of the pillared cow byre and thatched walls and mossy-roofed barns and a crude little chapel-of-ease in a hamlet of that name, I could never work with any degree of topographical accuracy. That didn't interest me at all. What I wanted to say was what I *felt* about my countryside, and particularly at that moment of spring when the swallows come back and the naked fans of elm trees begin to thicken. So I composed my own Alington, placing elms just where I wanted them and entirely changing the landscape beyond the farmyard. All my teacher objected to was the trees. 'Go and look again', he urged. 'You've never seen treetops shaved to those shapes.' But I had, of course. I had lived with elms all my life. There were more elms in North-West Wiltshire, and finer ones, moreover, than almost anywhere in England. I contrived to let the design stand, and he kept his patience.

The delicious sensation of running my needle through those sixty-three square inches of smoked wax ground was positively healing, and I was as excited and lost to the world as when I went wild with Michaelmas daisies in my infant school. I still have the meticulous record of the long series of bitings, first in the slow, penetrating Dutch bath and then in fierce, bubbling nitric acid. I had to lay a second ground, with further needling and biting, before the etching was as good as I could make it, and I have this record too. They are a tribute to sound teaching.

One night a publisher and dealer in prints came to see me. I do not know where he had seen this etching – I cannot remember whether it was at the RA – but he said he liked it and begged me to print an edition of forty proofs, for which he would pay me £1 apiece. I was horrified at the idea at first, and resisted. Moreover, I had no press, and the art school one was already over-used. But after a long struggle I agreed to get them printed by David Strang, the only firstrate professional printer still working. They were not ready until the autumn of 1927, but they were well and sympathetically done on fine paper, and I think most of them were shipped to America.

With the £40 I earmarked an excellent second-hand double-geared press at the redoubtable firm of Kimber. Wilfred C. Kimber's, at Tankerton Street Works near King's Cross Station, was the mecca for etchers then, but is, alas, no more. I sometimes look through his thick, enticing catalogue of fifty years ago and am dismayed at the way we have come. The range of sound and well-prepared materials and superb tools, at prices which now seem absurdly small, and which were all ready to hand in those days, was bewildering to a young etcher. Kimber could supply everything any engraver could desire. I penetrated the dark and oily Tankerton Street Works to see the press that would be mine when I could find a home for it. It was practically new, with nineteen-inch rollers and a yard-long iron bed, and I pictured the large prints I would one day pull from it. I read the 'unsolicited testimonials' about it from men I knew, and I felt safe.

There was W.Y. Rhind, too, of Gloucester Road, Regent's Park. I longed to know what Y stood for, but have never discovered. His catalogue I still cherish, long after his death, and a bottle of his stopping-out varnish and a pat of his dark etching ground I almost fear to use, knowing there will be no more. His catalogue advertised materials 'all of the best English make' and 'used by the most eminent etchers', and displayed a reproduction of a very crude etching of a moustached gentleman in a high collar and smart tie and

[39]

spotless overall in the act of taking a copper plate from the acid bath. Was it Mr. W.Y. Rhind himself?

T.N. Lawrence and Son were the source for fine handmade papers on which to print, and I began to collect these as people collect stamps. Mercifully the Son still flourishes at his blood-curdling address – Bleeding Heart Yard, in Hatton Garden – and a few good paper-makers continue their subtle craft. But how glad I am that at this time I began to collect old papers whenever I could find them in junk shops and second-hand bookshops – fly leaves of tall eighteenth-century tomes, early lawyers' casebooks, and the manuscript sermon books of nineteenth-century parsons. I dip into my store still. It is good to hold up to the light those mellow sheets with 'J. Whatman 1800' showing clear on the wove surface. Everyone knows the name Whatman, but who was Budgen who was making a perfect laid paper in 1796? And what do we know of C. Wilmot and R. Barnard, whose thin and lissom pages bear the dates 1819 and 1828? Their papers have gilded edges, for they come from painting books evidently once the pride of industrious young ladies: in one I found a nosegay of moss roses and pinks and ferns painted most painstakingly, and in another a not very convincing pencil copy of an engraved ideal pastoral landscape. I love to finger these crisp papers of earlier centuries. They are now ripe in tone yet still a gentle, subtle white; and their firm creamy texture is of a quality we do not know today. I think that, blindfolded, I should still recognise them by feeling them and by listening for their peculiar sound when shaken in the hand. Their watermarks, though always beautiful, personal, and inventive, can be so incisive as to mar a pale passage in a print, and I sometimes have to go to great lengths to avoid this. My mother, however poor, always bought providently and in bulk, and I have followed her. I little knew in the twenties, when I amassed papers and materials I did not really need, that a time would come when they would be superseded or become obsolete, unobtainable, or no longer considered of any worth. I take a rich old paper from my store today as though it were a wine of rare vintage, and on those occasions when I spoil a sheet with a faulty print I could weep at the waste.

In 1925 Lawrence Binyon's book, *The followers of William Blake: Edward Calvert, Samuel Palmer, George Richmond and their circle* was published, and I used to have eager, hungry sessions with it in the local reference library. The reproductions of Calvert's minute wood engravings took me into an ideal pastoral world of poetry that enthralled and enchanted me, and the early sepia drawings and late etchings of Samuel Palmer left me dazed and intoxicated. Why I did not immediately rush to see the originals I do not know, but I brooded long over this book, and the revelation of it remains with me, no less startling and shaking, today.

Then, late in 1926, came that astonishing exhibition at the V. and A.: *Drawings, etchings, and woodcuts by Samuel Palmer and other disciples of William Blake*, which I positively haunted. The first item – the self-portrait of Samuel Palmer as a young man, which his son had lent and which is now in the Ashmolean – I found strangely poignant: never before, I thought, had a man's portrait so mirrored his work. I knew that the Shoreham drawings, so heavily charged with feeling, could only have emerged from such a poet. I went back to the exhibition many times, until my familiarity was so complete that I found it hard to believe there had ever been a time when I knew neither Calvert nor Palmer.

During the Christmas holidays Heather and I met in our lane and walked in our woodland, and the reunion was particularly sweet because the whole length of our elongated island now separated us. Heather, with a First Class Honours degree, was now the senior English mistress in the sedate girls' school under the shadow of Alnwick castle on the North-East border of Northumberland. I talked ecstatically about Calvert and Palmer, and I lent her the V. and A. exhibition catalogue.

We had begun to draw, as truly as we could – and she drew with greater accuracy than I did, taking fewer liberties – everything we specially loved in the places we knew so well. Even on those January days of pale sunlight, when the hazel copse was deep in dead leaves, we drew some of the 'stowls' – as the many-branched nut trees were called – and the first green flowers of dog's mercury. And we stood in the cold to draw gate fastenings of local smiths' and wood-joiners' work, and the shapely straw finials on ricks of corn. We little knew that we were recording the passing of an age-old culture, that technology and the obscenity of another war would warp and ultimately destroy the intimate features of farming England, that within twenty years most of these gates as they decayed would be replaced by mass-made tubular metal ones and the wooden stiles would go for ever. The meadow flowers would be ploughed up – and flowerless leys would take their place, and there would be neither time nor desire among money-lusting farmers to take pride in making a handsome rick. We worked feverishly and with immense thoroughness: it was as though we sensed – though we did not – that the vast change was upon us, that the end was near, and this was our valediction, and we must lose no time. I remember our outraged sorrow at the paving and tarring of the first white road and the removal of the fine gate that had always swung across it near the farm. For us this was a huge calamity – this overlaying of the limestone with alien granite chips and tar, so that the landscape seemed invaded by some sluggish black and monstrous snake. But slowly and mercilessly, mile by mile, holiday by holiday, the white lanes were covered, until none save a few cart tracks were left.

When I turn to those drawings of the late twenties now I am amazed at the untouched world that was their source. Great hoop-raved hay wagons of splendid form and stance were used on every farm. The wells and well-houses in the stone villages had not yet become obsolete objects to be arted up for tourists to admire, and no people came in motor cars to feed ducks on the ponds. Few of the vast barn roofs of graded stone tiles, with noble finials at the gables, had been replaced by that arch enemy, corrugated iron. The gear and tackle of dairying, of hedging and ditching, sowing and reaping, were still good to look at and quiet in use. Horse ploughing was still an art. There was time, it seemed, to give work that extra thought and care that raised it to the dignity of workmanship. Though I hardly think we two, in our early twenties, could see the situation as clearly as this, yet some instinctive urge drove us to lose no chance to record in sketchbook after sketchbook the things that made up our small world.

On a day in the summer holiday – it was the fifth of August, I remember, and the countryside had emptied itself into the market town for the annual flower show – I sat all day in the farmyard of my Alington etching, absorbed in drawing an open hovel or shed built in a corner of the stone-walled yard, with its third wall made of bundles of straw, and its roof of heavy thatch. The cowman had made it as a store and a place to sit in at midday. Van Ostade in seventeenth-century Holland had nothing more native and primitive than this to delight him! And as I drew I found myself 'seeing' above the haha wall the graveyard and church I had drawn a week before in Biddestone, two miles or so away. And I wanted shocks of corn around the hovel so that it appeared to be not where it actually stood but away in the distant wheat field. It was a still, hot, perfect day, and I worked till the setting sun – all Palmerwise – burst in a great shaft across the hovel in a moment of trans-figuration. At home that very night I roughly composed *Martin's Hovel* as I wanted it. I had recently drawn a bramble-covered gate, fastened by a cow's horn, and I placed this across the foreground, and let the outrageous beam of light strike right across the design, illuminating the gate post and the quilted straw roof and the bowed shocks of corn. It was Palmer, Palmer all the way!

When next month I brought my design to the etching room my teacher protested at what he called 'that blasted searchlight', and said the whole thing was impossible in England today. I showed him many meticulous pencil studies of the hovel and church and gate and shocks of corn. He became very interested in them, and his attitude changed. He steered the plate through that long London winter and, to my surprise and pleasure, pulled a print for himself, which, after his death, I found he had bequeathed to his favourite provincial art gallery.

My good printer despatched sixty proofs in March 1928, and I paid him £6-10-0 for his labour. The dealer sold them in America at five guineas apiece. His ways were strange. He wrote from New York to say that thirteen had been 'accidentally lost', and begged me to send more, which I foolishly did but was never recompensed. It was hard to believe in this mysterious loss. Now I longed to be free to etch and to be my own printer; and I longed to live in my own country once more. I still loved teaching my eager Greenwich children; I was given such warm encouragement in all I tried to do with them that I was rarely downcast; and each time I pondered on the future and dared to picture myself in Wiltshire, free to etch all day, I felt the tug of these deprived and avid little boys. Here I was surrounded by friends and shown wonderful understanding, and my income was safe, if small. Nevertheless I made the decision to leave teaching at Easter and become a full-time student at the art school for the summer. I remember how my colleagues took me to dinner at Gennaro's on the last night of the spring term, and I still refer to Lumsden's *The Art of Etching* which they gave me then. I returned sometimes to that monolith of a school building to talk with my old class and chat with my successor about them, but I spent most of my days and nights preparing for my flight from London. At the end of July, on a night of dramatic storms, I staggered to Paddington with the last of my belongings and caught a late train to the West. For many miles I watched the movements of stupendous clouds massing for a lurid sunset, and by the time I reached home the sky was clear again, and a full moon as large as Samuel Palmer's came slowly over the wooded horizon.

5

Youth should dwell in a land of health amid fair sights
and sounds and receive the good in everything.
PLATO, *The Republic*

Our reunion that summer was of tremendous significance for us both: I had come home and Heather had left her northern fastness for the gentle coast of Wales. We met almost daily and talked long as we drew. It was in my mind to celebrate in a small etching the work of a woodman, and as we sat in a hazel copse at Thickwood, making studies for it, we decided to search for some old cottage or small house to make our own, declaring that it must be built of stone with thatch or graded stone tiles for its roof. So we travelled the near countryside looking at every house for sale, but, strange as it now seems, they were all unlikely places, and there was not one that we could see ourselves living in. So we took the advice of Heather's architect uncle, Vivian Goold, who generously offered as a wedding gift to design a house for us and supervise its building if we could find a piece of land we liked.

The village where my mother was born, and where my happiest days as a teenage boy were spent, had belonged to a dissolute fox-hunting squire whose untamed horses roamed the common and whose word was law. You were supposed to salute him if you met him; indeed, my grandmother once warned me that if I ever failed to show this mark of respect and deference she would be turned out of her house. I had often met him, looking like William Cobbett, riding to hounds, but I always felt more inclined to shake my fist at him for his blood lust than to touch my forelock. I told no-one of my dangerous behaviour, and my grandmother was never evicted. And now, with the squire's death and the sale of his estate, most families in the village were able to buy their houses. I do not remember how much the Post Office in The Barton cost, but a perfect thatched cottage where the infants' teacher lived was sold for only ninety pounds. Several parcels of land were for sale. One was a field of one and a third acres, enclosed by old mixed hedges of hazel, hawthorn, maple and holly, where I had often gathered nuts. But I had never entered this field. My aunt and I had often stood at its fine old gate, but she would say, 'No, we never go there. They say it's holy ground. An old chapel was here long ago.' And when I took Heather to see it, and we stood in the long grass looking through the gateway across meadows and woods to the downs, and the tall elms roared in the wind, and owls hooted, we sensed its secret feeling. It took in a sharp bend of the lane, and at this corner there was a wall instead of a hedge – a beautifully made one with well chosen corner stones, looking more domestic than the loose stone walls we were accustomed to. Here, but a few hundred yards from my mother's and grandmother's home and the ancient moated house of my grandfather, in this silent secluded place, we decided we would live. For me it would be a return to the place where I belonged, and from here Heather could see the stretch of downland where her forebears once farmed. I had already spent my savings, so she paid the hundred-and-fifty pounds for what the sale catalogue called *Old Chapel Field* with her own.

I despised engagement rings. As a betrothal gift I made her a workbasket of plaited rushes. I shaped it like a corn rick, nearly three feet high, stitching it with fine linen twine and a packing needle. It was the work of several months, and I suffered many blisters on my fingers before it was done. I lined both the basket and the conical lid with stout linen. All round the basket I stitched pockets to hold reels of thread and hanks of tape, and there was one for long knitting needles. I made the lid a receptacle for mending, and I decorated a darning mushroom and a button box.

I had bought a portable wooden workroom which my father nobly erected for me in the garden at home; he also made me a far better steel printing table or hot plate than the one I had been used to, though there was only paraffin for heating it. The press was duly installed; and with my bed and my books and papers there too this little room quickly became an ideal habitation.

I began work at once, etching two small plates that autumn and a third early in 1929. All three were poorer than *Martin's Hovel*, and showed the marks of haste, which I knew to be the result of pressure from the publisher. I needed to earn, and resistance was not easy. But I felt ashamed. I caught myself just in time, and vowed I would work more slowly and – what seemed

[46]

still more important – would give my thought only to what I longed most to express.

It was in October that I began a large design – thirteen inches by eleven – called *Christmas*. One night of perfect moonlight, Heather and I stood by the ancient market cross in Castle Combe, the village I used as my source, and drew the tall Flemish gables, the great barns, the inn, and the cross itself. I remember the snores of one of the sleepers coming from a mullioned and dripstoned window of a cottage near by. It was an uncanny feeling, working through the small hours in that empty village where the moonlight lay in sheets of silver so bright and constant that we drew as easily as by day.

I needled this plate slowly and with immense care. Sometimes I paused for a rest, when my mother would usually sense that I had and would urge me back to my bench. 'Let me have a go', she once said, and she straightway needled a few lines in a conveniently dark passage of the design! I was ready to begin the complicated biting by the end of January 1929, but it was not until the first of April that I considered the state of the plate fit to be called final.

I was now put to the test of printing the entire edition of fifty impressions myself and alone; without a clean helper to handle the printing papers and the sheets of tissue and blotting paper it is extremely difficult to avoid soiling the proofs as they are peeled from the bed of the press. I spoilt several sheets of expensive paper; I had no old sheets large enough and had to rely on the best now obtainable. I was persuaded to try a greenish-toned laid paper for a few prints, but I never cared for the result, and the rather insistent 'laid' lines were disturbing. This first major feat of printing occupied me – and every inch of my work-room – for almost a month. I had no press large enough for flattening the prints, and I was glad to use the heavy dilapidated volumes of the illustrated Bible on whose pages I had loved to draw as a child! They proved excellent.

I sent a print to the Royal Academy, and on varnishing day I took a richer, more subtle impression with me, hoping it might be possible to change it. A spare, serious, gentle man, with the straight and kindly glance of a sensitive doctor, came up to me, smiled, and asked what I was carrying under my arm. When I showed it to him and he compared it with the one on the wall he at once made the change, and I blessed him. I did not know until someone called him by his name that at last I had come face to face with the hero of my teens, F.L. Griggs. The modest bearing of this great etcher and his winning voice and smile completely held me. He liked my work. This was wonderful to me. He asked what other designs I had in mind, and I told him about an even more ambitious plate, *Harvest Festival*, and the small one called *Wiltshire Woodman*; and he showed the sort of enquiring and total interest one would give to a friend but hardly to a young stranger. I went home elevated and strengthened, and still more determined to follow my own way.

Already in 1929 the overseas market for English engraving was crumbling, and the hideous word 'slump' became common. Although the entire edition of *Christmas* was sold, this was the last of my plates to be published. True, in 1930 the XXI Gallery held prints of *Harvest Festival* and *Wiltshire Woodman*, but not one was sold. It so happened that in the summer term the headmaster who had given me such a stern and memorable training as a student-teacher asked me to fill a temporary gap in his school, 'just for a few weeks', he said. I hesitated at first, but almost as soon as I began teaching again I knew without doubt that this was my work: it excited me, and called heavily on my resources, and filled me with pleasure. In July the master whose place I had taken retired, and in September I became a permanent member of staff.

I shall never forget the acute contrast I felt between my London school and this. The unlovely one-storey building had been designed with no greater imagination, though it was far cleaner and as light as a greenhouse. Twenty-five years had done nothing to weather its livid brick. Trains passed within a stone's throw of its windows. In contrast to my tolerant and liberal headmaster in London with his obvious concern and his open smile, this grave distinguished man who had given me my start in teaching seemed even more severe and unbending and – certainly to the children – more unapproachable and forbidding than I had remembered. He wore a bow tie and had a perfect carnation in his button-hole, held in a silver tube of water to keep it fresh, and as he greeted me on that first morning he carefully shook out from its folds an overlarge white linen handkerchief, with very great ceremony. I was soon to learn that he did this solemnly every morning as an example of the standard of cleanliness he expected from every boy and girl. I knew there were many here who could not afford a handkerchief a

CHRISTMAS

day. But what large, plump, highly-coloured, glossy-haired, well-clad children they seemed! Those London waifs I had abandoned were altogether smaller, leaner, and poorer than these. And there was a settled calm and a slow pace here; and the drawling West Country speech, with its pronounced 'R' sounds, seemed almost akin to American after the Cockney voices I had become used to. The day began and ended with The Lord's Prayer, and when I listened to 'Ow-urr Vaathur which aa-urt in heavun' I realised how much I had forgotten about this rural community and how much I had to learn. A number of the older children made long journeys to school by bicycle from villages where at that time their parents – probably without much evidence – felt they were not receiving an adequate education. This was a long-established practice here. Some would walk quite three miles to school, and all brought sandwich lunches which they ate in any odd corner: there was no provision at all. At that time probably about half the parents were agricultural workers and the rest were in light industry.

At first I was responsible for a group of eighteen girls and twenty-five boys of about eleven years of age. The headmaster held the advanced view that children who were considered dull should nevertheless move up the school with their own age group. Every morning I taught my class English, arithmetic, and what were then called Scripture and P.T., and every afternoon I taught art and craft, each group in succession, but only, alas, to boys. The timetable, which hung for all to examine and was duly signed by HM Inspector, called these sessions 'Drawing', for the notion that drawing and painting, designing and making, represented one broad field of human endeavour was not understood in schools in the twenties. 'Handwork' – if it existed at all – was a quite separate and special occupation. But I was allowed and encouraged from the start – arrogant, confident, and passionately believing as I was – to do what seemed to me right.

One of my bibles was the collection of papers on art and labour by W.R. Lethaby which he called *Form in Civilisation*. I believed every word of them – as indeed I still do. I had lettered extracts from them and hung them like texts in my etching workshop: 'Design is not abstract power exercised by a genius; it is simply the arranging how work shall be well done.' 'Art is not the affair of a few but of everybody. It is order, tidiness, the right way of making things, and the right way of doing things.' I had read J.W. Mackail's *Life of William Morris*, and that giant of a man was my hero, though it was not until five years later that I read his lectures and essays. But had he not said, 'If you want a golden rule that will fit everybody this is it: Have nothing in your houses that you do not know to be useful or believe to be beautiful'? My parents knew nothing of the teaching of Lethaby and little of Morris, yet our home in a large measure bore it out. My college and school in London and my present school, like most others, fell far short. No-one seemed aware of children's sensitivity to their surroundings or to the mark they made on them. I remembered with acute misery the evil dried-blood colour of the shiny wall behind the desk where I sat when I was six, and how when no-one was looking I used with my fingers to enlarge a portion that had peeled away to reveal more of the healthy white plaster beneath. I remember there were no less than three large photographs of Queen Alexandra in tight chains of pearls in that classroom; and a hideous bullock or buffalo head in mangy disrepair stood in a vast glass case upon a dusty cupboard; and the Conscience Clause, darkly varnished and mounted in an Oxford frame, had pride of place over the black and smoky fireplace.

I longed to have a thorough spring-clean in my classroom, and a bonfire of obsolete charts and papers, and so create a simpler, more workmanlike setting. Surprisingly I was now allowed to do all I wanted. The traditional green and brown walls and woodwork could not be changed, but I brought a Verwood earthenware jug of flowers, and most of all I think the children enjoyed the civilising, unschooly effect of a hanging textile or two which I placed where they seemed to be needed. They in turn brought offerings which I'm afraid I had sometimes tactfully to decline, but it was heartening to me that together we had started to make a fundamental change: this classroom henceforth was to be both a shipshape workshop and a pleasant place to be enjoyed.

Slowly it was dawning on me that the major craft throughout the school must inevitably be book production: the making of books for our own use and pleasure, hand-writing and formal lettering, and block-printing. I had learnt bookbinding at an art school near my own, where I had been taught by simple, direct methods, and with but little apparatus, so I felt on safe ground. I let 'cardboard modelling' die, and the headmaster's cherished

[51]

'object drawing' now became the handmaiden of picture making. We set out to enjoy ourselves.

Scale was our great problem: nothing ever seemed big enough. The room was small, the desks had sloping tops, and at first there was no bench or table. The only paper was in small drawing books which we carefully dismembered by extracting the staples and opening each folded page to a single sheet. Brushes and palettes were small, as were the tubes of watercolour. The struggle to obtain more appropriate, enticing, sympathetic materials and to extend their range continued for some years but it was most acute before the thirties. Teachers generally, no less than manufacturers, have been slow to believe in children's powers, yet at this time there must have been many lonely, scattered teachers trying in their various ways to provide honest basic materials for their pupils to use. I collected paper and card of all kinds and sizes – wrapping paper, plain-backed wallpaper, and cardboard boxes from which nice panels could be cut. We used watercolour, distemper from a local ironmonger's, and waterproof inks – mostly of distressingly crude colours until they were muted with a little Indian ink and watered down somewhat. And it was with these that at first we made our patterns, prints and pictures.

It was harder, in our limited space, to establish book production. I made a tentative start with the making of very simple books in which we practised writing a formal hand based on Edward Johnston's script that he called 'foundational'. He was one of my heroes too, and his book, *Writing, Lettering, and Illuminating*, one of my bibles. We followed him closely, which was a lot for my rigidly copperplate headmaster to countenance, but he did. However, I felt I should go slowly, especially as a number of girls and boys had begun to copy and adopt my own everyday hand-writing – a quite heretical act which the headmaster tactfully passed over. Cutting blocks and printing with them had for the present to be restricted to work on paper, though I was privately experimenting with possible methods and materials for block-printed textiles.

In my etching room I was absorbed with work on a new plate. Harvest Festival in village churches before the days of flower-arrangement societies was a ripe, pagan, riotous affair. Marrows, cabbages, chrysanthemums, parsnips and dahlias were crowded together in window splays with trails of smoky traveller's joy; great shocks of corn were brought to the altar steps, with loaves and enormous apples, and more sheaves were bound about the pew ends. It was all wonderful to draw, and I made my design that autumn, drawing in Draycot Cerne church and at Biddestone, with perfect pleasure. My mother and my younger brother and friends posed for the figures I wanted, and I worked at the composition throughout the winter. By Christmas *Wiltshire Woodman* was finished, and my workroom was full of the smell of printing.

In early January we walked to Old Chapel Field, and stood picturing how our cottage might be placed within its four hedges. Again the wind raged in the shaking elm tops, and we realised for the first time that we were on a ridge. But hartstongue ferns were still green in our hedge banks; the grazing horses belonging to the farmer who rented the field from us nosed us in a friendly way, and we found our first celandine.

1930 was a full year. We made tentative and impracticable plans for the house, which our gentle but firm architect persuaded us to abandon. His master was Annesley Voysey, and the cottage he envisaged was clean-lined and sturdy with thick outer walls, a great central chimney stack and a steep, heavy roof. Though he provided for beautiful traditional freestone mullioned windows, and two large beams to support the upper floor, he made no attempt to copy the older houses in the village. He made meticulous working drawings for two fireplaces and door latches and handles, insisting that all this work would be done by hand. He gave his very best, and he used to say later that he liked the house better than any other he had built. In the late thirties I sometimes met Voysey's son, and I told him about our cottage, and he showed his father the plans. Voysey lived till 1941, and I have always regretted that he never saw this modest offspring of his inspiration.

The plans were ready by July, and Heather's aged grandmother dug the first sod in early autumn. Sadly, we could not afford a roof of stone but had to content ourselves with clay tiles made by hand a few miles away. Fortunately, in the neighbouring village of Rodbourne we found a one-man brickfield where beautiful sand-faced two-inch bricks were made, and one day we two went to choose what we wanted for our fireplaces and the main chimney stack and the smaller one for the etching room.

The brick-maker, whose name was Tanner, seemed to think it natural that we should select from several firings just those we liked best, for he had made them all with love, and he handled each one with care. We made neat piles of plum-coloured and grey ones; a few were dark purplish-brown, and the bulk were muted reds and ochres. It was like collecting pebbles on a beach.

During the long months of building I paid several visits a week, walking the three miles from school at the end of the day, to inspect the work, checking it as well as I could with the plans and detailed drawings, and sometimes insisting that this should be unpicked or that altered, for the builder tried to save money where he could by not entirely conforming to the contract. He talked constantly of 'the slump', vowing that he would lose money on our house. Indeed, many people warned us that the slump was upon us and this was the worst possible time to set up house. But it was pleasant to sit beside the young man who was building the large brick fireplace in our living room, and to feed him with those glowing and individual bricks we had chosen, one by one, suggesting where each should be set. He was a rare craftsman. He was proud enough of his finished job to cause me to photograph him sitting in the chimney corner.

There was a memorable visit to Gordon Russell's workshops in the then unexploited village of Broadway in Worcestershire. I had seen some of the woodwork of Ernest Gimson and those who were associated with him at Daneway in Gloucestershire and were now continuing that great tradition after his death. But we had taken out a mortgage to enable us to pay for our cottage – a rather indecent thing to do in those days – and so we had to spend very carefully. Gordon Russell was inspired by Gimson as we were, and he designed furniture that we could afford. In his workshop we chose the oak planks for our double bed, which cost less that five pounds! Our greatest extravagance was a long roof-tree table, also of English oak, which his foreman – R.G. France – had made three years earlier; it cost twenty-one pounds. The rush-seated chairs of English ash were twenty-five shillings each, unpolished; and the armchair was one pound ten. Michael Cardew, in his old country pottery at Winchcombe, made good slipware that was positively cheap; and in London there was the first Swedish exhibition, where we bought inexpensive kitchen china, industrially produced, that was

WILTSHIRE WOODMAN

a revelation at that time. It was at a very ordinary local shop that we bought three marvellous Khelim rugs at thirty shillings apiece.

Working in North London at this time there was a Dutch silversmith named Adrian Harlaar to whom I took designs for spoons which I had copied freely from early English ones at the V. and A., and he made us six teaspoons at three shillings and fourpence each, six dessert spoons at six shillings and eightpence, and four table spoons at thirteen shillings and fourpence each! His workmanship was impeccable and his silver pure and luminous and with a lovely surface. Sadly, a smash-and-grab raid on his workshop destroyed his health, and he died soon afterwards.

But now teaching was daily becoming more engrossing, more exciting and demanding. I was beginning to discover that – contrary to accepted opinion – children's imaginative powers which are so abundantly evident when they are young do not in any way diminish as they grow older. In this school of some three hundred pupils from three to fourteen this was clear for all to see. By twelve or thirteen their interests were changing, and they relished grappling with more complex methods and techniques and using tools demanding greater skill; indeed it sometimes seemed clear to me that some of the oldest boys revelled in practising a particular skill just for its own sake. But the paintings, in particular, of the fourteen-year-olds were as fresh and spirited and certainly as deeply felt as those astounding pictures by children half their age. That medical-sounding word, puberty, was now much used in educational writings. I cannot say that I ever observed any dramatic changes, fallings-off, disturbances: I saw only development and inevitable change. I suppose the graph was a zigzag one, but it took an upward direction, and my only sorrow was that it was cut off at fourteen – long before it had reached its climax.

I was becoming interested in tempera painting, and was beginning to teach myself to use earth colours tempered with egg yolk, and had come upon Lady Herringham's translation of Cennino Cennini's *Book of The Art*. In the first chapter I received a shock from which I hope I shall never recover. In this earliest of all technical treatises on painting, this fourteenth-century Paduan says that the painter 'must be endowed with both imagination and skill in the hand, to discover unseen things beneath the obscurity of natural objects, and to arrest them with the hand, presenting to the sight that which did not before appear to exist.' This, surely, was what I saw happening among children before me almost daily. The release, the power, the directness all staggered me. In their paintings, and in their writings too, these unsullied, uninhibited children showed little or no concern with fantasy or with invention: rather, through the language of the imagination they would transmute the ordinary into the arresting and memorable. Theirs was the capacity to disclose and celebrate what already existed. In some measure this of course was what my less favoured London boys had done: the fish-and-chip shop and the Thames barge were the only material they needed. Here in Wiltshire the material was much easier on the eye, and life too was far softer and more comfortable, yet it was still the simple everyday things and happenings that consumed the children and became the substance of their art. They would probably never hear of 'significant form', though that was what they dealt with! I would look at my own designs for etchings in some dismay, contrasting them with the direct finality of a boy's work, and the lines would come to me:

> But he beholds the light, and whence it flows,
> He sees it in his joy.

I was fortunate in being able to talk about these things with several sensitive and understanding visitors. There was a woman education officer called Esther Hill, whose knowledge of art and craft may have been slight but who sensed intuitively that all the hard work and sustained application these children were bringing to painting pictures, printing patterns, and making books were shaping them as people. She asked me to speak to a teachers' conference and show some work. I cannot remember the event. She was a great ally, and I hope I did not let her down. I was so fiercely sure by now that all children were essentially artists and craftsmen that I'm afraid I fought all those who said this was nonsense. Then there was the director of education himself, Keith Innes, who entered my classroom looking like a magnificent Viking. He was soft-spoken, with a most winning manner, and my class was as spellbound as I. His understanding was complete and his encouragement wholehearted, and we talked long together about what we had yet to discover about children. Then one day there came into my room a tall, sad-looking, gentle art inspector from the Board of Education, called

Robin and Heather Tanner, 1931

Reginald Green. He told me he too was an etcher, and we compared notes on grounds and acids, inks and papers, and our heroes among the great painter-etchers. It was a most propitious start to a long and fruitful friendship. I remember how knowingly he moved about the crowded classroom and talked to everybody, making each boy feel noticed. I cannot say that my austere headmaster often showed respect for the proper dignity of any child: he tended to regard them all as units that make up a whole rather than as distinct and unique personalities. But this perceptive visitor found every individual worth his attention, and of course the children readily stripped themselves bare before him and greatly regretted his departure, even though he took with him a heavy portfolio of their precious work. This they found very hard to bear, but I assured them that one day it would be restored to them, and after many weeks it was.

The early months of 1931 were bleak and uncharitable, and my walks to Old Chapel Field were cold and muddy. I think I shall never forget the shock and shame I felt one evening on seeing, across the valley from the high meadow outside Birds' Marsh, our screaming roof tiles that had just been laid. In the brickyard they had seemed a harmless brownish red, muted and pleasantly varied; now on the roof a mile away they burned in the setting sun, a flaming, spotted vermilion. I felt I could never be seen entering that house, and I pictured the wrath of our nearest neighbour who lived in the fine grey farmhouse across the lane, and who, we had already learnt, felt outraged that anyone should dare to build a new house in the village. But Heather's uncle was not dismayed; he assured me that Nature was quick to mellow handmade tiles. I could not believe him, though he was of course right. The south-west rains soon drained out the strident reds; friendly lichens patterned the roof with greys and browns, and we no longer felt guilty or ashamed. The month of March that year was so wild that the lane was littered with elm branches, the uncut grass was grey, gales howled through etching room, living room, and kitchen, and the cold was alarming. A careless plumber allowed the hot water tank to freeze solid and burst. One night after the men had gone home I stood alone in the unfinished, untidy emptiness and felt almost afraid to move from room to room. I had always been frightened of the dark, but now I tried to tell myself this was my home; I should come to love the country dark, the harsh newness of the house would disappear, its naked walls would be clothed, and it would one day become part of this ancient pasture.

At our next meeting we read the Anglican marriage service, which seemed to me quite abominable. I loved drawing churches, and we both recognised the poetry of the *Book of Common Prayer*, but I had no use for a Church that was 'Established' – which to me meant that it supported war and preserved class privilege. Nor did I feel we two could not be trusted to live happily ever after without swearing this before a parson. But to save bother I agreed that we should be married in the ancient church in Corsham, near Heather's home, provided we were spared an address by the vicar. To this arrangement he agreed.

[59]

So we were married at Easter, very early on Saturday, the fourth of April, 1931, in the presence of our parents and a few other relatives. Heather wore a favourite dress I had designed for her three years before, of wonderful wool and silk dyed with madder and woven by her aunt: a tight bodice and full skirt, with collar and cuffs of unbleached linen. At her school they had said she looked like Jane Eyre in it. I wore my favourite old tweed suit and a shirt of natural shantung silk my older sister had made me. I bought no wedding ring. My brave sweetheart was taken for a fallen woman by the contemptuous fellow who sold her the ring, though he proffered her a set of six cheap spoons that went with the purchase. That faithless vicar harangued us after all, which brought me near to mutiny. But we had a good meal of my mother's cooking afterwards, and then walked home.

6

The lines are fallen unto me in pleasant places;
Yea, I have a goodly heritage.
PSALM 16

It was late afternoon when we reached our naked white walls and harsh roof, looking painfully new and unsheltered in the open field of tousled hay grass. The builders had left only the day before, and their rubble lay in untidy heaps. Their muddy footprints sullied the parquet floors; the beams were dirty, and there was a mountain of work to do. Only the kitchen was finished. My younger sister Grace had painted it as gay as a caravan, as a wedding gift, and my stalwart younger brother Leslie had lit the range and made log fires in the living room and studio to dry out the plaster. We called at the farm to buy milk and to ask for a daily supply, wrote homesick letters to our parents, ate our supper by the unfamiliar light of an oil lamp, and candles lit us to bed. And what candles they were! We had been given the two beautifully made brass candle holders that Heather's grandparents had used, each with its ample, splayed, oblong tray, its neat device to raise the candle as it became spent, and – what still gives me the greatest pleasure – the elegant, faultless handle built for one's thumb and longest finger to hold and balance securely: we never spilt wax.

We woke to the call of the chiffchaff, and gathered a bunch of our own primroses for the breakfast table. And then we set to work, I to etch four plates to illustrate an essay by Virginia Woolf on the River Thames for, of all things, *Nash's Magazine*, and Heather to scrub the wood-block floors, patiently yard by yard, with endless buckets of water and soap. It was a hard honeymoon, and cost Heather a 'housemaid's knee', but it won us forty pounds, which we sorely needed, and the living room was now beautifully habitable. My older sister, whose profession it was, had made our curtains perfectly, and my father had fitted ample drawers for our precious silver in the built-in dresser. Getting the floors to take a polish was a long and

[61]

arduous job, but slowly the pine blocks absorbed the beeswax and turpentine and mellowed to a warm, smooth surface. At the end of our first week we lit a great bonfire of builders' rubbish and etching rags and papers, in which we accidentally cast our marriage certificate; we found it among the outer embers at the end of the day, charred but just recognisable!

The walk that I had loved so much as a boy was now to be my daily journey to and from school, and a decade had hardly changed it. My usual way was to follow Morrell Lane, the broad green glade that runs steeply from the corner of Old Chapel Field into the valley, gradually narrowing with undergrowth and then becoming wide again where it ends at a pair of stone cottages. A gate spanned it here, with a squeeze-belly stile, and an ash tree on either side. Then I crossed Jackson's Lane, plunged through another shorter, deeper one called Lovers' Lane, then over a stile and steeply up to the great chestnut trees outside Birds' Marsh. Here, at the gateway where my father had once seen a ghost funeral, I would stop to look back at our red roof on the opposite ridge, persuading myself each day that the colour was becoming less insistent; certainly the shape was good, and as the trees thickened it became more bearable, until I began to love the sight of it there, nestling among the foliage. Going through the wood was always the climax, and on those first scented spring mornings and evenings it seemed like walking in Eden; the earth was hidden by ferns and anemones, wood sorrel, moschatel and primroses, and the thrusting grey leaves of bluebells. Then came the last three meadows before the still countrified outskirts of the town that brought me to my school under the railway embankment.

Heather would come to meet me on my way home, and we would watch the pretty antics of red squirrels, gather fallen branches for firewood, and out in the open again try to distinguish between the songs of blackcap and garden warbler. By the time we reached the head of our green lane we were always heavily laden: a basket of fircones, a splendidly lichened branch or a collection of snail shells to draw, besides my pile of school books and our precious firewood. Our homecoming each day was memorable.

I began to keep a diary about weather and the passage of the seasons, which has now reached its fifty-sixth year. The first entry, for October 12th, 1931, runs: 'Holly berries in Morrell Lane already burnt orange, and both ash trees at the gate nearly bare, their leaves suddenly fallen in a yellow heap. Saw a dark grey badger in Birds' Marsh, and Heather found his excreta by the pond. Greater stitchwort, skullcap, wood betony, sheepsbit scabious, tormentil, still in flower; and one plant of wood anemone in full bloom next to a vivid orange-antlered fungus called, we think, *Calocera viscosa* – a beautiful sticky horn. It is like a fern almost. I drew it. Amethyst agarics and tufted mushrooms. Queer pale green brittle discs, half an inch in diameter, under the oaks. What are these? Nuthatches in the elms tapping, cracking nuts, almost as loud as woodpeckers. Verdigris fungus on pine needles, bright as a thrush's egg when young, and becoming opalescent as it ripens. Devil's inkhorn spilt over the grass. Drew a fine spray of wild honeysuckle. All our hazel nuts now gathered, though many were shed and lost before we could get them. The first moss appearing on the roof of the etching room! The Irish ivies we planted now reach the stone frames of the windows.'

By December my walk home was dark and mysterious, and I was glad whenever I was met by a stream of scented smoke as I entered Birds' Marsh and found the woodman still at work beside his fire. Usually I met only the middle-aged son of our village thatcher returning to Chippenham from helping his father, and his customary greeting was, 'Dark in 'ood'. It was so regular that we privately called him 'Darkinood', though one dusky evening he stopped and said, 'Missus doant venture vaar at noight, then?' Like me, he would collect a good bundle of firewood, and sometimes the woodman would reserve a specially sound log for him and place it near the entrance to the wood, with his name, 'SAM', written in capitals on a scrap of paper beside it – a privilege which we scrupulously respected. Rarely was I prevented by rain or gale or snow from making my daily journeys by lane and meadow and woodland. I hated riding a bicycle, and there were no buses, but I also disliked walking along roads. So even when rain was heavy and mud was deep I took the country way. I would carry my shoes and wear wellington boots, changing at the last meadow, leaving my wellingtons under the hedge, where they remained safe until evening.

Throughout that first autumn I made countless drawings of plants that held me on my way back from school: sprays of ripe blackberries, clusters of hazel nuts, a trail of polished black bryony in heavy fruit, plump ears of wheat, sprays of fleabane and tormentil, and the grey feathery seed heads of the wild clematis. I was obsessed by all this wild autumnal richness, and craved to celebrate it on a sheet of copper: it was line, not mass and colour, I felt, that could best express these forms and textures. I would gather them all together in a pot in one of our windows; and beyond I would have Sam's father thatching the corn ricks at the manor farm; and away beyond under a mellow sun I would have a great field of wheat still in stook, and rows of heavy elms, and a church tower rising among woods, and yet more woods fading into the downland distance. It would not be 'true to life', as they say, but it would be true to the life I dreamed of. This was the ideal and perfect world of my imagining: when one who saw my design said, 'But I've never seen any real place like that!', I wanted to reply, 'But don't you wish you had?' This, for me, was 'the real and eternal world'. The autumn sun shone, with never a cloud, upon wheat and oats that were never blighted and leaves and berries without blemish. No poles and wires nor any 'dirty devices of this world' cut across my landscape to mar its beauty. I loved ordering my own world, where my word was law, and where the wicked machinations of principalities and powers could never desecrate nor destroy. Escape this certainly was. But for me it was escape into reality from the growing exploitation and mismanagement of the land. It was this subtle, fragile beauty of England, so delicately balanced, and already being assailed, that I lived for and longed to perpetuate. I worked long at my *Autumn* design, which grew alarmingly big because I could not bring myself to reduce the true size of any plant: that seemed sacrilege. A hazel nut could only be the size of a hazel nut, and a diminutive blackberry would no longer be a blackberry. I finished needling what was more than a square foot of copper by the end of the year, and began biting it on New Year's Day, 1932.

It was during that first autumn, too, that a stranger entered my classroom who was to be a great example to me. This small bald man wearing a superb tweed suit and figured silk tie found me with a group of eleven and twelve-year-olds in the throes of block-printing with potatoes upon fine cloth. He told me his name was Edward Walsh, and asked mine. I gave him my surname. 'But your first name?' he asked. 'Robin,' I replied, a trifle hesitantly. 'You look like one', he said, smiling. 'Are you married, Robin?' and I told him I was married at Easter. Then he laughingly said, 'You look as though you were!', and we were friends. I wondered who he could be: if an official he was a singularly unofficial one. He sat among the absorbed block-printers and marvelled as I did at the precision with which they inked their blocks and placed them unerringly upon the cloth. 'They're born craftsmen, aren't they?' he whispered, and he watched intently, saying no more until the end of the afternoon. The headmaster then joined us, surveyed the printed stuffs critically but with obvious pleasure, and bade the visitor a formal goodbye. It was only then that I learnt that he was a Board of Education inspector. 'Where do you live, Robin?' he asked, and when I told him he wanted to know if we had started to make a garden. I said we had barely begun, and that we were sadly ignorant and inexperienced. He said he would be glad to give me plants from his garden, and that this was the best moment for planting. He took me to the little manor house below a fold in the downs at Cherhill where he lived; we had a perfect country meal in the kitchen with his gentle wife; and then he dug from his mature and lovely garden plant after plant, packing them with care and writing a label in his distinguished hand – both Latin and English names – for each one. I came home that night in triumph, and this was the real beginning of our garden.

But what we had not realised at that time was that our strange light soil was strongly acid. It had puzzled us a great deal, for it was quite extraordinarily fine and loose, without any binding matter or stones of any kind. The only solid objects we turned up with the spade were shards of old earthenware with finely combed slip decorations, and the little bowls of clay pipes. When I set two stout stakes of willow as posts for the clothes line I dug the holes very quickly, but I had to find stones to pack into them to make the posts firm. I should have known that our soil was without lime, for in the wood I walked through daily there were luxuriant tree rhododendrons, and the common yellow azalea seeded itself freely. And had not John Aubrey, who was born but three miles away, called this 'a woodsere country, abounding much with sowre and austere plants, as sorrel, etc.'? Sorrel grew four or five feet high in our own hay grass, and our foxgloves were a tremendous size. Alas! the chalk-loving plants from that beautiful downland garden languished with us, and only a few survived. But we had learnt our lesson, and when at last we found time to plan our garden we chose more appropriately.

There were already frequent inroads upon our quiet life. First, I was persuaded to spend twelve winter evenings teaching English ecclesiastical architecture to a WEA class in the industrial town of Swindon some twenty miles away. I still have the notes and charts and diagrams I made each week, and I am amazed at their meticulous detail and the way in which I contrived to choose all my examples from churches near at hand. I would arrive at this featureless town by rail at about six with my imperial-sized portfolio, always to be met by two staunch members of my class. One, a ragged-looking visionary and true socialist, was Reuben George, the mayor; the other, Mr Whiting, tall and neat and shy, was also a socialist, and our talk was free and seditious. Always the mayor insisted on carrying my heavy portfolio. We must have looked a strangely assorted trio as we walked through the usually wet streets to Euclid Street school, where our class was held. I have always considered an umbrella a thoughtful invention, but they shunned any cover.

There were twenty-four of us in all, and except for three women members and my two guardians every one was a railway worker. Some came in their overalls, straight from the workshop.

I found that my best way of teaching was to draw on a blackboard every architectural feature as I described it, and this the class loved. But I was never allowed to rub off any sketch until every member had copied it in his notebook. In my innocence and enthusiasm it had not occurred to me that my blackboard work would be regarded as an entertainment; the class found no less than four blackboards and easels for me, and I was of course very happy. Everyone worked hard, and we never wanted to stop. There was always a rush to catch my late train, but I never lost it. I was not allowed to carry my portfolio; only when I reached Chippenham station did I find it a burden, so I used to leave it in the parcels office and collect it next day in the lunch hour. The long walk home was refreshing, and I thought constantly of those eager men and women who had lapped up all I had to share with them.

Sometimes on Saturdays in the following spring and summer, when the course was officially over, we arranged to visit village churches together. Everyone came. The mayor and his wife brought a tea urn, and others provided crockery, and we all brought sandwiches. The game was to survey the church and try to build up its architectural history, suggesting rough

[66]

dates for every feature. I was the judge but there were no prizes. Instead, with the prior consent of the parson, our bell-ringer members rang the bells, we sat in the church in silence for a few minutes, and then enjoyed a tea-party in a field or the school or village hall. They seem to me now to have been extraordinary gatherings, taken with immense earnestness yet full of harmless pleasure.

Then on alternate Saturdays I was called for by two elderly schoolmasters, Messrs Inkpen and Watkins, and driven to a distant village school to teach a group of teachers the crafts associated with book production which my own children at school were enjoying. I marvel now that these men and women – most of them heads or teachers with much experience – made long journeys after a heavy week to learn how to write a formal hand, make patterns by divers means, bind books, and use paint, and that they were so kind to this obsessed young assistant master. They were wonderful to teach, and as biddable as that band of children I had taught under the railway arch when I was seven. But some had far less skill than they, and this sobered me. Even making a single-section quarter-bound book would have defeated a few if I had not been there to see the job through. Others were deft and accomplished, though they were usually alarmingly uncertain in their choice of colours and distressingly derivative in whatever they designed. So I dared to limit their palette – for the most part ruling out strong bright colour – and to restrict their choice of materials generally. They took this good-humouredly. It was a shock to me to realise that the world of greyed and muted colour in bark and lichen, shells and feathers, stones and flints, was little heeded by them. Colour meant only brilliant hues: grey was hardly a colour at all. They teased me about what they called my 'love of mud', so one Saturday I set up a grey and brown display – all manner of natural objects such as horse chestnuts, dead leaves, wood, undyed wools, a limestone tile, seed heads, beans and pebbles. They were arrested by it and saw the point at once, and said I had won! And certainly when they next printed with blocks they chose to explore whites and greys and blacks, producing what they called 'expensive-looking' results which were admired by all.

I learnt far more than I taught on those twelve Saturdays, and I made many friends, some of whom came to see me in my classroom. Always it seemed that they could accept children's craftwork far more readily than their pictorial compositions. Lettering, making books, cutting blocks and the like were straightforward enough, and if certain prescribed methods were followed the results were predictable and could not be other than satisfactory; but the world of picture-making was baffling and obscure: there seemed nothing to hold on to, and by what criteria would the results be judged? To say that judgement was not necessary would have been useless. After all, none of these men and women had been thought of as artists when they were children, and they were afraid of giving their pupils what they called freedom; so I ought not to have been surprised that they found my positive assertions unacceptable.

That series of Saturday sessions was to be the first of many during the next few years, and I hope that as I gained experience I was able to speak more convincingly about this 'divine spark' in children – this gift of conceiving an idea and giving it shape, without instructions or even hints from a teacher. Sadly, I found that to show paintings that had been done in my classroom helped me hardly at all: only seeing these very ordinary children actually at work under very ordinary conditions was convincing. So I'm afraid we had visitors, week after week. But no-one appeared to mind, least of all the children, who were articulate about what they were doing and organised the distribution and collection of materials and all the cleaning and storing at the end of each day with commonsense and skill that amazed me.

My work with teachers now took me to all four corners of Wiltshire, and I made time to see what I had never seen before – a thatched barn like a cathedral, small churches built of chalk and flint, and primeval earthworks on the Downs; and I became familiar with the silhouette of Stonehenge late on Saturday evenings, sometimes in frightening storms, sometimes against a dramatic sunset.

There were weekend courses too, each well planned and organised, where to my delight I sometimes worked alongside that sage, ripe, kindly inspector who had given me plants for our garden. We took short walks together, when we talked about gardens and the humorous foibles of people, and I shook with laughter at his stories of innkeepers, shepherds, and country parsons he had met. His calm, unhurried approach was only matched by that of a colleague and friend he usually brought with him,

Frank Wright – a very rare person who hardly seemed to be living in the present, so deep was his feeling for the past. When I first met him he showed me a brand new, unused prehistoric bronze spearhead which he thought must have fallen from some sort of munition carriage and which he had found two feet below the downland turf. His pockets bulged with ancient treasures which he himself had come upon. He would talk in a sad, hollow monotone that was little more than a murmur, holding us enthralled as he clothed each object he drew from his pockets with its own particular story. There was also a woman inspector called Jenny Mack, who took part in these courses, introducing teachers to spinning and weaving. Her large form was always hung with those handwoven magyar jumpers and unshaped skirts that weavers in the twenties and thirties made. Her explosive enthusiasm and her dedication to young children were an inspiration to me, though she could be alarming in her sudden prejudices and unexpected reactions. Everything about her was outsize and extravagant, not least her generosity. When she came to our cottage she described her own, at Shaftesbury built on what she called 'a frightening precipice, with the whole of Dorset below', and she invited us to spend a day with her. Cheerfully she came to fetch us in her motor car and drove us wildly there and back, a journey of a hundred miles. All these inspectors seemed extraordinary characters to me. Each was unlike any other. Each held passionate beliefs, and was a master in some chosen field. I revelled in their humanity and their enthusiasm, and I loved their eccentricities and the almost careless way in which they broadcast their knowledge, scattering largesse with no motive save to share it. In a subtle way too they were careless of their reputations and were refreshingly unfettered by local loyalties and allegiances.

Our first summer had been wet and sullen, but 1932 restored our faith, and I was tormented by dreams of etchings there was no time to realise. In early July the hay grass in the meadow adjoining Old Chapel Field was cut, and I recorded the event in my diary: 'Wonderful haymaking weather. Late last night old Tucker, young Tucker and their men and Joe Gough gathered in the last load of hay. Two tired, patient horses were led by one man, and on either side of the great wagon two men raked and hoisted up their loads in easy rhythm, and young Tucker stamped and piled on top. Now around the edge of the field remained only one row of cocks, near Joe

[69]

Gough's cottage. Tilly Bubb lit her lamp and passed before the window. The Tucker children took their candle up to bed. The men in their light-coloured shirts and trousers tied below the knees worked quietly on; sometimes there was low talking and the clink of chains and the sigh of the hay being loaded. And then at last the procession moved across the still vivid field below the steep thatch and the dark elm; and the meadow was shorn and empty. Joe Gough got over his garden wall and went through the rows of lupins to supper; our kitchen clock struck ten; and a huge orange moon rolled over the horizon.' Here was a theme very near and dear to me, but I could do no more than scribble a rough design for the etching I might one day realise.

We both loved the approach of winter. With the stripping of the trees their anatomy was laid bare as for an engraving. To mark the differences between drooping ash boughs upturned at the tips and the wide-spread arcs of elms was a daily pleasure. The melancholy sunsets like old-time Christmas cards, the country dark, and the safe feeling within the house when wet winds were raging; 'a frosty night and an egg for tea,' as a neighbour said, or 'wolves outside, all cosy indoors', as Heather and her sisters chanted when they were young – all these we looked forward to. Mists and muddy ways we put up with manfully. Only the Beaufort Hunt marred the months of winter. On my way to school I would find the foxes' earths stopped, and I knew this meant there would be a hunt on the morrow; so when Heather met me on my way home we would un-stop every one we could, hurling away the boughs and logs that had been brutally stuffed down them. But we could not stop the slaughter. We saw no beauty nor romance in oafish men and their hard-faced women, dressed up for murder, tearing heedlessly over any man's property in their blood lust. I find this entry in my diary: 'January 28th, 1932. A soft, still day, with snowdrops in hundreds and hazel catkins loosening. Some elms thickening to purple-red. Heather disturbed at her work by the sight of the entire pack of hounds streaming through our garden and round our windows, and the huntsman attempting to call them off, while the mud-spattered "gentry" waited outside on the Common. She told them what she thought of their "sport", and ordered them off, but not before the starved and frenzied hounds had torn up the garden. January 29th: Earths in the wood rammed tight again this evening, but we managed to open them up, twelve of them. A fox with a huge trailing tail loped across our path.'

It was at about this time that the slow harassment of gypsies was beginning. The sight of a trail of bright caravans and piebald horses winding through the village was already becoming less common. A favourite resting place was the head of our green lane where the land slopes to the friendly South and there are great sheltering hollies against the wind. My diary for February 18th, 1932 records: 'Bitter, withering wind. Gypsies encamped in their favourite place. Strange to see the men and women sitting round a blazing fire in the moonlight at 11 p.m.; Birds' Marsh and the hollies intensely black behind the pale yellow caravan. The tenor voices of the men in conversation carried right to our door.' There has never been a policeman in our village, but the nearest constable was always quickly told of the arrival of any 'travellers', and they were usually hustled on next morning, leaving their clothes-peg chippings behind and the white tell-tale cuts among the hazels in the lane.

But we little dreamed then that these handsome houses on wheels – so perfectly evolved for their purpose and so much a part of the countryside – would in our day be almost banished from the roads and come to be looked upon as rare objects for collectors and museums. The kind we knew was particularly light and elegant, and beautifully poised upon its fine slim wheels. Its arched doorway with carved and gilded porch brackets and painted decorations, and the chamfered ribs along its full length, gave it a look of wellbeing and pride rather than of poverty. And its under-carriage and shafts were as cunning a piece of work as any good wheelwright would expend upon a farm wagon.

There were one or two great hoop-raved wagons on every farm, and these were light and elegant too, though their large dished wheels were far heavier than any caravan's. Their wide raves or side boards dipped from the front and then took a wonderful upward curve over the back wheels; they moved along the lanes as majestically as boats. Each had a fixed fore-ladder and tail-ladder which were tall and lissom, and allowed surprisingly high loads of hay to be carried safely. And wherever the body could be lightened this was most beautifully managed with a draw-shave; there was delicate chamfering along the edges of the hoop-raves, on the strouters that

[71]

buttressed up the panelled sides, and even beneath the wagon-bed where no-one would see the artistry. I drew it all, and I loved, too, to draw the smith's work, which was as truly wrought as the wheelwright's: the subtly curved middle-staff, the drag shoe and chain to lock the rear wheels, the splendid tyres, and the great hooks and bolts.

A familiar evening sight was the return of the huge timber wagon drawn by three or four horses, straining up Plough Hill and round our sharp corner with tremendous trunks of elm or beech to the timber yard that had once been my grandfather's. Stupidly I made no drawings of this mighty construction, nor do I know whether such a one still exists. Farm wagons now decorate the yards of country inns, or, like gypsy caravans, stand conserved in museums. Timber wagons were, I suppose, considered too large for either use, and all must by now have been broken up. But the clink of chains, the low rumble of wheels, the clopping of hooves, and the goading calls of the men are sounds of late afternoon in winter that I remember still, as keenly as I recall the raw, pungent scent of the bark and newly sawn wood.

Teaching children and adults now absorbed so many of my daylight hours and left so few weekends free that I had to postpone proving my *Autumn* plate until March, 1933. This was the first etching we printed at Old Chapel Field. I inked it at the window bench in the kitchen, where Heather also managed the damping of the papers. She prepared the press, and with her clean hands laid down the blotting and tissue papers on its bed while I brought in the warm plate and put it in position. Then she handed me the precious printing paper, which by now I had learnt to place fairly accurately upon the copper, and our hearts beat fast as I lowered the blankets, slowly turned the great wheel, lifted the blankets again and peeled off the impression. Fortunately, it seemed that it would not be wise to do further work on the plate; the few lines that were needed before a second print was taken I engraved with a burin straightway on the bare copper, and I think they were hardly distinguishable from the etched lines. We pulled only a few proofs, which Mrs Bernhard-Smith held in her XXI Gallery along with a few of my earlier plates, but none was ever sold except the one I sent to the Royal Academy that May. With it, too, I sent my first large water-colour. The subject was the deep lane – the old coffin way – that runs down Fitzurse Hill, the northern slope of our ridge. I chose that moment of early spring when the cart ruts and ditches were filled with water and fresh growths were springing in the hedges. It was bought for five pounds by Bury Municipal Art Gallery. I did not see it again until the gallery kindly lent it for exhibitions of my work in 1980 at Bristol City Museum and at the Ashmolean in Oxford.

At school we had reached a high moment of ambitious production when the headmaster decided to retire, and I was filled with apprehension about the future. This stern, austere man, with a reputation for repressive formality, had not only given me my head and encouraged me in what might well have seemed to him wild and unheard-of ventures, but he was beginning to speak freely of what he called the liberating influence of art and craft. Each new advance was a revelation that surprised and pleased him, and he did all in his power to help. I felt his departure keenly. He found a house in Lacock, the village he loved best, where he devoted his days to church music and to unravelling the history of the parish. His successor, though far less strong and given to self-advertisement, was generous with the official purse, so we suffered no material setback.

Much that was happening in my classes was old-fashioned in the sense that everyone – from the youngest to the oldest – really enjoyed drawing. Daily on my long walk I found things worth bringing into my classroom, and there was no need to draw attention to them. I was astonished to find that whenever there was a chance children would sit and turn these things about, examining and feeling them, and would use pen, pencil, brush or chalk to express not just their form and texture but the quality, the feeling, the very nature and personality of each one. Some made tiny, meticulous drawings; others swept their shapes on to the paper in large bold strokes. It seemed to me that both ways were right, so I tried to provide a very wide range of drawing materials. When they used colour too, some liked the tentative, transparent tints of water-colour while others relished the thick creamy solidity of such opaque paint as was available. It was lovely to watch children working with sensuous enjoyment, each in a world whose scale exactly matched him, and where there was harmony between him and the tools and materials he used. I was constantly shocked with delighted surprise at their immediate response: it was almost as though they identified themselves with what they chose to draw – this conker in its case, this marbled ivy leaf, or this bleached skull of a fox. I could not have said then why I particularly encouraged the drawing of natural forms. Partly of course it was because they meant so much to me, and these children with their roots in the country naturally responded to them instantaneously. What seemed clear to me was that although they would draw man-made things with zest and pleasure, these shapes and surfaces and colours from the natural world answered a special need and brought a peculiar satisfaction. A sense of wonder was very present among these children.

I think I was less surprised at their strong inborn sense of pattern, and I ultimately came to feel that it was for most of them their natural approach to art. As with all children, pattern had meant much to me from babyhood: a sound or movement or shape repeated was always satisfying. I remember how when I was two my mother would let me empty her button-box on to the kitchen table and arrange the contents in circles, stars and diamond patterns, alternating mother-of-pearl with bone, and dull with shiny. At six I would come home with other children running along the kerb of the pavement, two steps on and one step off, two steps on and one step off; and I liked laying a meal on a chequered cloth, placing the plates on the dark squares and the cutlery on the light ones. Bricks in a wall, panes in a window, boards in a floor, all patterns inevitable in construction fascinated me; and honeycomb and ferns and a halved lemon or cabbage were miraculous. All things balanced and symmetrical, sprigged and spotted, striped or latticed, and especially those all-over patterns with an ogee or lozenge foundation, delighted me. And when my mother let me loose with a fork on mashed potato while she worked wonders with one on pastry, how good that was!

I soon discovered that even the least endowed among the children I taught could be helped to make beautiful patterns, especially if the unit was not drawn but made; drawing a pattern could be both tedious and inappropriate, but cutting one as a block and holding it in the hand and printing with it was sensible and easy. Such an experience was often the starting point for those who showed few natural gifts, for through it they won a sense of prowess which often led them to venture on pictorial work with assurance. At the same time it was borne in upon me that what were then called 'artistic aptitude' and 'general intelligence' developed as one: the boy with a good mind was a good artist and craftsman. I learnt from

[74]

Cizek's Viennese children and my own Londoners not only that a love of pattern is universal but that it is not confined to strictly formal patterns: a picture is an informal pattern or design. And here were these bucolic West Country boys and girls with the same strong feeling. One would say, 'I should like to make a design out of boys playing leap-frog', and another, 'I must paint a design of the prodigal son coming home to his father'. This sense of a picture being an informal arrangement or pattern of flat shapes within a prescribed space was so strong that I could not have resisted it had I felt inclined to. Would children in Tokyo, Tuscany, or the Orkneys, I wondered, share the same view? I began to see that a child is a child the world over.

I was now responsible for the thirteen and fourteen-year-olds, and for them too design was paramount. These boys and girls were quite untouched by commercial vulgarity, but alas! they had seen hardly any good painting or sculpture, and few had travelled far beyond their own homes. Good buildings and well made implements they saw daily, and they accepted the generally sound standards of husbandry that prevailed as natural and ordinary. They liked to see a job well done, and would pursue it to the end: very few wilted by the way. It no longer mattered much that there was no provision in the timetable for the girls to draw and paint and enjoy craftwork, for I found myself gradually breaking through the boundaries of 'subjects' into a wider field. My mornings were spent with English, arithmetic, the study of the Bible and whatever else seemed appropriate. I seized the opportunity to share my love of Gothic architecture; we made our own loose-leaf books for the purpose, and we often visited churches near enough to be reached on foot. My class was quicker and better at arithmetic than I: it seemed to me to be a somewhat overrated accomplishment. We read a great deal of poetry and prose together, with emphasis on what was modern then; and every day everyone wrote. We were required to read the Bible daily, and this led to searching discussions. Constantly I presented Jesus as, above all, a Jew and a pacifist, and I did not hide my horror at the appalling conduct of the God of the Old Testament. I think the marvellously poetic language of the Bible moved these boys and girls as it moved me: we all came to know long passages by heart, only because we wanted to read them so often. Of their own accord they – and the younger children too – chose as many themes for painting from the Bible as from their own environment. These two, the Bible and Wiltshire, were the great sources of inspiration.

Like the Sienese and Florentine primitives, these children put their biblical characters and events into a contemporary setting. A ten-year-old called Edwin Pearce painted *The Feeding of the Five Thousand* in a way I shall never forget. His crowd was kept from mobbing Jesus by a cordon of policemen, all wearing immaculate boots. This boy's father was a shoemaker, and he drew carefully stitched toe caps and shoelaces tied in bows for every figure. A thirteen-year-old set *The Nativity* in a fine stone-tiled cow byre with great pillars, for which he made careful studies in his village; and his Joseph was a handsome farm-worker in pullover and wellington boots. *The Triumphal Entry* was by way of the splendid old balus-traded bridge over the river, but a few hundred yards from our school, that a foolish local council wantonly destroyed thirty years later. The shepherds watched their flocks by night on the Wiltshire Downs, and in one Christmas picture a white horse cut in the chalk was given a prominent place. Sometimes these designs were strangely dramatic and moving. A boy who had never seen Rembrandt's great etching of Abraham about to offer up Isaac used the same elements and in a similar way – a winged figure shielding the child with his right hand and staying the father with his left, and all happening in a great shaft of descending light; but the angel had a rustic head, and the father was in workman's corduroys. Another composi-tion, by a twelve-year-old, showed David and Goliath as himself in white shirt and shorts and a huge dark fellow wearing boxing gloves, with the two camps – identified by different colours – cheering and hooting as in a boxing match.

But many of these biblical pictures were lyrical and tender, especially those designed for panels of embroidery or appliqué or for decorations in books. Moses was a prize country baby in a sort of coracle on a pond among bullrushes, with sleek cows drinking nearby. And *The Flight into Egypt* showed a curly-haired young Joseph reading the white signpost at a typical Wiltshire crossroads, and Mary dressed like any young woman in the thirties. Jacob's ladder was a growing tree, and, like the sculptures on Bath Abbey which the designer may well have seen, the angels descended upside down. Not that it was strange to put things upside down. We often displayed

[76]

pictures in this way, contesting that it is a good test of a design: if it holds together and still 'tells' in that unfamiliar position, it must be good.

Only mountains and sea really defeated them. *The Stilling of the Tempest* and *The Miraculous Draught of Fishes* were both painted as cartoons for murals which were never begun. Both were stirring designs: no mawkish figure in a nightgown, but a virile Jesus with a flashing Jewish eye and commanding stance and the disciples in both were portraits of friends. But the sea was a timid convention derived from the muddy Bristol Channel. For mountains and rocky heights we drew pieces of coal and limestone, which greatly helped, though I never felt that what was outside the children's experience came over with any force. When they drew haymaking scenes these were as true as my diary entry about the Tuckers and Joe Gough, and they knew as much about harvest festivals and woodmen's work as I did. They were at home with wagons and horses, barns and cows.

So when three bright-eyed eleven-year-olds came with the proposal that they should 'make a pattern of summer' to fill the entire back wall of my room I agreed at once. The space was about eighteen feet long, and they said they would take the design to a height of five or six feet. I knew the work would take some months to finish, but I was not in the habit of setting limits. Many of the hundreds of pictures that were being painted in the school took a month or more. It was never possible to keep a group working together. But what did that matter? I found it far easier to organise classes where some children were working away independently at ambitious projects while others were needing my help with, say, the handling of a gouge or the stitching of a multiple-section book.

The main design for *Summer* was the work of a boy with the unusual first name of Milton, whose knowledge and skill astonished me. I still have his squared-up drawings that show an uncanny understanding of animal forms – prize bulls, butting goats, and heavy cart horses. In much the same way as I worked to compose my etchings, Milton Kilmister created his own world. It was a patchwork of meadows and cornfields, thick with elm trees and full of activity. There was an idyllic school, with children playing outside, undisturbed by a bull feeding near them; and there was a procession of four horses drawing a hay wagon into a farmyard. He and his two assistants drew

[77]

Summer *by Milton Kilminster, Roland Chapman and Raymond Badham*

the design on the pale grey distempered wall with no fuss at all, while below them children were at work at English or arithmetic in heavy dual desks. There was no disruption. My fears that the flat decorators' oil paints they used might prove difficult to handle or maintain in workable condition were unfounded, and none was ever spilt. Milton allowed his helpers a good deal of freedom of interpretation, but there was to be no attempt at modelling the forms: all were kept flat, though the textures of the various surfaces – hay, wool, or stone – were cunningly rendered. The mural was not finished until summer was long past, but when the day of triumph came we all rejoiced. 'It looks as though it has always been there', was one boy's comment, and another said, 'I can't remember what that wall looked like before', and we decided, one and all, that these were perhaps good tests for any piece of work.

Autumn *by Denis Noyes*

Now there was great eagerness to attack a second wall, and I gave the job to eleven-year-old Denis Noyes. He was a very different person from Milton Kilminster, preferring to work alone and obsessed with drawing figures, especially boys. They were all about his own age, powerfully athletic, and never still; they jumped, sprinted, danced, climbed, fought and somersaulted, and their calves and insteps were tremendous. I was not surprised therefore when Denis showed me his cartoon —a central apple tree laden with fruit that boys were picking and gathering, one tumbling out of the tree: on one side boys sawing wood, and on the other a group playing, and one boy diving into the river. It was a vast enterprise, but he saw it through to the end, and it was a fine decoration.

There was only one wall left, as the fourth was taken up by windows, and here Edwin, the shoemaker's son, now 13 years old, painted *Spring* in a

Spring *by Edwin Pearce*

panel fourteen feet long and five feet high. In many ways this was the most distinguished work of all three I suppose, though we always avoided such comparisons. Edwin's design was three years further advanced in both idea and technique than his *Feeding of the Five Thousand*, and it showed the same sense of humour and amusement at human affairs. He used the neat little park near his home as the setting, and he chose a windy day with a rainbow spanning the design, and crocuses blooming everywhere; a nurse was wheeling twins in a splendid pram, one of the babies holding a bundle of balloons; a boy was flying a kite, while two others were working a slot machine under a budding tree; and this group was balanced at the opposite end of the panel by an old couple on a seat under a similar tree. White fan-tailed doves were flying round their dovecote. Needless to say the nurse, the boys, and the old couple all wore immaculate polished shoes, painted with loving care. Edwin was a boy of few words. He worked steadily but swiftly, and with extraordinary sureness, knowing exactly what he wanted; and when at last his wry, Stanley-Spencerish painting was finished he showed little excitement, though to the rest of us it was an astounding revelation.

By now I had brought these children to a point where they would stop at nothing. They were so fearless and competent in handling tools and materials and so undaunted by scale and complexity that they were ready for enterprises far more ambitious and demanding more sustained concentration than the school could provide or I could easily face. I never hatched up work for them to do. They had an insatiable appetite for what they called

[80]

'real jobs', and one day a group put a new and serious proposal before me. It was a boy whose father was a foreman on the Great Western Railway who, with several others, came to let me know that he had told his father that he considered the dismal brown waiting room on the Up platform of our local station was a positive disgrace, and he had arranged with him that we should tackle it. There would be four murals, one over the fireplace and one on each of the other walls; he had worked out the sizes, and he showed me the excellent preliminary cartoons he had prepared. One mural was to be of an excursion train taking children to the seaside; another, children swimming in the Avon; a third, the river in flood at the town bridge, as happened every autumn; and over the fireplace the annual local flower show. I at once thought of all the administrative difficulties there might be, but when I asked where we should borrow ladders and store materials, and wondered what the public would do while we were in occupation, they replied with such commonsense and wisdom that I felt ashamed. I said I must consult the headmaster and the railway officials, and so put off my decision. But I'm afraid they showed by their looks of dismay that they knew I had already decided against it. Fortunately they soon became so immersed in other worthwhile ventures that I think they forgave my surprising lack of courage, though whenever I enter that waiting room – which, except that brown has given place to grey, is just as it used to be – I have a bad conscience. The murals at school were obliterated long ago, but had I not been afraid there might be spirited paintings lighting up those waiting room walls today.

There were only a few boys who wanted to draw mechanical things like trains and motor cars and the still unfamiliar aeroplane. Martin Spearey was one of these, and he produced very strange compositions of aeroplanes that he made transparent so that he could show their engines and controls in minutest detail. The figures of pilots and mechanics he dismissed summarily, lavishing all his care on the machinery. He also had an eye for a handsome building, and was so outraged when a perfect eighteenth century house in the High Street was pulled down to make way for a scarlet Woolworth's store that he made an unforgettable painting of the demolition, now preserved in the collection of children's work by the Wiltshire Libraries and Museums Service.

Martin's attitude to drawing was unique in the school. He showed the entire construction of whatever he chose to draw, and he would sometimes superimpose one view of it upon another; on the few occasions when he elected to draw a portrait he would show profile and full face in the same drawing. Picasso never seemed strange to him! Another boy, Philip Bird, rarely attempted any figurative, representational drawing. The conventions that served him as a seven-year-old he clung to at fourteen, refining and modifying them but still making them serve his ends. He painted panel after panel in glowing, luminous colour, always of subjects that asked for a strong pattern and what today we should call 'abstract' treatment: Daniel's dream and the seven days of the Creation are two that I remember. It was deeply interesting to me to watch this growth of personality in children's drawing from their infancy onwards. More even than in what they wrote I think each one's peculiar approach emerged through his art; what he accepted and rejected, what for love of it he repeated many times, the characteristic scale of his work, his attitude to detail, and his sense of colour were as clear as his own name.

Only occasionally was it possible for me to work at a drawing or painting of my own alongside a group: I was too occupied with organising the many activities happening all at once. But the older pupils, certainly, always knew what I was etching or painting. When I had finished a piece of work I brought it for them to see, and if an etching I would bring the plate as well. A few boys wanted to etch themselves, and I let them. We laid grounds on copper at Old Chapel Field, and they made their own etching needles from gramophone needles set in sticks and neatly bound with thread. When the great day came for proving their plates we had a celebration round my press, and they went home in triumph with their fresh, delightful prints, too excited to leave them in my workshop to dry.

Even in the realm of formal pattern-making children's personalities were rarely hidden, and they themselves knew one another's designs with certainty. Apart from that lovely method of combing or drawing patterns in a wet ground of paste and colour, much used in the seventeenth and eighteenth century, our work was with blocks, and these were of boxwood, potato, and linoleum. For small things like book covers and folders and for printing borders and spots and sprigs on textiles I found sticks of boxwood with square or circular ends ideal. I let a few of the most competent boys use engraving tools on them, but the majority filed their patterns with needle-files. We never destroyed a block. The most unlikely unit if cunningly arranged was capable of producing a good pattern, if only as a background texture on which to print a second block. We soon built up a collection of sticks which the children called a library. That is how they regarded it. It was for common use. They borrowed what they needed for the work in hand. Endless variations and combinations were made, which it was a constant surprise to see: the possibilities hidden in a square inch of boxwood seemed limitless. We printed on white, toned, and coloured papers, and on both tough and fragile ones: selecting what was right for the job was always a serious matter. The nicest medium was tube water-colour mixed with clear starch and applied sparingly with a stiff flat brush. Pressing the charged block firmly upon the paper with a slight rocking movement was a knack that was soon mastered, and everyone saw the need for a sympathetic printing pad made from a wad of newspaper. These small but vital matters were taught by child to child. The experts among them held block in one hand and brush in the other without ever putting either down. It was a clean, rhythmical, craftsmanlike process. No patterned sheet was consi-dered finished until it had been rubbed with colourless wax polish, which gave it a pleasant, smooth surface and also made it impervious to paste if used in bookbinding. Whenever I acquired a block-printed paper from Florence or scraps of early printed stuffs from old garments or worn-out patchwork quilts I brought them to school to be enjoyed.

For work that could be finished in one session we often used potato. Its pleasant surface, firm yet yielding, and quite extraordinarily sympathetic, is perfect for printing on paper or fine cloth, and it is extremely easy to cut with gouges designed for work on linoleum. I encouraged free cutting direct upon the potato without any planning on paper, then testing the pattern and maybe developing it until it seemed nicely workable: the tools dictated the pattern, which was essentially one that was cut, not drawn. Beautiful results came with over-printing, using transparent colours; indeed we rarely used an opaque medium, as this obscured the native vegetable texture. Inks and dyes and water-colours were available, and Indian ink gave a useful range of greys: a drop or two in water made a good silvery colour. Some of the most satisfying potato-printing was done on natural shantung silk which cost about three shillings a yard. I have pieces which are still as fresh as when these children printed them with oil-bound inks diluted with turpentine.

Linoleum-cutting seemed a natural extension of designing with potatoes. There were no new techniques to learn nor new tools to master, and the firm, cheesy substance was pleasant to plough through. I had thought we might cut blocks up to about twenty square inches, but the older boys had more professional ideas and began to design on a far grander scale. I had shown them some of William Morris's cottons printed with single blocks – *Brer Rabbit*, *Anemone*, and *Marigold* – and if he could work to that size why couldn't they? Kelmscott was only thirty miles away, and the birds and plants that inspired him there were common here too. Phyllis Barron and Dorothy Larcher – surely the greatest designers and printers of textiles since Morris – were now working at Painswick in Gloucestershire, and I had bought a length of Dorothy Larcher's *Old Flower* design, printed in galled iron on natural linen, and several pieces of cotton printed by Phyllis Barron in stripes and spots. In my small collection too were early nineteenth century English chintzes with charming renderings of fruit and flowers and garlands of leaves. It is hard to say how far the children's acquaintance with this work influenced their own and their attitude to the craft, but I am certain that in a subtle way it moulded their taste. Some of the most perniciously vulgar printed textiles of all time surely filled the shops in the early thirties, but I never found a child wanting to emulate them. The poetic feeling that informed their paintings was as potent in their block-printing.

There was the *Boy and Bird* design that was unmistakably by Denis: an athletic figure dancing among foxgloves, with a bird flying into his arms. I still have a white bedspread printed by Edwin in blue with a block called *Christmas*; angels holding wands of holly float among loaded Christmas trees in a starry sky. It is a beautifully rhythmical design in which it is difficult to discover the units, so cunningly are they locked together. When, many years later, Phyllis Barron saw it she was filled with admiration, declaring, 'Well: I don't know if I could ever do it'. There were the rugged designs called *Horse and Foal* and *Feeding Cows* by a Kington Langley boy called Bert Winch, who knew his cows and horses well, and also knew how to exploit the possibilities of linoleum to say what he wanted to say. In *Feeding Cows* a white cow grazes with a black one and a third that is piebald. The clearing away of large areas of linoleum for the first, the clean engraved white line on the virgin surface for the second, and a combination of both for the third, represented a well thought out plan; and further 'colour' and sparkle are achieved by the pretty counterchange of white line-engraved plants and grass on a black field, and black ripples and flowers on a winding white stream.

Bird's Nest, by Jasper Wood, comes nearest to Morris perhaps, with a thrush alighting on her nest among hawthorn blossom, her mate singing among the foliage. It was printed in a cool green on undyed cotton for curtains; the designer deliberately created a strong transverse rhythm of white branches and flowers which looked well when hanging in folds. Every pattern was made in the first instance for an express purpose, and this lent force to the designs. Edwin's *Footballers*, an ambitious piece of work involving two blocks, printed in two colours on a half-drop plan, was intended for the central panel of the designer's own bedspread. There was to have been a border of spectators running round it, but this was never finished. The unusually complicated cutting was managed without an error, though one of the eyes of a footballer – a little isolated island of linoleum – broke off during printing. Undaunted, Edwin drilled a hole where the eye once was and plugged a piece of matchstick into it to act as the eye, and it stood up perfectly to several yards of printing!

The business of printing wide and long pieces of cloth in restricted space and without any special apparatus was solved by the children themselves. A heavy, solid table was the prime need, and we were able to borrow one. We padded the top with carpet-underfelt and an old blanket, and this made a resilient and sympathetic printing surface. We mounted the blocks on thick laminated plywood so that they could be easily manipulated. A heavy coal hammer served as printing hammer, its handle shortened, and cushioned by screwing a rubber shoe heel into the end. Unfortunately it was not possible to print and steam-fix in the professional way; we had to be content with oil-bound surface inks, which when thinned with turps however gave a good impression without stiffening the cloth, and they stood up to washing very well. Only the quality and range of colour were disappointing. The ink was rolled out on glass with a gelatine roller and applied to the block very sparingly. Laying the block down accurately upon the cloth worried hardly anyone. Some printers worked singlehanded, others in pairs, one inking the block and the other placing and hammering it. What might have been tedious and mechanical was turned into something satisfying and good, and if at the end of the day the work was not finished there was no question of leaving it overnight. Steadily the printers continued, sometimes to the consternation of the caretaker. I remember waiting till six one night to see four yards of a pattern called *Town and Country* at last completed and hoisted on a line across the classroom to dry.

Strangely perhaps, linoleum was used for making pictorial prints only after some months of printing patterns. These children had no use for the trite little 'lino-cuts' so fashionable at the time. They had explored the techniques of cutting and engraving pretty thoroughly, and now their pictures reflected this experience. A quiet thirteen-year-old who was a fast runner made a large line engraving of a boy crouched ready to run: the poised body, taut with a sense of urgency, was marvellously expressed in fluid white lines on sheer black. In *Angels and Shepherds* another boy used only his pen-knife to cut the black shapes of sheep and kneeling shepherds upon a white ground, and the white form of an angel with stars in a black sky. When Denis was cutting his *Boy and Bird* he fell in love with a V-shaped pecking tool, and he became so obsessed with the effects he could get with it that he also used it to break into the white lines of his *Picnic* picture — toothing the rays of the sun and the outlines of his three characteristic boys, and creating also a grassy texture with it. I watched him at work, trying to collect the tiny triangular bits of linoleum he was pecking out. From time to time he would make a rubbing of his block to see how it was progressing – a sensible procedure followed by many other boys.

But it was when block-cutting, writing, lettering and bookbinding were brought together in a single piece of work that these children reached their full stature and produced what seemed to me real and satisfying craftsman-ship. The younger ones made simple books with patterned covers which they filled with writing, lettering, and pictures, but the older ones liked to embark on books that would perhaps take some months to complete. They would turn to this work as occasion arose, and sometimes would make a great burst and concentrate on it at the cost of all else. What they liked best was to have a big job in hand that they could pursue slowly and with immense care. A twelve-year-old lavished all he had on a half-Imperial-size calendar with bold numerals and a linoleum-print for each month. *The Book of Ruth*, which was never finished, was small, with stick-printed borders to every page and telling illustrations printed from blocks. All was in black and buff paper, and the result was very rich. *The Story of Jacob*, which, like *The Book of Ruth*, followed the text of the Authorised Version, had tall pages with generous margins and occasional ornamented capitals. There was an anthology of poems about animals; there were carol books and recipe books, a village history, an alphabet of flowers, and an original one-act play. And in each there was a harmony between the scale and form of the book, the work within it, and the cover. Whenever I was able to bring to school books from the Golden Cockerel Press they were eagerly devoured and at the same time critically appraised. It was this innate sense of standard that so impressed me. I remember the disgust of a boy who had mastered the binding of multiple-section books when he discovered that an otherwise well bound book that I had bought had what he called a 'false' headband: it had merely been stuck at the head of the spine. Now I had taught him how to sew the headband as an integral part of the binding, an exacting operation which he had managed perfectly, and he found it hard to believe that commerce could stoop so low.

During his last term at school Edwin Pearce saw through a monumental enterprise which arose out of his love of the *Apocrypha* from which I sometimes read aloud. Tobit, Judith, Susanna, and Bel and the Dragon were very real to my Form, but it was the poetry of *The Song of the Three Holy Children* that he loved best. He would go about chanting to himself, 'O all ye beasts and cattle, Bless ye the Lord: Praise and exalt him above all for ever. O all ye things that grow on the earth . . . O ye ice and cold . . . O ye lightning and clouds, Bless ye the Lord: Praise and exalt him above all for ever.' And it was this incantation with its profusion of capital O's and B's and L's that he chose to celebrate as a book. He folded ten Imperial sheets of heavy paper, folio, not stitching the sections until the entire work was complete. Each tall page held one couplet with its appropriate decoration below. These and the capitals were in vermilion or blue on alternate pages; the capitals were cut in linoleum, but there was not time to cut the decorations too, so they were painted. I am amazed to see that the more generic themes, such as 'ye powers', 'all ye winds', and 'ye waters above ye heavens' were attacked with as much confidence as the more concrete ones. The settings of course were local. Elm trees falling in a gale and a country woman's umbrella blowing inside out made a convincing design for 'O ye winds'. He took 'O ye fire and heat' very literally, making a pattern from flames and a school thermometer, all in vermilion. 'Ye that are holy and humble of heart' were Wiltshire farm people, one bearing a yoke and another driving to market in a pony cart, which was then a common sight on Fridays. 'Ye children of men', too, he interpreted literally, as boys in their school running clothes taking part in a relay race.

Finding stout enough boards for the cover of the book was not easy until the designer himself discovered in an obscure cupboard the very first attendance register of the school, with millboard covers of superb quality, and these he used. He printed the yellow linen for the full cloth binding with a *Holy Child* block in vermilion. It was a masterly achievement. That was more than fifty years ago, and the boy who conceived it from start to finish, so nobly and with such obvious relish, must now be in his middle sixties. I have the book still, and when I turn its pages and mark again their imaginative freshness and boyish naiveté I find myself wondering if this man still draws or designs or binds books or enjoys lettering. If he does none of these things I cannot but believe that in some field or other he is a craftsman, and that in his home he has some decent things about him. For by the time he and his fellows had reached their early teens they had had so much experience of choosing, of selecting this and rejecting that, that they had become discriminating people. I trusted their judgement and good sense. In retrospect I realise though that I cast an enormous amount of bread upon the waters, and perhaps it is as well that I have not sought to 'find it after many days'. If, as I believed then and believe now, children are potentially artists and craftsmen, they need to be taught by adults who are likewise creative; and the artist-teacher must somehow find his satisfaction in the act of communicating, of teaching, sharing, and giving, but with no expectancy of return.

What had become abundantly clear to me by the early thirties was that every boy and girl I taught was unique, with gifts and graces peculiarly their own; and that it was my privilege to create a setting or environment or, one might almost say, a climate in which these startling powers could emerge and flourish. Without the nourishment and fostering and sometimes even the protection I as a teacher could provide, these children could not have found themselves and come into their own: there lay my reward. I was the agent, so to speak, who could promote all manner of creative activities as ordinary, necessary, everyday work and play, in which everyone had a part. And I saw then as clearly as I see today that children come to the arts as their birthright: they are the most direct means through which they learn and grow. One day Harry Peach, the inspired founder of Dryad Handicrafts, came to see me – a ripe, humble man with a massive knowledge of architecture and domestic crafts, and I shared these thoughts with him. He was sure that if only we could discover and disclose it every person has the capacity to create, devise, and make good things. He went further. He quoted Morris's dictum: 'Every improvement in the standard of work men do is followed swiftly and inevitably by an improvement in the men who do it'. We laughed together and said we hoped he was right! He talked with ten-year-olds as though they were grown-ups, and they discussed their work with him as with an old friend. Before he left he asked me to describe for others the work we were doing, suggesting that I wrote first about block-printing and then about lettering, and that both books should be well illustrated. I think I began work on them quite soon after his visit, though they were not published until three years later.

My walks to and from school continued to be a solace and an inspiration. However hard the day I recovered my peace of mind on my homeward journey, and I would recite Keats' words: 'The setting sun will always set me to rights – or if a sparrow come before my window I take part in its existence and pick about the gravel.' There were dark days in winter when my pace was slow, a hard frost gripped everything relentlessly, and a criminal wind made the land look dead; and we felt under some awful darkness as of a pestilence or curse. I wrote in my diary: 'Found frozen white violet buds in the lane this morning. In the wood I watched two starved red squirrels, ready to eat anything, nosing among iced leaves, and attempting to gnaw old cones and frozen twigs. At last each found a wretched acorn, sat up prettily and enjoyed them, and then rushed on. Boys and men sliding on

Shepherd's Pond in the moonlight. The Plough would be a perfect group of stars for an etching, arching over a dark barn or thatched cottage as it is tonight.'

When the thaw came we planted a group of young aspens which looked well with our already sturdy trees of beech, lime, ash and hornbeam we had set two years before. Our postman, Edgar Wilkins – a gypsy-looking man who liked us and was always reliable and good to us, and whom we trusted – helped us plant hazels at our north-western extremity, where we hoped one day a thick copse would check the hilltop winds. The Irish ivy up our walls was growing fast, and its large shining leaves were good to see in any weather. We were becoming cosy and sheltered at last, and in but three years the roof had weathered and its colour softened so that the house began to feel old.

The spring of 1934 was early and dry. Hazel catkins were blowing loose and woodpeckers were drumming in the first week of January, and by mid-February we were wakened daily by the dawn chorus. A wren had begun to visit our bedroom, taking great liberties as he found he was safe, until he would take no notice of us if we walked past him. Our bedhead was his favourite perch, and to this day we have not been able quite to erase the marks he left. In the bathroom he would slip on the polished floor, with obvious embarrassment. I began to make drawings of him and planned to etch a wren one day.

But this spring was a sad one for us. The ways of 'Nature' are strange and unpredictable, and at the end of March Heather was taken to the cottage hospital a few miles away for an operation that meant we should have no children. But our joyful reunion at Whitsuntide and above all her renewed health seemed sufficient compensation. I cannot say that what might have been a disaster for us actually proved to be one.

In January I had finished a large water-colour of a rickyard, with aisles of ricks on staddle stones, the studies for which I had drawn last harvest time with our friend, Paul Drury. In it I had tried to distil the essence of autumn, and because of its size it had given me a fresh challenge. Now too I was becoming increasingly aware of the rare quality and luminous colour of egg tempera, and following the erudite papers of the Society of Mural Decorators and Painters in Tempera, Heather and I prepared a large mahogany panel – having slaked the plaster for two years before mixing it with parchment size of our own making for the gesso foundation. Painting with raw umber and terre verte and the exquisite potters' colours – vernalis, Perigord orange, and potters' pink – upon the ivory-white, ivory-smooth surface was a rare pleasure. My portrait of Heather, surrounded by woodland flowers, was a poor one, but it gave me the long practice I needed. I had worked out the design in such detail that I could take up the painting whenever I found a chance. By August I had finished the background of primroses, anemones, bluebells, and rosettes of spotted orchis leaves, and in the Christmas holidays I completed the portrait and sent the picture to the Society of Painters in Tempera. It was kind enough to accept me as a member, praising my painting of plants and offering tactful suggestions regarding the portrait!

It was a busy holiday. On New Year's Day, 1935, I worked at a design in ink and sepia for an etching to be called *Wiltshire Rickyard*, using the conical-topped corn ricks and barns and gateway of my large water-colour, but changing the season from autumn to spring. The huge horse chestnut was now in bloom; and instead of the bare ash beyond the rickyard I put the tall square tower of one of my favourite churches. I focussed the light upon it so that all the elements in the design converged on it and settled there beneath the wooded hills.

Next day I surrounded myself with drawings of our venturesome wren and of clumps of primroses, and designed the small etching *Wren and Primroses*. It excited me so much that I straightway laid the ground on a plate I had by me which happened to fit. But then the new term started, so I postponed the needling until a weekend in February, carried out the very straightforward biting in early March, and pulled the first proofs at Easter.

It was a strangely disturbing term. My etcher art-inspector from the Board of Education had been a regular visitor throughout the past three years, and we now knew each other well. Usually he would bring a colleague with him, but one day he came alone, looking even sadder and gentler than usual, and he spoke little until school was over. Then we sat for a full hour in his car, while haltingly and slowly and with obvious difficulty he made the suggestion – as though it was a most improper one – that I might find it interesting to be an inspector. He had been told, he said, to put this notion to me, and I mustn't hold him responsible. I must say it came as a great shock to me. He drove me to Old Chapel Field, and over supper the three of us talked over the horrid possibility. 'But wouldn't they banish us to the far industrial North?' we asked, and he agreed that that could easily happen, though to comfort us he added that such an exile was usually brief. Wisely, he gave no advice, though as he left he said, 'Wouldn't it be good to work together!'

It happened next day that that wise and warmhearted man – the inspector who lived in the little manor house at Cherhill under the downs – paid one of his frequent visits. He guessed or knew what had happened. 'Don't worry, Robin', he said. 'You've met so many of us that you know the worst already! But if you join us and they send you to Hull, don't give up Old Chapel Field.'

Heather and I together made our decision. I filled in some forms, wrote a letter, composed at my headmaster's request my own testimonial which he signed without reading!, and a few weeks later I spent an enjoyable hour one day at Whitehall over an interview. There came a moment when an elegant and fascinating woman called Miss Phillip, who was a chief inspector, asked if I would like to ask questions. So I said, 'But would you send me to the industrial North?' and with a smile she admitted that that was quite likely. Then I said, 'I ought to tell you that I am a pacifist, and if war ever came I should register my objection to it and lend it no support. Should I not be an embarrassment then?' She replied that in a free country we are surely all free to obey our own beliefs. In a week or two the blow fell. I was asked to work in the city of Leeds as an inspector from the middle of September.

Misgivings assailed us throughout the summer. Turtle doves purred in our hedges, the lawn we had made by mowing the ancient pasture was shaping well, and a lifetime's happy work to do lay at our very door. Why then had we said we would desert it for this unknown city nearly three hundred miles away? At school we were engrossed in work that could never be finished by the end of term, and there was dismay among the older children when they heard of my plans. On my last day they gave me a handsome suitcase of raw-hide which they had caused a local saddler to make for me, and one of the best scribes had lettered my name and address inside the lid. I use it still. These boys and girls had taught me so much, and

I hoped I might be able to share it with the schools of Leeds. They had demonstrated beyond all doubt their innate powers and their love of work. If there were meaning and purpose behind what was asked of them they would always throw themselves and their all into doing it. Mostly I had led them and they had followed, though in some important ventures they had taken the lead and I had followed them. They knew what I could do better than they, but they also knew what they could do at least as well as I. There was not one who was not, in some way or other, an artist, a craftsman. They had proved to me how potent a force is the quality of the environment in education. Our school had just been redecorated, and a kindly Local Education Authority had invited me to suggest how it should be done. The children and I together had had long discussions and had experimented with colour and texture and materials; and I think we effected a minor revolution. I shall never forget the response of the children generally to the change. Jam jars of naked bluebells, jam jars of crowded tadpoles, and all the sordid litter of classrooms of the period had already disappeared, and now there was a desire to make every room positively a good place to be in. Books had been habitually stored in piles in pitch-pine cupboards: desk tops wore a patina of dirt. We scraped the cupboard doors and the tops of the desks, revealing most excellent wood, which we polished with bees' wax and turpentine. We were hoping soon to have bookcases. The children's respect for the inherent qualities of materials and their pride in shipshape surroundings were heartening. But we had only just begun when I left. I still remember my feeling of emptiness on that last afternoon, and when Heather met me in Birds' Marsh, that was deliciously cool on this blazing July day, I could talk only of this. I should never teach children again, yet I had only just started to know something about them and how they might best be taught.

In August we journeyed to Leeds to find a place to live in. I had seldom travelled further North than Cheltenham, and as we approached Birmingham I thought I had never seen any work of man so mean and haphazard. But when we reached Sheffield it seemed that Birmingham was a comparatively bearable Southern place. The belching nightmare squalor on the way from Sheffield to Leeds positively froze all feeling in me. The desolation of slag heaps fed by buckets on wires strung high across the wet wastes; the imprisoned pockets of rural landscape, now sullied and choked with dirt; the occasional sight of straight streets of faceless dwellings with pitiful back gardens; blasted trees, a few soiled sheep, an unkempt pony — they all seemed too shabby, too sordid, too unloved to be real. Then came Leeds. We remembered Paul Drury's story of his father's bronze nudes supporting the electric lights in City Square, and here they were — an incongruous, Maillolesque company in this confused and blackened city.

We asked a man the way to one of the addresses we had been given by a house agent. He called us 'love', and said he was going near this place, and we all three boarded a tram. At the terminus, when he could have given us directions, he came with us; out of simple kindness he went out of his way to help, doing far more than we had asked, and we suddenly felt less homesick and that we had come to a friendly city. And we had.

7

For the bed is shorter than that a man can
stretch himself on it; And the covering than that
he can wrap himself in it.

ISAIAH (Ch. 28)

We returned to Leeds in mid-September. Our postman had tethered his
goat on our grass and said he would keep a friendly eye on Old Chapel Field
on his daily visits to tend her, and my older sister would come from time to
time to open windows and see that all was well. We left in searing anguish
very early on a warm green morning, and within eight hours we had started
our curious makeshift life in a semi-detached house in Headingley, called
The Gables – though it had no more than any house must have; it had rather
absurd lattice windows and a pathetic shabby rockery. We were to occupy
but a part of it and the rest remained empty: I think the strange owner
regarded us rather as caretakers. Quickly we made the living room look like
ours with furniture and all we needed from home, and we told ourselves the
exile could not last long.

No-one could have had a gentler initiation into the vaguely defined work
that I was to do; my mentor, Arthur Peters, was the kindest man I have ever
known. The North was his home; he recognised at once my homesickness
and suggested I should spend my first day at Adel, in the only countryish
school within the city boundary. He knew I should find comfort too in the
remarkable Norman church nearby, with its millstone-grit carvings, so
unlike the limestone work of Wiltshire. Everywhere the trees were thinning
and the gutters were filled with shrivelled leaves. The air smelt of varnish
and vinegar, pear-drops and burning paint. When I walked over a patch of
sullied grass to the school I wept inwardly at the far-off vision of bright
viridian herbage at home. But it was a good day. A shy headmaster warmed
to me when I told him I had never been a headmaster: he found that hard to

believe at first, and I think he felt I could not be the genuine article. But when he came with me into the church in the lunch hour and saw my delight at the marvellous sculptural decoration of the capitals and the unique Norman door-ring of a monster swallowing a man, he lit up and became excited. When I said how much pleasure his children must have had in drawing the carved centaur with a bow, and the horseman with his lance, he was suddenly incredulous and said they never had, assuring me that it would be far too difficult for them. I didn't press it: I felt I must bide my time. He was at any rate quiet and considerate with his children. We parted friends. When on that first Saturday he happened to see Heather and me making drawings at the church he talked happily with us and said he had been thinking . . . He would let his children have a go!

This was perhaps a false start. My days were now to be spent in getting to know as many schools in the city as I could. Most were within a twopenny tram ride from 'home', and some were in pleasant places, but many were swamped by factories and warehouses, and few were the sort of buildings in which children should spend their days. I shall never forget Jack Lane school. Was it in Hunslet? Perhaps it no longer exists. In this appalling slum a band of brave teachers brought daily joy to sadly under-privileged infant children. I walked through disgusting fogs, that left an indigo-coloured slime on railings and bushes, to reach schools which I hope have by now been demolished. Men earned a living by washing down the fronts of houses. Even in our favoured little cul-de-sac on the outskirts of the city, where we sometimes heard the cuckoo, this was a regular practice. The filthy residue of a bad fog would somehow seep into closed cupboards and drawers. In Holbeck the women, trying to take some pride in their drab dwellings, scrubbed their doorsteps and the very pavements we walked on. The struggle against dirt was never-ending. I used to carry a pocket mirror and remove the thick smuts from my face before entering a school. When, thirty years later, I paid a brief return visit, I was astonished at the marvellous change: the black buildings now almost white, and the trees looking alive at last and suffering no premature autumn.

Day after day I met more and more teachers, and evening after evening I wrote my impressions. I was free to say and write what I wanted: I had nothing to lose. My allegiance was only to the truth as I saw it. If I had power

I wasn't aware of it. I now belonged to a traditionally feared or even hated race, and knew that respect or prestige would come to me only as I earned them. It was a lonely position. No-one really wanted me: I had to work to make myself wanted. I argued with myself that perhaps the compensation for being bereft of a group of children of my own and suddenly becoming a nobody was having time to help schools if my help was sought. I found that on a first visit I could never offer help; indeed it quickly dawned on me that I could be no missionary, and that I could be of no use in any way until I was known, accepted, and, in short, liked. What was clear was that it was I who was daily under inspection by those it was my job to inspect. In and out of staff rooms it was this young man from the South-West who was being discussed, and what he said was quoted – often out of context. But the generosity of the schools to me was heartwarming, and it was not long before they asked me to address the multitude on some of the things I stood for. It was the teachers of the youngest children who most nearly shared my convictions, and the quiet woman from the local education authority who led them was a most perceptive and dedicated ally. There was comfort too within the Education Society, where university and training college and teachers met. The fight for a saner education for young children was on, and many voices were heard – Susan Isaacs, Margaret Lowenfeld, Charlotte Bühler among them. Dorothy Gardner had started her play centres in the darkest parts of the city. It was inspiriting to be a part of this movement.

At the end of October we spent a few days at home, where the elms and the grass were still green and the air was soft and the house kind and enclosing. We determined that, come what might, we would contrive to have a sight of it once in every month. Edgar Wilkins was clearly enjoying giving an eye to Old Chapel Field in our absence. His goat, Bluebell, was still tethered in the open glade, and sometimes, he said, he slept there alongside her. In June he had scythed the hay grass for us. We met him at the gate as we arrived. He had just been evicted from his old tied cottage and was indignant about it. He told us that he had dug up all his snowdrop bulbs and planted them in our copse, and had even taken up the willow clothes-post he had put up in his garden. 'Look! I've planted him in the middle of your field, and he'll make a fine tree one day', he declared. How true that was! Today its great spreading dome is hung with wild honeysuckle and ivy; longtailed tits find it a perfect nesting place; tree-creepers, nuthatches, and woodpeckers haunt it, and on occasion, when an owl takes up his stand conspicuously on a stout branch, all the birds in the garden, large and small, set up a frantic din as they mob this great immovable bird. We always know when the owl is there because of the alarming, cacophonous noise: natural enemies and friends all join in it – magpies and thrushes, tits, finches, wrens, robins, blackbirds, blackcaps and garden warblers all swoop as near as they dare, while the sphinx-like owl merely blinks at them. After our return North we met wintry weather which lasted many months. Blocks of blackened frozen snow were a permanent feature at intervals along the streets, and the sky hung low and sinister and dark. Sometimes it was as though Heather and I had lost our identity and we wondered where we were. But I had brought back with me a grounded copper plate and many drawings of wild hedge flowers, so at weekends I was able to sit at our brightest window and escape with my etching needle into the hedgerows of spring. In late December I bit the plate in my own workroom at home, and the smells of the acids mingled with the scents of Christmas: all seemed right and normal once more. I pulled a first proof, and found that a second ground for further needling was necessary, so I spent the first days of January 1936 bringing the design to its final state before we left for Leeds. I longed to take an impression, but I had to wait until Easter for this. Then all went well and *Hedge Flowers* was chosen as my diploma print when some months later I was elected an Associate of the Royal Society of Painter-Etchers.

But it gradually became clear that I must forsake etching until the day of our release: it was impossible to embark on the long and complicated process at this great distance from my studio and press, and moreover my new work was becoming more and more demanding, so that there was time only to draw and to paint in water-colour. We owed much to Mary Glasgow, a colleague who had an Austin Seven motor car; with her we penetrated the lean, spare, open country of the dales. In Buckden at the head of Wharfedale we were given a good Yorkshire supper, bed and breakfast in a spotless cottage for eight shillings and sixpence each. The wonderful bird-cherry was white in the hedges, and I drew and painted butterwort, cloud-berry, grass of Parnassus, and the mealy-leaved *Primula farinosa*. I made hasty paintings – sometimes under an umbrella – of hard, wild, upland places with names that fitted them. I loved drawing the old roads – the walled coffin way zigzagging up from Bainbridge in Wensleydale and over the moors, and the primitive green road from Askrigg to Muker in Swaledale. This of all the dales I think we loved best. From our bedroom window at the Cat Hole Inn at Keld – which is no more an inn – I painted the clustered hamlet under the stark grey heights. And I tried to paint the frothing beer-coloured water of the rushing Swale itself, and its wanton waterfalls and boulders and sapling ash trees taking root in impossible places. The pastures were thick with mountain pansies, and curlews called. It was a country less mauled by the twentieth century than our own, less cluttered too, and as indigenous; yet I could not think of it as a source for my etchings. I found finely forged gate handles to draw, a magnificent ashwood hay rake and other old farm gear, yet something came between these things and me. I was a stranger in a strange land. I could admire and love this Northern world but it wasn't in me to feel a part of it. Yet oh, the solace of those clean, empty places after the squalor of Leeds!

There were now three of us young inspectors, as Bill Elliott had joined us, and our benign senior colleague must sometimes have found us difficult to hold. We would frequently lose him, so that instead of sitting long over an indifferent lunch in Betty's restaurant we could explore the city. We instituted what we called 'constructive lunch hours', when we went in search of 'glass dumps' – those ingenious domes of crude glass imprisoning cut paper flowers and beautifully disposed bubbles of air, which glass workers made for their own amusement; or we would go to a news theatre in City Square, or pore over the incredible water-colours in the Art Gallery, or try to find beauty still in the once splendid abbey of Kirkstall. We owed a lot to each other.

There were many days when I was alone. Sometimes I peddled my wares, taking a portfolio of Wiltshire children's work to schools that were beginning to believe that boys and girls might have powers that they could set free. But that was a poor and unprofitable method. Even in infant schools teachers were wary and slow to accept what seemed to them strange, untried ways, and the teachers of older children were so set in their attitudes and methods that it seemed they would never change. All I could do was to appreciate and foster any faint sign of growth and be thankful wherever I found a happy atmosphere and an interest in discovering some of the ways in which children learn best.

Sometimes I was asked to speak at teachers' conferences and meetings in other parts of Yorkshire. On a foul day in February I travelled by train through the inferno to Sheffield University at the request of the National Union of Teachers to talk to Sheffield teachers about 'Child Art': that was the title I was given. 'Child Art' was now a controversial topic; reverberations from London, where Marion Richardson was bringing zest and colour into the lives of thousands of young children, were heard in the North; wild claims were made by some, and there were passionate denouncements from others. I could only speak about my own work with children. In the lecture theatre where I was to give my talk I spent the afternoon and early evening setting up a display of prints and paintings, block-printed textiles and books, and I was flushed with excitement when I surveyed it, for I thought it was beautiful, and I felt I had my Wiltshire children there with me. I was left alone until six-thirty, when the theatre quickly became packed. The crowd swarmed round my exhibition, and left the textiles I had so carefully hung and the books I had arranged all in disarray, so I deliberately took my time to restore order before I began to speak. Then I told my simple story, illustrating my points by referring to particular pieces of work. But I was howled down by angry teachers who protested that this was not the work of children. At first I lightheartedly laughed them off, but the more I revealed of my story the more violent became their refusal to believe me. It was nonsense to pretend that children were artists, they shouted: I had cooked up all these paintings myself! They jeered and stamped when I described the making of *The Song of the Three Holy Children*, and a crowd of men at the back of the theatre made a great groan when I showed the *Christmas* bedspread and its beautifully cut block. I stood my ground, but with difficulty. It was only the insult to the spirit and talent of my pupils that hurt me: I wanted to have Milton and Edwin and Denis and the rest there to be vindicated. I fought on till I had said all I had intended to say. A tactful chairman tried to thank me, and my last words to my audience – and I managed to smile as I said them – were, 'One day you will believe. Remember tonight when you do!'

I was left alone to dismantle the exhibition. As I was folding the abused

Boy and Bird and *Feeding Cows* two schoolmasters about my own age came quietly back and, with great sensitivity, helped me pack. 'Don't you worry about them. It was grand', they said. 'One day they'll learn.' We went out into the miserable night, and they accompanied me to the station, and over our glasses of beer we were able to laugh at the foolishness we had witnessed. I still bless them for their understanding, though I have never seen them since.

My faith was restored when some weeks later I took part in a course for teachers of young children which a group of inspectors had organised in Chester. When the first speaker began I felt I was looking at a martyr about to be burned at the stake. He stood, lean and erect, his greying hair seeming to wave like flames and his all-seeing eyes magnetising us all, his long fingers gripping the lapels of his jacket of lovat tweed. His book of notes lay closed before him. 'Children move – because they must', he declared. 'Children speak – because they must. They touch, explore, make, and this is how they learn and grow.' He uttered these simple truths as though for the first time, in the loud authoritative voice of a prophet. 'Children never stand still. They change. A child is a different child every day. No two are alike or ever will be. Children live only for the present. Our job is to help them fulfil to the full their present stage of growth.' The conference listened, awed and intent, as though to a doctrine that was shockingly new – as indeed it was to many present. For exactly an hour, in the simplest words, this passionate, almost fanatical man, Christian Schiller, pleaded for an education in which the nature and needs of children rather than the convenience of teachers would dictate its content and method. I listened enthralled. Everything my Wiltshire children had shown me was confirmed. I felt happy and bold next morning when I showed the conference the work I had displayed at Sheffield and told the story I had told them. It was an easy hour. A few who doubted were anxious that I should remove their doubts. And this dynamic man, with his visionary countenance and sinewy, gesticulating hands, leapt to help me. He was electrified by the paintings and craftwork I showed, and with a vitality I had never seen in any human being before he asked questions about them and became deeply involved in my story, so that by the end of the session we were firm allies. I did not know then how much he would teach me nor how often and with what satisfaction we should work

[101]

together for more than twenty years, fighting and sometimes losing the battle against official philistinism, fighting and sometimes winning. I learnt more from him than from any colleague. No man has influenced primary education in our time as much as he.

I returned to Leeds reinforced and mightily encouraged, and although my senior colleague, who was himself a conformist, expressed doubts and fears about what he considered the extremist views I had shared, he left me free to sow what seeds I could. More than that, he encouraged me and bade me accept as many invitations as I could to speak to groups of educationists. I must confess that I accepted more readily those that took me to the South or West. Every year in July the Board of Education held a number of courses for teachers simultaneously in Oxford, and it was good to work there with my old art inspector, Reginald Green, and other artist colleagues. The cramped working conditions at Norham Gardens and the crude standard of living in Balliol College did not prevent us from making headway with a group of teachers gathered from far and wide. We block-printed and made books, and we drew and painted in the countryside and in Oxford. It was all very calm and leisurely, settled and pleasant, but I missed the fiery call and challenge of Chester.

Work at courses kept me in the South-West until October, when we returned to face a second desolate industrial winter. Always the blow of returning was softened however by the hospitable welcome, with a Yorkshire tea, from our neighbours – on one side a young editor on the *Yorkshire Post* and his family, and on the other an elderly university lecturer on dyestuffs and his wife, who always seemed glad to have us back. And by now I positively looked forward to almost every visit I paid to the schools. I was among friends, who though perhaps not prepared to go the whole way with me were at any rate eager to test fresh ideas and broaden the field of their teaching. To this day I remember vividly many talks over excessively strong tea long after the children had gone home; or I would find myself sitting next to a schoolmaster on a tram, and unable to finish our discussion on the journey we would stand arguing about 'centres of interest' or children's art in a cutting blast straight off the Pennines.

I journeyed far afield to inspect art and craft in training colleges and secondary schools, and much appreciated the bonus my visits gave me of seeing for the first time the cathedrals of Durham and York and the sumptuous sculpture in Beverley Minister. But I trudged also through Rotherham, Barnsley, Dewsbury, Batley, Morley, and Ossett, and cursed the greedy capitalists who had raped this once lovely land. I was rarely moved by any of the work I was shown in the schools, and I was not able to contribute to its advancement. I returned from these long days dispirited, for I saw the need for the revolution that did not come till many years later, and I was powerless to help to bring it about. Unfortunately, in Leeds I was becoming too closely identified with art and craft: some schools looked upon me as a luxury, I fear, and expressed surprise when I showed interest in children's work in language and number. I think what the schools appreciated most was that I had all the time in the world to give to their problems. There was no hurry. Because I was far away from home, and thus relieved of many responsibilities, I could devote all my waking hours to them. Only occasionally at weekends did I feel free to draw.

Heather and I had entered upon a major piece of work together – a book called *Wiltshire Village*, that she would write and I would illustrate, and Collins would publish. Since I had begun in the twenties, with her help, to draw the farms and cottages, the gates and stiles, wagons, wells, and the flowering plants of North-West Wiltshire, I had amassed a vast number of drawings; and she had made many notes about people and their work and seasonal changes. Our plan was to epitomise the character and life of the region in a village of our own invention yet true in every detail to one or other of those we knew so well. It was with a strange sense of foreboding at this troubled time in Europe and disastrous change in rural England that we set out to record the ordinary and typical as well as the more noteworthy while they yet remained to be recorded. Heather was to write in her foreword: 'To call back yesterday would be foolish even were it possible; but in order that what was noble in the yesterday that still lingers might not pass unhonoured and unlamented this book has been made.'

On Sundays particularly I would make my pen drawings while Heather wrote; she would try out some paragraphs on me and I would submit my illustration to her. We worked extremely closely: the words and the drawings must be one. I found it comforting to draw our old fingerpost at the crossroads near Castle Combe, with its oil lamp at the intersection of its arms; and I so loved drawing the cheese room and press of a farm we knew well near Westbury that I determined one day to celebrate it in an etching. There were straw rick finials to draw, a local smock and sunbonnet, a foot plough, and the tools of our thatcher and basket-maker. Our progress was slow, but the work gave us a strong sense of belonging and of purpose, and we cherished it. And as there was no pressure of time upon us we could work at our own pace.

Late at night on the first of July 1937, we arrived at Old Chapel Field for a few days with Mary in her Austin Seven. The air was heavy with the scent of elder and honeysuckle; our postman had scythed the hay grass, and my sister Olive had put flowers on the scrubbed kitchen table. We beat the bounds in the half-dark, and were soon asleep under our brooding brown roof. Next day we found a hundred different wild flowers on a long woodland walk in hot weather. Then back to Leeds, and the usual heavy post of brown official envelopes to open; but among them the glad news that I was to leave Leeds and work in Gloucestershire in the autumn! My mother was very ill, with no hope of recovery; the long journeys between North and South were wearing; and I do not think we could have lived this double life much longer: so the relief was overwhelming. At the end of the month, on a sullen morning as uncharitable as winter, we said goodbye to the friendly people and left the dark city for our own country.

I bought a motor car and was taught to drive as part of the bargain. Until I had passed my test a young mechanic accompanied me on my journeys to Cotswold schools, teaching me en route and employing himself in his own way until I could join him for the return drive.

I followed in the footsteps of an elderly inspector of extraordinary independence and with an appetite for history so consuming that it governed his whole way of life. He rejected the motor car, and chose to reach the schools by bus, on foot, or even sometimes on horseback. The official school files I inherited from him told me far more about this gentle, ruminative, penetrating man than about the schools he visited. He transformed their ugly manila-covered files into enticing local histories. On each he wrote these words: 'To that Colleague who succeeds me, Pray . . .' and then followed his injunctions, begging his successor first to visit the church and to take note of this or that particular feature, to be sure not to miss seeing the tithe barn or the wagon works or to walk the old bridle ways. The derivation of the place-name was carefully unravelled, and there were notes on old families, on surviving customs, native plants, and unfamiliar birds. Often too there were references to the old school log books: 'Pray, read the valedictory words of the retiring headmistress in 1905,' was one such entreaty. And this is what I read: 'Today, I, Eliza Gainey, with great relief, retire from this school. For 35 years I have been the dustpan – nay, the dustpan and brush – of the vicar of this parish.' My colleague, who was always indefatigable in his researches, added a note to say that 'on retiring this weary woman married a well-to-do farmer, and never set foot in church again.'

My last meeting with him was in a drab boarding house in Stockport where he lived on leaving Gloucestershire. My *Harvest Festival* etching which I had given him was the only picture on the walls of his room. We talked long about his beloved Cotswold churches, and he told me how when he had first entered a particularly remote and ancient one that he now loved best of all a grave gentleman in antique dress had led him gently from nave to chancel and up the belfry steps, lovingly describing in biblical English every detail of the building. 'And then he vanished', he said, declaring positively that this was a ghost.

The first school I visited was in a remote Duntisbourne valley much loved by F.L. Griggs. He had etched the tiny church with its saddleback tower rising above the turf and stone walls of the hillside, and it was good to be there. I found the older children reading *As You Like It* from Blackie's Plain Texts, after which they were required to repeat exactly what they had read, which they did with incredible and meaningless accuracy. It was very strange and not a little unnerving. The next lesson was Nature Study, when the teacher read from a book called *Mother Nature and Her Children* a chapter about molluscs and shellfish, and she showed little monochrome pictures. Again came the uncanny 're-narration', as it was called, and again with quite extraordinary results. Wreaths of berried black bryony draped the hedge outside, and I had just found the large bleached shells of Roman snails in the wet bank. But when I talked to the children of these things they were uncommonly shy, and some were silent. Their teacher – a very dear person whom I came to know well and liked very much – explained 'the system', as she called it. Every school was struggling with *As You Like It* today, and every school today was learning about molluscs and shellfish; and it was clear that within this prescribed, confined and confining practice the results were striking. Outside it the children were inarticulate and unenquiring. The dead hand of PNEU (Parents National Education Union) lay heavily on the schools of this beautiful countryside: its resources, its history, and its whole indigenous character passed them by. A foolproof method kindly designed to help families abroad serving 'the Empire', the often untrained governesses teaching small groups in large country houses, and the unqualified teachers in private schools was sadly inappropriate here. True, the 'supplementary' teachers at this time – of whom there were many, particularly in rural schools, and 'monitresses', who were not supposed to teach but often did – found PNEU a blessed prop and stay. Indeed an authoritarian director of education, now retired, had decreed that there must be adherence to both its substance and its prescribed method, and examinations set and marked by the Union were taken regularly. It all seemed singularly un-English and feudal to me: it stifled initiative, it bored, and it drained the colour out of life.

The second village school I entered I found empty. The foxhunting parson had ordered the children and teachers to come and see him at the meet that morning. 'Oh, but Canon always wants us to be there', explained the servile headmistress afterwards. For the first time I used my power.

I arrived at my third school too early, but even after I had enjoyed the lettered memorials on the walls of the church against which the little one-teacher school was built I could still hear the droning of hymns and prayers in the classroom. I sat in my car and waited, for in those days HMI did not enter until religious teaching had ended. I listened. The teacher asked in a loud voice, '*Who* were the Jews?' and the children shouted in chorus, 'The Jews were the *wicked* people who crucified Our Lord.' Six times the question was repeated, and six times, on this perfect autumn morning in this perfect Cotswold village, I heard from those innocent, mishandled children the anti-Semitic reply. It was a difficult start to my day. I greeted the teacher – a singularly loud, humourless woman who spoke patronisingly and tactlessly to the children – and told her who I was. 'Then you can help me', she shouted. 'Come here all you who are left-handed. Stand by the stove.' And

[106]

nine of the twenty-one gathered round the fire guard, looking guilty and ashamed, and the teacher threw them a look as though they were lepers. 'And this gentleman can see that most of you are boys', she growled. 'Boys suffer from the disability more than girls', she told me. 'Now what would you advise me to do with them?' Here was my chance. Being left-handed myself I stood with the lepers, and I told the teacher and the children that I too 'suffered from the disability', and that it was of no consequence whatever whether we are right or left-handed; that the world is made up of different people – left and right-handed ones; black, brown, and pinko-grey ones; Jews, Gentiles, Muslims, and many others, and none are better or worse than their fellows. Throughout the day I wrote on the blackboard a good deal, ostentatiously with my left hand, though I could have done pretty well with my right. And before the day was over I was able to tell the teacher what I had heard – and what any passer-by could have heard – as I had sat outside the school. She was surprised at my alarm, but she spoke quietly now, and said she would think about it.

My colleague was a tired, lame, elderly, scholarly man, much loved by the schools, whom I met but rarely. At the end of any day we spent together he liked me to drive him up to Painswick Beacon and there to read him the *Sonnets* of Shakespeare. When I expressed my horror at the stifling effect of 'the system' and the ways of autocratic parsons he smiled wanly and reminded me that I was young. He died the following year, and the schools deeply mourned his loss. His place was taken by a man with a malady that restricted his activities, though he struggled to lift the yoke from the schools. But his greatest passion was clocks. He chose a house full of corridors, he said, so that he could display his clocks to advantage. There were more than a hundred, and he knew them all by name and tended each one with loving care. They cuckooed and chimed and played hymn tunes, and some had figures that danced or popped in and out or clanged a loud gong: every quarter of an hour in this over-inhabited house some event in the vast clock family took place and the walls trembled. Next to clocks he loved statistics, by which he proved to himself all manner of things which I am afraid had little relevance to the way in which children's time was being used. It was clear to me that 'the system' would continue until it died a natural death.

When, on my round of first visits to country schools, I sometimes felt defeated – unable to find some spark of life – I used to picture how my friend Edward Walsh, the inspector who had made me tell him my first name at our first meeting, might face the problem. Sometimes I longed for him to be there to help me remove the ancient barrier of distrust and fear of the unknown that still existed. I did not need to picture how nearly a century ago Matthew Arnold had dealt with similar situations, for I had read his reports, which made this clear. He saw his job in a purely inspectorial way. His prime concern was to see that money devoted to the education of the poor was properly spent. He tested and appraised, and within the limits of 'The Code' he made suggestions. He found infants 'an inconvenience' that 'clogged and impeded' the progress of the older children, so he advocated separate infant schools. To his eternal honour he fought the monstrous 'Revised Code' of 1862, with its intimidating system of grants based largely on annual examinations. But the development of educational ideas and any change in the relationship between children and their teachers, or teachers and inspectors, were no significant part of his work. Who then was I, a young ex-elementary school teacher, to want to challenge the status quo or share my beliefs about children with these settled, easy-going schools? Yet had not Arnold said that the whole purpose of culture is to make the best that has been thought and known in the world current everywhere? And the children in the schools were surely being offered but a tiny morsel of the best. I had been so stirred when first I read Arnold's report to the Queen after his visit to Europe in 1865 that I had copied a passage into my commonplace book: 'The aim and office of education, say many people, is to make a man a good citizen, or a good Christian, or a gentleman; or it is to fit him to get on in the world; or it is to enable him to do his duty in that state of life to which he is called. Of course it is none of these! And the modern world more and more discerns it to be none of these. These are at best secondary and indirect aims of instruction; the prime direct aim of education is to enable a man to know himself and the world.' Surely then I was not over-stepping my duties if I saw my work as a balance between inspecting, in the narrow sense, and trying to promote advance. But it was an alarming responsibility. I was let loose in the schools for good or ill. No-one told me what to do. I could leave them better and happier than I found them or the reverse.

[108]

There were teachers then, as there have always been, whose spirit transcended the cramped atmosphere of the time and led them on to great triumphs. I often remind myself of what English education owes to the vision and courage and skill of these men and women – for the most part anonymous and unhonoured – who, decades ago, anticipated the ways of teaching current today. 'Family grouping', the 'open plan', and 'the integrated day', to use contemporary labels, were present then – often of necessity in the close communities of village schools. I remember a teacher on Severnside whom I first met carrying into school a load of logs for winter fires in the open grate of her tiny infants' classroom. The children helped her, taking them two at a time and stacking them in piles of ten in the corner of the room, and I shall never forget their delight and satisfaction when they discovered that there were exactly a hundred logs in the load. She had sheep in her orchard, and would bring a lamb to school which sat on her lap while the children gathered round and talked about it. She grew cider apples, and would bring baskets of Bess Poole and Morgan Sweet at their best moment of ripeness for the children to eat. She lived such a real, full life and was so free with her possessions that the children lived a rich life too; there was always so much to do and talk about, and so much to write and read.

I remember another pioneer in a Forest of Dean village famous for its plums. I arrived on a somnolent afternoon to find the class of infants with their heads down on their uncomfortable desks apparently asleep. 'Are they resting?' I whispered when I had told the teacher who I was. She led me into the stuffy little cloakroom and pointed to a row of empty medicine bottles on the window sill. 'Well, technically, they're inebriated', she smiled. 'You see, everyone here makes plum wine, and the mothers say it is very good for their little ones, so every child brings a full medicine bottle with sandwiches for the midday meal. I can't do much with them in the afternoon!' But she did. Like her colleague with the cider orchard she shared her whole everyday life with these boys and girls, and they were truly educated.

There were moreover concerned teachers who fought for more civilised conditions in the schools. In some there was no drinking water on the premises, and many had only primitive earth closets. I took a parson to see what was provided for the children in what he was proud to call *his* school; but when I showed him the wooden seat with its two holes, one small and one larger, over a couple of buckets, he protested, 'But my dear sir, you attribute a sensitivity in these matters to our country folk which they certainly do not possess.' As for the teachers themselves or visitors like myself, there was often no provision at all. I found my own in lanes or woodland, or I was given the hospitality of the school house.

I came to know many school houses, for as I became well acquainted with the teachers they liked at the end of the day to sit over a cup of tea in their homes and talk. It was then that we exchanged cuttings of plants or I gave advice about a new carpet or admired some improvement they had made in the house. I felt that these occasions, perhaps more than the hours spent in school, were when we made real progress together. The loneliness of their work and their singularly ill-defined place in the village community made them look upon a visit as a real event, and they were loth to bring it to an end. There was little communication between schools, and scant encouragement from any other source.

I also came to know the homes of school managers and the rectories of more enlightened parsons. My visits to the school in the beautiful if self-conscious village of Stanton in the North Cotswolds always ended with tea at a perfect house, where its owner – a frail old lady in a lace cap and magnificent jewels – would sit with me at an open window and feed nuthatches with pine kernels from her long translucent hands.

At Sapperton, Mrs Ernest Gimson was always told of my visit, and she would ask me to come to the remarkable thatched house that Ernest Gimson built. Talk about the school was usually brief; in that austere, woody room where we always sat, with her husband's and the Barnsley brothers' furniture fitting it so perfectly, and Griggs' etchings on the white walls, our talk was soon about these artist-craftsmen and their work at Daneway; and we rejoiced in the example of Morris and Emery Walker, of her husband and her near neighbour, Norman Jewson, but also of fine craftsmen still at the height of their powers.

For me, the greatest of these were the textile printers, Phyllis Barron and Dorothy Larcher. I combined a first visit to the school at Painswick with a first visit to them. Heather and I had slowly added to our collection of their work that had so influenced the children I taught, and we wanted to buy more. It was Barron – as she liked to be called – who met me at the doorway of their great stone house. She stood, large and handsome, in clothes of her own printed stuffs, with beautiful buttons, I noticed, and wearing brogues that looked like men's. I loved her fine, authoritative voice. 'I think education is horrible. I never really learnt to read, and I still can't spell', she said. 'Whatever do you do in schools?' At that moment Dorothy Larcher brought coffee in exquisite eighteenth century china, and we sat drinking and talking and laughing about 'horrible education' in a room that seemed to me more harmoniously and subtly beautiful than any I had ever seen. Hangings, covers, cushions were all their own; every detail of every thing was perfect, and the room was a wonderful expression of their attitude and way of life. Dorothy was small, yet there was a feeling of power about her as great as Barron's: the 'marriage of true minds' was wonderful to sense. Barron brought out what she called a rag bag of printed silks and linens and cottons, and she pressed me to take some to show to teachers. There were a few scraps that Dorothy did not want to part with, and she made a little heap of them. 'You can't go about making yourself little nests,' said Barron, but I was glad I wasn't allowed to add those bits to my collection. 'You etch', said Barron. 'You know, I hate etchings. I used to watch Therese Lessore at the smelly business; but of course she did give me the idea of block-printing by nitric acid discharge. She showed me how when she splashed spots on her indigo smock they bleached out pure white. Yes, I owe that to etching. But all those wan, empty places Griggs etches give me no pleasure at all.' I also learnt that she hated my hero, Morris, largely because in his later years he had allowed what she insisted was mass production, and because of some unfortunate encounter with his daughter, May. Yet we had responded acutely to each other at this first meeting, and had gone a long way together, and there started a friendship that was to be fruitful beyond anything we could have guessed then.

Later that year she asked to see the stuffs my Wiltshire children had printed and the book I had written about them, and she began to take a critical interest in children and schools, seeing all manner of possibilities with the freshness of an artist from outside the official world of education. Her directness and simplicity were a shock and a tonic to me. Not for some years did she actually join me in teaching teachers, but I knew already that I had met a born teacher.

1938 was an anxious year. After a blinding illness my mother died at the end of January, and was buried near her mother, with a simple oak headpiece like hers, which I designed and two of my brothers incised. Nearby is the grave of my grandfather and his wife, with its carved stone cover and a grandiose iron railing round it. The three graves still tell their tale plainly for those who can read it.

Spring came with a tenderness and splendour we had never known before. It was easy to believe that according to the records March was the warmest for a century: the sun shone golden every day on daffodils, primroses, celandines, and every flower of spring. But the haunting beauty of this fabulous season was made poignant and bitter by the news that reached us daily from Germany. The stories of the unspeakable treatment of Jewish people revealed by the *News Chronicle*, the *Manchester Guardian*, the *New Statesman* and *The Friend* – virtually the only journals to publish the truth instead of supporting 'appeasement' – were more than confirmed for us by Heather's older sister who was teaching languages in the Baltic port of Stettin. She was doing her utmost to help Jews and aid their escape. Knowing we had offered asylum to any refugee she entreated us to 'give a holiday' to a boy of eighteen called Dietrich, who was being harassed and hounded, and whose life was threatened by the Nazis. As Quakers we knew the procedure and made immediate application. Our book, *Wiltshire Village*, was almost finished, and Collins gave us advance royalties on it, so we were well able to guarantee the maintenance demanded by our Home Office. But the deliberate dilatoriness of this exaggeratedly official department amounted to cruelty – that peculiar, gentlemanly, English brand of cruelty by delaying tactics. The brave, laconic, urgent letters from Dietrich, who knew hardly any English, were terrible to receive – when there was no progress to report. It was not until April 1939, after countless reminders and jolts from us, that a permit was granted. Only the advice of the German refugee who had taught German to Heather in Leeds – to try for a permit for Dietrich as a farm trainee – had saved him. We had persuaded a reluctant farmer in our village to agree to give him a start, and now suddenly, because work on the land was urgently needed, the permit came through in three weeks. It was given not to save a life but to win labour.

He arrived on the day he was due to be put into Dachau concentration camp. I was to meet the train from Harwich at Liverpool Street station in the small hours, and he was to claim me from a photograph. The weary, bedraggled trail of refugees limped past, but I was left unclaimed. In terror that the Nazis might have seized him after all I rushed to Woburn House, the headquarters of the German Jewish Aid committee, and there in the whirl and turmoil I got a kindly official to shout, 'Dietrich Hanff! Dietrich Hanff!' At last he heard his name above the din and came smiling up to me – a cropped, sallow slip of a boy with 'prune-dark eyes' and all the sorrows of persecuted Jewry in his sensitive face. He looked so young and so defenceless that I felt a great surge of protective love for him. We went by taxi to the office of our publisher, where I had to discuss some details about the illustrations in our book, and 'Billy' Collins was so moved at the sight of Dietrich that all he could do was to order food and drink for him. These were the last things he desired after his buffeting journey, but he saw the kindness behind the gesture, and did his best. In the train he slept soundly with his head trustingly on my shoulder. My youngest brother had made furniture for his room, and he was soon at home in it. But whenever I recall those first weeks I see him standing at the windows, looking pensively into the spring garden, not wanting to venture far; I watch his sorrowful, peaceful absorption in the music of his beloved Bach and Beethoven; and I hear him wrestling extraordinarily skilfully with a strange language and contriving to communicate to us the hopeless plight of Jewish people in Germany. His parents, his grandmother, his brother with his wife and child, all were trapped there. We applied for permits for his mother and father to come to England, but restrictions being ever tighter they were not granted until the outbreak of war. This was the end. When the Nazis started their 'liquidation' in Stettin all Dietrich's relatives were taken to Lublin and murdered in the gas chambers of Piaski.

Where life had seemed complete for us two it was now a perfect harmony of three. Heather and I would whisper during the night about this mysterious happening: why of all the thousands of refugees who might have come to us should it be this boy? We shared not only similar social and political views but even the same sense of humour; and although he was a city boy with untrained hands he found he was at heart a countryman, and his response to craftsmanship was immediate. We took winter walks in Birds' Marsh to mark what he called 'the progress of Nature', for it delighted him that there was no dead season. He watched me making studies for a small plate called *Lesser Celandine*, with a background of wild strawberry leaves and a white violet. At last I etched the *Wiltshire Rickyard* design that I had begun four years earlier and I pulled a first proof for the 1940 Royal Academy exhibition. But already the whole of life was becoming darkened by war. It seemed that a high wall was slowly closing in upon us, and all that was good in the world was being smothered. We swore however that we would not let it swamp us: I began a commonplace book which I called *Memorable Speech*, and which is still a constant companion.

We also began work on the studies of woodland plants suggested by the publisher of *Wiltshire Village*. Heather would dwell on the long history of this strange company, the derivation of their names, their characters and uses; and I would draw each one – not as a cut specimen but growing in its own setting. I began at once. I drew winter aconites and stinking hellebores in the snow; in early spring I made studies of wood sorrel and the rare asarabacca and yellow gagea; and, as the season advanced, that strange witchy limestone flora of the dark beechwoods – broad-leaved helleborine, herb paris, the bird's nest and fly orchids, and the parasitic toothwort and yellow bird's nest. It proved the greatest solace to me throughout those dark war years to explore with my pencil the gentle intricacies of twayblade, the subtle forms of wild columbine and martagon lily, and all the patterned veinings and flower symmetry and infinite variety of textures in the generally unnoticed, the self-effacing plants, like sanicle and dog's mercury, cow wheat and enchanter's nightshade, spurge laurel and moschatel.

Wiltshire Village was published as war broke out, so it was hard to rejoice at its kind reception by reviewers like Robert Lynd. We sent copies to our friends at Christmas, little knowing that when the edition ran out there would be no more, for the bombing raids of 1940 destroyed the blocks.

It was possible at this time to buy great treasures from the antiquarian booksellers of Bath and Bristol at little cost. I bought the first edition of James Sowerby's *English Botany* – the entire thirty-seven volumes at which he worked from 1790 to 1814 – for five pounds. I suppose those three

WOOD SORREL

thousand hand-coloured copper plates were quite the most comprehensive national collection that had ever been made in any country. Their astonishing truth makes them by far the most reliable British flora: whenever I need to identify a flower I turn first to Sowerby. And I turn to him also for the refreshment of his clean, astringent drawing, the unerring beauty of his colour, and his uncanny identification with the personality of each plant – its growth and stance, and those features that make it unique. Sowerby is an abiding influence.

While he was working at his incomparable engravings of plants Thomas Bewick was engraving his little miracles on boxwood for his *General History of Quadrupeds* (1790) and the two volumes of the *History of British Birds* (1797). I bought both works for £1! They were early nineteenth century editions with the wood engravings wonderfully sympathetically printed on good paper. Like Sowerby, Bewick remains my constant companion. He renders fur and feather and sleek hide with startling skill informed by astonishing knowledge; but it is the cold Northern landscapes, with their intimate and unflinching realisation of hard country life and the details of ferny hollows and water, that hold me even more than the engravings of animals and birds. A whole world, astoundingly articulate and complete, is held within each tiny vignette; there is no more to be said.

As 'the war effort', as it was called, gave excuses to farmers to despoil the countryside, and as the old life we had known for so long was further threatened, we clung more passionately to it; and one of our most enduring comforts was the *Diary* of the Rev. Francis Kilvert from 1870 to 1879, which William Plomer had edited and Cape published in three volumes in 1938, 1939 and 1940. Kilvert was born at Hardenhuish, little more than a mile off; his mother and her ancestors had lived in our village; and much of the diary was written in his father's parsonage at Langley Burrell, a few meadows away on the opposite side of the valley. I read entry after entry, hungrily and with excitement, for here were loving and vivid descriptions of places I had always known. On my way home from school I used to pass a clearing in the wood near the keeper's cottage with the mossy stumps of old trees ranged like stools under the oaks, and now I read how Francis Kilvert and his friends, in true Victorian style, had picnicked here in 1874. On the twentieth of June, 1932, I had written in my diary: 'Today we found the

ASARABACCA

richest coloured dog roses we have ever seen, growing among the hollies at the top of the field below the Ridge – deep red, almost carmine when in bud, and very flushed and dark-veined even when fading'. And now I read what Kilvert wrote on a June day some sixty-six years before: He had walked to 'the top of the long green meadow near the double-roofed grey house which stands upon the Ridge' and there noticed a rose that had twined round one of the hollies growing there. 'The spray was starred with blossoms,' he wrote, 'not pale pink or white flowers, but roses of a deep rich red fit to twine round Ettie's lovely brow or wreathe in her dark clustering curls'. Ettie's brother lived in the double-roofed grey house and Kilvert often walked from his father's parsonage to see his sweetheart when she stayed here. But the romance was short-lived, and he never passed the Ridge without a feeling of great sadness. On a spring day in 1876 he wrote: 'I went on past the head of the steep green lane in the site of the old Chapel and burying place where my great-grandfather was laid to rest . . . I lingered some time leaning over my favourite gate, the Poet's Gate, and looking at the lovely view. From time to time I looked back through the fringe of trees at the chimney stacks and double gables of the Ridge and half expected to see dear Ettie coming round the turn of the lane . . . At length twilight began to fall on the wide and beautiful landscape. I turned away with a sigh and a heart full of sad sweet tender memories, and passed over the village green among the pleasant friendly greetings of the kindly village people. I always seem to feel at home among these people in the village of my forefathers.' So when my aunt had said to me as a boy, 'No: we never go there. They say it's holy ground. An old chapel was here long ago', she was right. And the mysterious domestic looking wall at the corner must have been a part of its boundary. Were the saplings of ash and aspen that we had planted standing above the grave of that eighteenth century squire, Kilvert's maternal great-grand-father? That this parcel of land should be so immortalised somehow made it more dear to us, and it further strengthened my longing to crystallise in designs on copper the essence of these ferny lanes and sloping fields.

It was not until six years after the publication of the *Diary* that the field of the Poet's Gate came into the market, and we bought it. 'The wide and lovely landscape' remains as Kilvert knew it, and the field gate is now a fine traditional one made by a young local woodworker, bearing an incised inscription dedicating the meadow to the memory of Francis Kilvert. But it was not until many years later that by a happy chance we were able to read the family papers of his great-grandfather, Walter Coleman. It was in 1778 that he had planned to build his chapel or mausoleum and laid down his curious regulations regarding the burial of his family and its use for 'divine service or meditation by any Society or Persons professing Christianity (except Roman Catholics)'. In his will two years later he wrote: 'I do order my body to be decently and privately interred in my Chapple . . . and do give £50 to finish it, and I decree that the body of Sarah Stevens, now buried at Kington St. Michael, be brought and placed as near me as possible.' She was his twenty-two year old wife's aunt. Her niece Elizabeth had married Walter Coleman at Calais a few months before the birth of their first child. He did not live to see his mausoleum completed, and was buried with his ancestors at Kington St. Michael, though an entry in the Parish Register records his removal to 'his own Chapple at Kington Langley'. His widow refused to pay for the last load of building stone when urged to by her lawyer, and she re-married two years later.

So we presume that Walter and Sarah lie beneath the camellias and azaleas and ivies of our own planting, near a part of the retaining wall of the chapel, which is all that remains. If the ghosts of Walter and Sarah walk they are friendly ghosts. Goldcrests and long-tailed tits, garden warblers and blackcaps and the neat little turtle dove have all nested above them, and the place is as undisturbed as ever it was.

The winters of the war were as hard and long and brutal as the war itself. Sordid human misery was matched by weather of unremitting violence and severity. On January 28th, 1940, heavy rain froze as it fell, and all through the night we heard alarming crashes as the elms all round us cast their branches. By dawn every tree was distorted and mutilated. Even the smallest twigs in the hedges were crystallised inside thick ice, and every grass blade stuck out grotesquely like a fat glass finger. Rose hips and hazel catkins encased in shining ice were sinisterly beautiful. When the wind rose there was a loud tinkling and jangling in the trees – a high, shrill chime we had never heard before and never wanted to hear again.

In those barren months with not a sign of spring, people talked of invasion. A farm labourer in the Home Guard, stationed in the lane at a road stop 'against the enemy' – the obstacle chosen being a superb mid-nineteenth-century hay wagon – expressed the stupidity of it all: 'Got to sit by one o' they' was all he could say. Already, aliens had had to face a tribunal, and at one of these Dietrich had been declared exempt from internment – but not for long. On a day in early July I returned home to find that police had searched our house 'for bombs', had confiscated Dietrich's parents' letters, and a book of playful verses Heather had written for him as possible codes to the enemy!, and had taken Dietrich into internment. When a country gives way to hysteria it no longer remains civilised. Dietrich was treated abominably. From the filthy disused cotton mill in Bury, Lancashire, where the internees were herded he was allowed no communication with us; only a letter of Heather's printed in a smuggled newspaper, condemning the inhuman attitude to internees, told him that we were fighting for his release. Later he was sent to the Isle of Man, where – after a determined struggle over permits – Heather visited him and was even allowed, under military guard, to take him out for a meal. The exaggerated precautions, the darkened windows of his place of confinement, the ridiculous restrictions, and the cunning coercion to get these refugees to join the Pioneer Corps were all part of the national panic. The only alternative condition for release was food production. This was arranged for Dietrich to do. But he could not return home for the absurd reason that we had become a 'protected area' because the headquarters of the Admiralty had been evacuated to Bath. So friends of ours at Filkins near Lechlade offered to employ him, and at last he was released.

We were to meet him in Oxford and drive him there. But where in Oxford? We were slowly driving towards the most likely place, the railway station, when we suddenly saw him, looking unkempt and unshaven, resting on the seat that stands at the junction of the Banbury and Woodstock roads. In her excitement Heather leapt from the moving car, and there never was a more joyful reunion. He was now speaking what he laughingly called Emigranto, but almost by the time we had reached Goodfellows at Filkins his English had returned.

At the end of 1940 Heather fell desperately ill, and did not return from hospital until March. In those days a hysterectomy was a dangerous and hazardous ordeal, and I am haunted still by the memory of sitting by her bed in a tiny room at our Cottage Hospital, watching her colourless face as I regulated, according to the doctor's instructions, the flow of the blood transfusion that saved her.

Another hard winter followed, and with it a further deterioration in human standards. War was made the excuse for wanton vandalism by farmers. In my diary I wrote: 'The field across the lane where Dietrich found the frog orchis, and the big meadow beyond – that has the richest variety of flowers in the village – have both been ploughed. This year the spotted orchids stretched for nearly a quarter of a mile, and white-flowered bugle and the melancholy thistle flourished as never before. Good oaks are being felled everywhere, and many beautiful young elms and ashes that cannot possibly be of use as timber are being ruthlessly cleared.' The sandy ploughed land proved hopeless for growing wheat, and was soon a shabby acreage of weeds.

With the exhortation to gardeners to become more self-supporting we had greater sympathy. On a hot July day I drove to a village in South Hampshire to buy a white Saanen goat called Elfenbein and her captivating kid called Heidi. They bore the journey amicably, appreciating the sprays of ash leaves which I gathered for them from time to time. It was dusk when I led them into our little green glade. Elfenbein shunned the pretty wooden shelter my brother had made for her, and settled down under the great willow tree. I need not have been anxious about the first milking. Heather held her and fed her while I performed the unwonted act. Instinctively I pushed her udders upwards rather than down as I gently squeezed them, and she warmly approved, allowing nearly three pints of marvellously rich milk to squirt down into my can. We bore it in triumph through the dark, and declared we had never tasted such good coffee as we made next morning. Soon we were making butter by shaking the cream we had skimmed in a glass jar. Heather made a good cottage cheese from the skimmed milk, for this was still as rich as cows' milk; and from the whey she made yet another, pressing them both under flat irons. We felt we were living in luxury. But no-one had warned us that goats do not graze but browse; nor that they are fastidious to a degree; nor that they become most sensitively attached to their owners. Every time I drove away, Elfenbein, on hearing the car, set up a pitiful bleating; and if she saw us walk out of the garden that too was more than she could bear. She loved an unchanging domestic life. Heidi would sometimes come indoors, when she liked nothing better than to sit in Heather's lap. But it soon became clear that, as we were allowed no ration of concentrates to balance the diet of green food and roots we could provide, we should have to part with them; only owners of a herd could obtain rations. We found one who was ready to take our lovely white-tasselled pair. He was a gentle person who sensed our anguish at parting. Like traitors we led Elfenbein into his trailer, and Heidi playfully followed. Elfenbein stood erect and stared straight ahead, never turning to watch us: it was as though she were going to her execution. And as the van slowly drove away and disappeared round the bend of the lane we were filled with grief and dismay, and wept together.

It was hard to concentrate and apply ourselves to the work in hand. It happened that we had bought several thousand bulbs of the single snowdrop from one Dorothy Eyre who lived near Chepstow and whose name became a household word with us. She was constantly offering large quantities of bulbs and ferns at a very cheap rate because, she said, she was about to sell her property; but this continued for many years, and we bought more and more! As I knelt in our hazel copse, planting snowdrops with my hands in the damp and easy sand, I found my fingers touching cool, soft, rounded forms that sent up the most deliciously concentrated aroma of mushrooms as I pressed them. Truffles! I called Heather, and we gazed in amazement at our rare and scented find. We were afraid to disturb the little colony, and hastily covered it, since when we have never discovered more.

Our friends in cities made us a repository for their treasures – their love letters, an unpublished novel, their paintings and drawings. We never revealed to them that after a raid on Bath a stray bomber had shed the last of his load where the melancholy thistle grew, shaking the house and opening a fissure across one of our floors.

At the end of 1942 Dietrich was grudgingly allowed to return home to live, although confined to a five-mile radius; and when he was not working in the garden Heather coached him for the London Matriculation examination, followed by Intermediate Arts of London University. He was drawn to teaching as a profession, and after the war he spent periods in Bristol schools.

As the months dragged on we felt more and more confined, impotent, and isolated. How often Heather and Dietrich and I wished we could 'join in' with the majority, feel moved by the feeble rhetoric of statesmen, and be carried away by the smug fervour of the times! For we knew we were witnessing the supreme folly of civilisation. Every government was uttering monstrous lies, which most people believed. 'In wartime', said Churchill, 'truth is so precious that she should always be attended by a bodyguard of lies'. Everywhere, now, the prime aim was mass murder: killing was extolled and honoured. If a few people were ennobled by their wartime experience the majority were shamefully degraded by it. We lived from day to day in a claustrophobic world of bewilderment and despair, for there seemed no end to the dark tunnel through which we groped. I had not been asked to relinquish my work, only to declare my willingness for military service. Instead I registered my conscientious objection. As a civil servant I had of course to be punished for this, and the penalty took the crude form of losing all increments to my salary as long as the war lasted. It seemed an odd price to pay, yet it was perfectly in keeping with the mindless ways of officialdom then. My seniors at the Board of Education resented it, and did what they could to show understanding of my view: they would have been surprised if I had acted differently. In cases of trouble over schoolmasters who refused military service they often asked me to help, and in Bristol schools, where I now spent much of my time, there were young men whom I was able to counsel and advise. Ever since our marriage Heather had augmented our small income as an examiner in English for the University of Cambridge. Now too she worked for London as well, and without her help we should have found it hard to manage on my frozen salary of £480 a year.

Night after night the Western sky pulsated with the fires of air raids over Bristol twenty-five miles away, and the morning journeys through the bombed and littered streets were a hideous nightmare. On a wild March day I arrived very early in the poorest part of the heart of the city to find a secondary school for which I had great admiration reduced to an unrecognisable smouldering ruin. The headmaster, in dungarees, was trying to salvage soaked books from the wreckage. By some strange chance his own desk was the only thing in the school left unharmed. He took me to see it. Not a paper had been disturbed; there was a letter I had written him a few days ago and there, too, was his handsome little eighteenth century mahogany letter press I had often enjoyed handling when I had sat talking with him there. 'Now you'll take it', he insisted. 'I always call it yours. Take it, please, before the next blitz comes.' And I cherish it and use it still. In 1973 I pressed the entire edition of the little plate, *White Violets*, in it, remembering as I did so that large-hearted schoolmaster, now long dead, who gave it to me as we stood in the sodden, twisted remains of his beloved school.

He and many like him contrived, with extraordinary ingenuity, to provide as stable a life for their children as they could. Although life now was ragged, makeshift, and temporary, and there was little rest, yet sanity prevailed in most schools, and the teachers – particularly those of the very young – far exceeded their normal duties; they resisted squalor, they improvised, they would not let themselves be frustrated. They turned towards the arts. This was an almost universal gesture against the dehumanising influence and utter futility of war. With a bizarre assortment of such materials as could be found they and their children worked zealously with their hands. Nothing brought such a satisfying sense of building up in the midst of destruction, of creating where all around was chaos. Indeed, my most indelible memory of those lean, grey years in the Bristol schools is of a positive life in the arts. There were appalling problems everywhere, and there were weeks of anxiety and despair, yet it was this clutching at the arts as to a lifeboat that I most vividly remember.

I spent some weeks helping groups of teachers at courses in the arts, organised by those more enterprising and far-seeing education authorities who saw the need for such periods of refreshment. One week I might be sleeping on a camp bed in a permanently 'blacked-out' schoolroom, the next in a cramped cubicle in an old training college, and the next in a comfortable hotel. When an artist colleague and I worked for a few weeks in the Village Colleges of Cambridgeshire and stayed in a Cambridge hotel I had a room overlooking a garden and the water. I was surprised the first morning on rising to find a dove comfortably sitting on my dressing gown which I had thrown over an armchair. As I gently persuaded her to yield up the garment I found she had laid an egg upon it. She continued to sit on the egg, quite undisturbed; she watched me shave and dress, and then I sat and made drawings of her. At breakfast I mentioned this event to the landlord, who became excited, saying that as his stock of doves was so depleted he would be extremely glad if he could induce a pair to breed. He suggested that I should change my room, but I assured him I was happy. When I retired that night my armchair was still occupied, and soon after I had got into bed my dove's mate flew into the room and settled down upon me. Every time I changed my position he protested with a gurgling sound, but was not to be dislodged. Early next morning he flew off, but the hen bird once more watched me shave and dress, turning her beautiful head jerkily as by clockwork. I made more drawings of her, and she even allowed me to stroke her. It was then that I discovered she had laid a second egg. I told the story to my colleague, who unfortunately told it to other guests, who asked to see the phenomenon. But I soon realised I must firmly decline. Night after night the mate returned and roosted on me, and morning after morning the sitting dove watched my ablutions – until the last day of my stay. Then a new chambermaid, on seeing 'a great pigeon', as she called it sitting in the armchair, drove it out of the window and threw the nearly hatching eggs out as well. But the sad story had a happy ending. Some years later Heather had occasion to stay in the same hotel, and was greeted warmly when it was discovered that it was her husband who had had the doves in his room. Evidently the pair had ultimately bred successfully, and the stock was well replenished.

The only etching I completed during the war was the small plate, *Lesser Celandine*. Our daily news was only of death and destruction, and most people were so consumed with finding enough food to eat that they had little time or interest for the new life that returned with each cold, late, wartime spring. Yet the celandine's polished brass, the pleated leaves of the wild strawberry, and the slender-stalked violet came back unchanged and as beautiful still as when Chaucer looked upon them. Here was pure, unalterable, final simplicity and peace in a raging world, and that is why I turned to them. The wild animals and birds were at peace also: only superior, civilised man was at war, and proud of his insane invention. Only he resorted to makeshift, ersatz materials to serve his substitute-world: the long-tailed tit wove her marvellous bag of lichens in our honeysuckle and lined it with tiny white feathers and hair as fastidiously as ever. The travesty man had made of his 'dominion over all the earth' was indeed both pitiful and despicable, and daily he was discovering more evil and more certain means of poisoning the very air we breathe. Even the rosettes of marbled celandine leaves were now in peril: at a touch of a finger the whole earth could be annihilated: nuclear horror was let loose on Hiroshima in August 1945, and the war was soon brought to an end – if end it could be called, for every war sows the seed of another. Heather's mother died in September, still unaware that the war that had clouded her last years was over. We were beginning to feel orphaned and old; so much had been taken from the goodness of life in five years, so much had been squandered, so much beauty irrevocably destroyed, and so many standards abandoned that it was hard to take heart and begin to rebuild and re-create. The first World War had brought a whole long epoch to a sudden and appalling close: the second clamped down on the damaged and sullied age that followed, and left it yet more deranged and demoralised. In but three decades more havoc had been wrought than in the three centuries before.

We mourned for a lost Eden. Farming was becoming a noisy, mechanised, stinking business. Wagons, ploughs, and the horses that drew them were all disappearing. Wood and stone were giving place to asbestos and corrugated iron. Care and grace, and the old slow pace and the old thoroughness and craft were all abandoned. The farm tractor was now king, and speed was all-important. Thatched ricks, cut-and-laid hedges, shocks of corn and cocks of hay, handmade wooden gates and stiles, were rare sights now. The stone-breaker was no longer needed since the white limestone lanes were tarred. Flowers that once were common had become rare, and only a few of the old mixed pastures escaped the zeal of farmers keen to sow 'leys' without a 'weed'. Those who never saw Edwardian England can have no idea of its beauty. Old photographs show this with great poignancy. True, the children pictured in them often look cowed and ill clad, and the men and women are bowed with labour, but that need not have been the heavy price paid for beauty and naturalness: the brash angularity of today, its harsh shapes and unsympathetic textures, its litter of poles and wires, its makeshift, temporary appearance, lie like an ugly palimpsest upon the old countryside.

My first and deepest longing was to make some assertion that goodness must be reclaimed, some celebration of the beauty of the natural world. I

LESSER CELANDINE

wanted to stamp out the base squalor of war and pursue my vision of the ideal world that could be ours had we but the will and courage to work for it. My sky should be cleared of aeroplanes and my landscape of pylons: my meadows should be filled with flowers again.

So I chose the idyllic month of June to celebrate in an etching – that untarnished time when spring runs into summer. And I chose to let a path run between perfect hay grass and moon daisies to meet a stone stile with a spray of unblemished dogroses growing across it. The stile Heather and I had drawn at Westrop a year or two before we were married: a monumental piece of work that still stands today, timeless and solid and perfect. And I let my path run through another meadow of hay grass, lit by sunlight streaming from a thundery sky. And I chose to let it end at a farmstead where the conical ricks are without flaw, the stone barns and gabled house are uncluttered, and corrugated iron is unknown. The square church tower gleams silver, and there is perfect peace.

It was a well-omened plate. My acids were now nine years old, yet they bit evenly and well; and the small print that at last emerged from my press in the autumn of 1946, though far from my ideal, made me eager to continue the craft. I little knew then that it would be twenty-four years before I should again have enough leisure to become absorbed in its exacting intricacies. My life as an inspector was to steal all my working hours.

JUNE

8

Enlarge the place of thy tent,
And let them stretch forth the curtains
of thine habitations! Spare not! Lenghten
thy cords, and strengthen thy stakes!
For thou shalt break forth on the
right hand and on the left.

ISAIAH (Ch. 54)

The first schools to shake off the restrictions of war and take a bold leap into the future were those for the youngest children. England owes more to that stalwart band of women teachers born in the early years of this century than it will ever know. The 1914–18 war robbed them of husbands, so they gave their lives to bringing young children into their own. Most of them were Fröebelians without knowing it: their vision of a good life for children tallied with his, though few might have read his writings. They were passionate and unshakable in their beliefs; they were clear-eyed and simple, and possessed of such true knowledge about the natures of children, their needs and their ways of learning, that they were able to create schools the like of which no-one had ever seen before, and some reached undreamed-of standards.

I suppose there are more eccentrics in England than in most countries, and probably more in the teaching profession than in any other. Vision and the courage to pursue it must inevitably single out a man or woman from the crowd, and every pioneer must face misrepresentation, stubborn opposition, and a certain loneliness too. Yet patiently and surely the chosen path is pursued, and in time those who spurned the way may come to follow it, and so advance is brought about. Most of those great eccentrics in our schools, from whom the best education of today has been inherited, have passed on unrecorded, but I would remember one here among the many I knew so well – a teacher of infants in Bristol.

This fearless, large-hearted woman, Margaret Gilvary, who never lost her childlike directness and lust for life, left her beloved Ireland in the late twenties and taught as an uncertificated teacher before training at what was then called Fishponds College. I first met her during the war at her nursery school in a comparatively new housing estate, and I remember the occasion vividly. An anxious-looking three-year-old clutched my hand, and he never left me throughout the visit, saying 'Daddy! Daddy!' as we walked about that serenely happy haven for children from two to five. She talked to me about Ireland and said my face reminded her of a Cox's Orange Pippin. Some might think that a bold thing to say to an HMI, but she was nothing if not frank and unguarded. She kept what can only be called open house at her school. Mothers, fathers and grandmothers called, and it was an education in the love of humanity to listen to her concerned conversations with them and to her shrewd advice and admonitions.

It was with a heavy heart and some misgivings that she left her nursery school in the spring of 1949 to open an infant school on another tradi-tionless estate, though it was here that, until her retirement nearly ten years later, she was able to make her greatest contribution to the education of young children.

A wise Local Authority consulted her about the new building, though its office must have had some shocks and surprises. She asked me to visit the school with her before it was quite complete. 'What colours would you have the walls and ceilings?' she asked. 'None!' I replied. 'Children's gay clothes and books and toys and flowers and pictures will come into their own in a clean, neutral setting.' We went to the dining hall. 'Of course, I shan't use it for that purpose,' she said. 'I want each group or class in the school to be made up of family units – brothers, sisters, cousins, friends – from five to seven plus; and I shall like to see these families eating their meals beauti-fully, taking as long over them as they please, in the rooms where they work and play'. She showed me the lavatories. She knew I would condemn the provision of a urinal for her boys, for I had often said what I thought about the uncivilised practice of standing in a row against a wall instead of being allowed to use a water-closet. 'Well: it will make a fine sand pit', she declared. And it did!

She and her band of courageous young teachers together made that school as beautiful as any I have ever seen. The force of the environment was so deeply felt by them that they spared no pains to create one which, both humanly and materially, was a comfort and stimulus and joy to every child. They poured into it their all. The meticulous planning of each day and the care lavished on the development of each boy and girl were extraordinary; and the effect upon the whole community was tremendous. But like all pioneers and prophets she had her detractors: a local doctor would advise parents against sending their children to a school where, he said, they only played and were taught nothing. In truth, the children's competence in using their mother tongue and in reading, writing, and handling number was very high, and more than that, their independence and poise and their eager response to the full life they were given were heartening to everyone.

It was my privilege to write the first report on the school, and on the occasion of the inspection I suggested that she might care to write something about the school for my colleagues and me to read. Here are extracts from what she wrote;

The parents of the estate were not good neighbours. Some felt superior to others. They quarrelled and tried to segregate their children; there was no social sense, no feeling of community. As we took possession of an unfinished building it filled with mostly unhappy, insecure, clamouring, indifferent and fully licenced children. But that first half-dozen youthful teachers and I gathered courage; we called a meeting, and 300 men and women came to see what we intended to do with their children, and I think we never looked back.

Now this is what I believe. Our main purpose is to civilise. We must give children a rich life, but calm, free from strain and pressure, in a place where they can live and grow joyously, securely, and cleanly. I believe in the discipline of good books; I don't worry whether they understand the meaning of all we read to them if I see they are catching a love of beauty and cultivating a rhythm in their lives. So we plan the day subtly, so as to give unbroken periods for work and leisure. Our whole job is to encourage learning. There is a clearly defined thread running through the day, but so fine as to be no hindrance; yet so consistent as to give security and build up stability. Above all, a school must be a welcoming, warming place, filled with wonder. We have to win the five-year-olds: then all is won. Steady, exploratory living, in a considerate and peaceful atmosphere, is all I crave for children.

We must be sparing of regulations, and even the youngest boys and girls must

[132]

be free to continue what they begin, and must be helped to see it through to a satisfying end. Industry has to be encouraged all the time, but there must be fallow periods as well: even what looks like idleness will perhaps be left untouched by the teacher in her wisdom. In a harmonious community children will assume unheard-of responsibility, and we must foster this. They will attack vast enterprises. Let them learn to choose and select.

I want to send out civilised, courteous, thoughtful, healthy, questioning, vital, real human beings, of high purpose, with self-control and a love of good things. In all we do we must be mindful of their needs and not our own, and of their immaturity and their weakness. We can afford to be prodigal with our most precious possessions: bring them into school, no harm will come to them. They will be a profound influence. Only the best is good enough for our purpose.

A day of sharp breaks, of chopped-up compartments, of competing and goading, is not real life at all. Every child has to be helped to do something well: it is in all of them: we have to find it. We have to do a lot of standing aside and watching, maybe, before we know how to find it. And this is an important part of our work.

All I aim for is the proper enrichment of these children's lives, the best growth of their powers, their generosity, their affection and compassion, their personalities, their judgement.

That credo of hers was shared by a growing number of infant school teachers, and now at last the belief that junior schools too should be liberated became articulate. For the first time in our educational history young men began to show a vigorous concern about children under twelve and a desire to teach them. That inspired movement, the setting up of what were known as Emergency Training Colleges throughout the country to meet the pressing need for teachers, was to make one of the most far-reaching contributions to primary education of our time – though not without discouragement. It was in these new colleges particularly, where many of the students were men returning from the Forces, married, and with children of their own, that a strong wish was expressed to teach in primary schools.

I remember how, at a conference of HMIs and administrative officials from what is now called the Department of Education and Science, I was howled down when I spoke of this keen interest among men and said I felt it was something to be warmly welcomed. It was asserted that no man worth the name would ever choose to teach anyone under twelve, that in any case men would be quite unsuited for the work, and that it would be a waste of public money to attempt to train them for what was essentially women's work. Christian Schiller and other allies were not present alas, and few would support me. I asked why we had ever bothered about the philosophy of men like Fröebel, Pestalozzi, Rousseau, Comenius. (Piaget was not yet a star in the sky!) I insisted that many of the best recruits to Emergency Training were men who were anyhow determined to dedicate themselves to primary education, and that to try to prevent them would be absurd. 'But no man will serve under a woman head', said one. 'Only a weakling would waste himself on eight-year-olds.'

But the primary-minded men in the colleges won – and Dietrich was one of them – and happily today they show that teaching young children is a challenge big enough even for the most distinguished among them. A primary school today without men on its staff is almost unthinkable.

In the late forties and the fifties a broader view of primary education was widely manifest: even the inspired ideas of the 1931 Report of the Consultative Committee were at last in some measure being absorbed. A change of heart and attitude was discernible in more and more schools; and there was a far greater expectation of achievement from those children fortunate enough to be given a chance to realise their powers. What was done in the best schools was neither new nor startling; life was simple, quiet, and meaningful; children were helped to advance at their own best pace in a non-competitive atmosphere where no-one was allowed to fail. To meet the needs and develop the gifts of every individual was the prime aim, and the ways in which this was achieved were – and still are – legion. Never before had the personalities of teachers and their powers of communication counted for so much. Never before had boys and girls of eleven become so poised and confident, so eager and enquiring, so well-informed and competent. There was a spirit of adventure abroad; fresh ways of coming to grips with learning were being explored and tested, and old ways gone sterile were discarded. The blind alley and the cul-de-sac were left empty: there was a great surge forward and outward into the light and the far open distance of the unknown. It was exhilarating to be working with schools and colleges at a time of such dramatic change and growth and achievement. We supported one another, and even sometimes I think we inspired one another. Certainly no-one struggled on in isolation and without sympathy. Progress was in the air. The vast amount of hard work to be done was accomplished with zest because it seemed right and inevitable. For me now there was much travelling, with long periods away from home to teach and lecture at conferences and courses. And because at last art and craft as a way of learning were coming into their own, I always carried with me great loads of exhibition and working material. The estate car I had bought for the purpose was always full.

After these periods of intense activity and community living there was always the blessed, restoring homecoming, with the long exchange of news round the fireside. But the burden of responsibility for house and garden and local affairs which Heather had to bear alone at this time was tremendous. Fortunately she had never known loneliness, and has always been, to use her phrase, 'too afraid to be afraid of anything'. Now her father's health was rapidly deteriorating, and as often as she could she continued to cycle to the old family home seven miles away to help care for him; it was a time of endless labour and searing anxiety.

The early months of 1947 were colder and more disastrous than we had ever known. From New Year's Day until mid-March we lived in a frozen waste of snow, over which there raged a brutal, paralysing wind. All life came near to annihilation: birds were pitifully tame, and it was hard to keep them alive.

At the end of February I was taking part in a conference at Yealand Manor near Carnforth in North Lancashire. A blizzard was blowing when I started very early on a Monday morning on the long slow train journey home. At Carnforth station I slipped on the frozen stairs and sprained my left ankle, so I was glad of the long rest in the train. Because of a national fuel shortage the compartment was cruelly cold and no food or drink were available. But I rejoiced when I arrived some time after midnight at Chippenham station, to hobble the three miles over the empty silent land to Old Chapel Field. My case was heavy and my ankle painful, and when I had left the town it was not easy in the murky dark and deep snow to distinguish between lane, grass verge, and hedge. Sometimes I found myself brought to a halt by fallen elm branches, or I would trip over a mound of frozen snow

[135]

and have difficulty in retrieving my precious suitcase – the one the children had given me when I joined the inspectorate. But when at last I gained the brow of the hill near home, and it was still just possible to discern the familiar shape of Shepherd's Pond, I was filled with joy. I had never been so happy to be under my own roof-tree as I was in the sinister early hours of that frightening March morning.

Next day a horizontal blizzard brought the heaviest fall of snow we had ever known. Our windows were glazed over, and deeply sculptured drifts blocked our doors. Then there was sudden sunshine which shone dramatically on the wings of snow along the hedgerows and on the iced tops of the trees and the down-sweeping branches of our white poplar that tinkled and crackled in the north-east wind. At night the full moon shone bright on trees of silver glass.

Then came the thaw, and with it a mighty gale that felled the two fine elms at the Poet's Gate in Kilvert's Meadow – a sad loss that we knew we should never become used to. I took my first walk down Morrell Lane, climbing over other fallen trees, and returned with plum-coloured blackberry leaves, grey in reverse, mustard-coloured kexes of ragwort, and a frond or two of cow parsley, and felt like the dove returning with the olive branch to the Ark.

Spring was late but poignantly beautiful and restoring. Dietrich left for college in May, just as the turtle dove had arrived. Summer was splendid and autumn bountiful. In October I set cuttings from Kilvert's bright dogrose in our garden. In late November a noisy, rasping cricket established itself on our hearth; it would sit at peace, with arms akimbo, looking out at us from a crevice between the bricks, and would screech so loudly that we ultimately bore it into the garden – only to find when it was too late that crickets cannot stand cold weather.

Although to etch was out of the question now, few days passed without some minutes for drawing. In boring official meetings a kindly colleague would always pass me a pristine sheet of HMSO paper, and at the end of the session would claim what I had drawn. It might be a nude, or an abstract doodle, or – more frequently – a plant or a tree. Sometimes on Sundays I was able to work at the illustrations and dust cover for a King Penguin book, *Flowers of the Meadow*, for which Geoffrey Grigson had written the text.

BUTCHER'S BROOM

Nicolaus Pevsner and the gently persuasive R.B. Fishenden used me as a guinea pig, for the method of reproduction was quite new to England. First I had to make a fine line drawing of each plant with a brush. A very faint reproduction of this was then given me to paint in full watercolour, and upon this was superimposed a firm printing of my original line drawing. When there was no faulty registering the result was convincing, though a number of the published copies were imperfect. For me it was a solace sometimes to leave the problems in the schools and take up the problems involved in rendering these likenesses of meadow sage, great burnet, chicory, sanfoin, meadow saffron, elecampane and other cherished meadow flowers that the war had brought near to extinction; and in 1948 the little book was published.

My younger brother had been deeply interested in my work for the book, and was eager to see it finished. But tragically this magnificent giant of a man – athlete and craftsman of quite astonishing power – was suddenly laid low by a tumour on the brain and felled as ruthlessly as our great elm trees. A year later, in one of the hottest of all Aprils, Heather's father – the most truly happy and contented man I have ever known – died also. These two had played a great part in our lives, and in a sense their presence has never left us. Daily we use the furniture my brother made, his bowls and platters of oak and yew, walnut, sycamore and burr elm. And the lifelong diary which Heather's father kept is so packed with everyday detail that to read it is to feel this wonderful human being is with us still.

When I joined the inspectorate I was assured that administration – in which I had no interest and for which I had neither aptitude nor training – was never likely to be part of my work, but increasingly now that position was being challenged. Only by standing firm and refusing to be diverted from what I knew to be my proper work was it possible to devote my whole time to inspecting and advising. The two were intermingled. I had never looked upon the 'Full Inspection Report' as a whip with which to lash the schools, or as some sort of punishment, or even as an examination. When I had got to know a school well, so that there was complete openness and trust between us, it was often the school itself that suggested or asked for a full inspection. If the school was large enough I would share the work with one or more

SWEET VIOLET

colleagues, and I think the event was anticipated with real pleasure all round. The schools felt cared for because of all this meticulous attention, and they found satisfaction in having an appraisal from people who had nothing to lose, no local allegiances to consider, but only a desire to share and to help. So I think of these many special occasions as happy and constructive ones; and I remember too the dinner parties in country inns or city hotels to which I would invite the head, to mark the end of each.

I inspected in order to advise. Indeed, 'adviser' would perhaps have been a more appropriate title than 'inspector'. Certainly the greater part of my time, especially on my many pastoral visits, was spent in listening, in sharing problems and interests so that I could identify myself with them, and in giving guidance and lending a hand.

Undoubtedly the most likely part of my own work to have any influence was the many short courses and conferences in which I took part from the last years of the war till my retirement in 1964. It seemed to me that these tremendous, concerted efforts paid even richer dividends than the inspection of schools. Educational ideas could best be shared in retreat, so to speak, away from all the responsibilities of school and home, in a pleasant place and in the company of others seeking refreshment, enlightenment, encouragement, knowledge, and practice. So it was that all over England there were courses of a fortnight or less designed solely for this, where the dissemination of ideas was made easy through discussion and visits to schools, and – perhaps most vital of all – through the personal practice of a craft or skill such as movement and dance, design, writing, scientific obser-vation and recording, or some other aspect of children's learning.

The first national course – for teachers and lecturers concerned with primary education – was hardly a success. The northern college where we stayed was still suffering from the privations of war. The gaunt, graceless building was cold, and food was meagre. I remember one classic evening meal when the course came near to mutiny. We each received on a large dinner plate a tiny horny slice of tinned meat and a slice of bread (cut up the day before, and stored in a chest of drawers which was the haunt of cockroaches). This was followed by a lemon. Lemons were not plentiful at this time, and the encouraging sight of bowls of them down the long institu-tional tables caused us to hope for pancakes. After waiting long for them to

[140]

appear, someone asked one of the maids what the lemons were for. 'You're to eat them', she replied. Now I happen to like eating a lemon as one eats an orange, so I reaped a full harvest that night. But I sent home for hazel nuts from our copse, and distributed them freely among the company to assuage their daily hunger.

The few simple ideas about educating young children upon which the course was centred are now so generally accepted that it is hard to believe how vehemently most members resisted them. Yet they co-operated wholeheartedly as adults – though not as teachers – in a final celebration involving painting, designing, speech, dance and movement: I think they were moved by it even, for it was accomplished and beautiful. But they would not accept that it had any relevance to their work in schools.

Undeterred, my brave colleague, Christian Schiller, the fiery prophet who had so greatly encouraged me at that course in Chester in my early days as an inspector, planned national courses in the major cities of England and in country places too. And while the substance of all of them was the philosophy underlying young children's learning, the working out was different for each. Every course was unique. Its particular theme was brought to a head through the study of poetry, music, painting, calligraphy, living and growing things, or some other great human activity. In one course all that was done centred on *St Joan*, in another *The Prodigal Son*, and in another *Green Grow the Rushes, O*. In each the culmination of a fortnight's intensive endeavour was a convincing and unforgettable occasion, and the work produced by individual members of the course in a wide variety of fields was often remarkable.

For every course there were carefully designed displays. These were primarily intended to give visual pleasure, though each had its special emphasis or message, so to speak: form, perhaps, or texture or colour. There were collections of baskets or pots or things made of metal; lettering and book production; woven or printed textiles; costume; sometimes there was an attempt to crystallise the design of a particular period or year; and often the display would be gathered only from the natural world of stone, plants, wood, wool, shells and the like. Always I was collecting – in junk shops, in the countryside, from Heather's old family home, and from many less likely sources – yet the range never seemed sufficient! Slowly the notion

[141]

that source material and its effective display are a significant element in children's learning was becoming accepted, and more and more teachers were beginning to realise the force of the planned environment in their schools. Learning to look and to see began at last to loom large. Learning how to make the least promising classroom good to look at, shipshape, and easy to work in was now coming to be seen as an art worth acquiring. And coming to terms with the essential natures of basic materials, and submitting to the disciplines they impose in their use was now for many an absorbing and satisfying study. Handling paint or clay or cloth, learning essential craft processes with proper tools, and so gaining respect for the qualities inherent in materials, were at last recognised as necessary accomplishments of every teacher.

Working intimately with men and women I had not known before, presuming to teach them, listening to stories of their work in scattered parts of England, and discussing all manner of ideas with them, I very naturally made many friends. I used to envy those colleagues of mine who, having worked so happily with members of the course, could now say a final farewell. Yet did I, ultimately, envy them? For these people, once strangers, who had found me vulnerable would usually in time find their way to Old Chapel Field, and many remain family friends to this day. This was one of the strange, surprising bonuses of the loosely-defined work I was doing.

In 1951, the year of the Festival of Britain, a course was held for educationists from West Africa (now called Ghana) as well as from England. I shall never forget with what ease and skill most of the Africans drew and painted, though for most this was a new experience; but they saw no point in displaying or preserving their work: a picture as a wall decoration was to them a curious notion. Nor shall I forget how unsubtle and elementary they made the English feel in the matter of rhythm. The theme for the final celebration was *The Flood*, and it was they who brought on the tempest with terrifying realism, first by rapping with their finger tips upon the floor and then by alarming drumming. One young man from Accra called Ayi-Bonte – the handsome son of a royal household – became almost a member of my family. We still have his glorious royal kente cloth, which he had renounced. Knowing our interest in textiles he was anxious on his return to send us some of the patterned cloths produced near his home by indigo discharge and indigo tying-and-dyeing, but what he sent, because he thought them 'smarter', was machine-printed stuffs exported from Lancashire, that were only a pitiful imitation of the indigenous cottons of his own country.

In retrospect I think my colleagues and I made light of frustrations, difficulties and disasters. We once arrived for a course in icy weather at a college in the North where the heating system had failed. We had not been warned. We spent that fortnight in our overcoats, pretending that the feeble, strong-smelling warmth of half a dozen little paraffin heaters was sufficient. But a London college where we worked for two weeks was so overheated that cockroaches brought forth their pink transparent young inside the corrugations of the tall columns of card I had used as the setting for an exhibition. It was almost impossible to shake them out at the end of the course, and on arriving home I found I had transported many with me. We worked for hours extricating them on the common outside our house before I was able to store away my precious roll of corrugated card!

My happiest memory of that vermin-ridden college is of my arrival. I was met by a smart, uniformed commissionaire in his middle thirties – a handsome person, but with a cast in one eye. As he helped me unload my exhibition material I was aware that he was uncommonly attentive, and at last he stopped and said, 'I suppose you wouldn't be a Mister Tanner?' I said I was. 'Why, you're *my* Mister Tanner!' he said. 'You taught me when I was seven'; and something – perhaps the cast in his eye – at once reminded me of his name. 'You're Willy Bull!' I exclaimed. And we had a joyful reunion. That ill-clad, under-nourished Willy Bull with the cast in his left eye, who always liked to sit in the front desk in that crowded, galleried classroom in Greenwich, was now this fine, immaculately dressed, indispensable member of the college domestic staff. We talked of other Deptford boys, and he begged me to meet some of those I had taught in his neat lodge at the college entrance. So one night they came – Reginald Mallett (who broke his arm on my second day of teaching and whom I carried in my arms to his home), Ivor Whittingstall, Victor Bostock (who loved drawing barges and ships), and Edward Lee (who wept freely at any sad part of the serial story of my own making which I used to tell). Willy Bull's pretty wife made us tea, and we talked of those lean years which had never seemed lean to them, and I marvelled at the miracle that had transformed those under-privileged, under-sized boys into these well-established, good-looking, happy men.

Weather seldom affected my journeys, though early in 1952 at the end of a course in another London college I was forced to leave my car – packed high with exhibition material – in the grounds and travel home by train, for snow had made the Great West Road impassable. Not until three weeks later was I able to drive out of London, and even then over the Marlborough Downs there was only a narrow passage for traffic through a wall of ice and snow.

Much as I loved teaching at courses I was always so eager to leave for home when they were over that after the final session, however late, I would pack my car in readiness for a very early start next day. One April morning I set out at half past four from the far North where there was still no sign of spring and snow lay on the hills. When I reached the highest point of the Pennines fog suddenly shut out the world, and I could only wait, wrapped in it, until daylight dimly unfolded the murky landscape. In the Peak district a few trees showed signs of swelling life, though the riven oaks of Chatsworth still looked dead. In Warwickshire there were budding hedges with a mist of green about them, but the North Cotswolds were still bare and grey. Then as I drew near home – with a sudden burst, as it seemed – all was Easter and spring, with sprigged trees and bosky hedges, flowery banks and roadside verges. I had come that day down the spine of England from winter into spring.

Summer was as perfect as spring that year. I had made a pictorial sketch, very roughly to scale, of a garden house designed to hold our tools, and with compartments for logs and coal. Placed under the spreading oak it would give shelter from the North, be easily reached from the house, and would, I hoped, mellow to a Van Ostade sort of rustic beauty. Our village builder was content with my 'picture', as he called it. We marked out the foundations together without any measurements; and old Monty Woodman and fifteen-year-old John Miles built it throughout the summer.

It was half finished in July when I left for a ten-day conference in Devon that was to be a deep and lasting influence upon me and ultimately upon Heather and Dietrich too. This was the International Conference of Craftsmen in Pottery and Textiles, and it was held at Dartington Hall. I had never seen the place before, and its quiet, grave, dramatic beauty instantly took hold of me. I walked through the courtyard, under the grey clock tower, and lingered in the great hall; then passed along the 'white border' by the tiltyard, climbed up to the top terrace under the sweet chestnuts, and stood beside Henry Moore's reclining earth mother with the wide Devon landscape behind her. This place seemed heaven to me, as it does still today. I had not then heard Leonard Elmhirst tell the story of the resurrection from ruins and the restoration of the Hall in the twenties, nor had I heard Dorothy, his wife, describe the foundation and the making of the garden. So perfect was the marriage between house and grounds, so right the scale, so inevitable each incident and vista that it seemed that this paradise must always have looked like this: surely *Cornus capitata* had always shed its parchment bracts on the flagged entrance to the garden, the tender trachelospermum had always trailed its scented flowers over the high wall, and the Davidia tree by the woodland walk had always fluttered its white handkerchiefs in the July breeze. Everything seemed perfect and in its perfect place.

My job was to address the conference on 'Children', and I sought in vain for any educationist among this galaxy of craftsmen that had come from all over the world to discuss their work and its place in modern society. Here were Hamada and Dr Yanagi from Japan, Bernard Leach and Michael Cardew, weavers from Scandinavia and England, and men and women from industry and science. But of all that great company two attracted me more than all the others, Hans Coper and Lucie Rie.

Their pots in the exhibition that had been staged for the conference had been an astounding revelation to me: the egg-shell fragility and perfection of form and texture of Lucie Rie's porcelain and stoneware, and its masculine counterpart in the unique forms and memorable textures of Hans Coper's work, set a completely new standard of judgement for me. Of course I still loved Cardew's Winchcombe slipware and the orient-influenced jars and vases of Leach that we had collected over the years. But here were two people taking a leap into the future, giving us more than a glimpse of a world of unheard-of beauty that could be ours. On the second day I accosted them in the garden. Lucie looked as fragile and beautiful as her pots, though I at once knew I had met a remarkably strong, brave,

[145]

tenacious character with the humility and dedication of the great. Hans was small and spare, with a handsome anguished face and exquisite speech. Neither warmed quickly to me, but they let me walk with them. And as we passed the great hall we exploded in laughter together as we heard a recording of my talk about children being played. I had not known it had been taped. We heard the drawling words, 'And I suppose you'll say to me, "You live in a fool's paradise". All right then, I do. Don't you want me to? It's as good as any other!' Then there was loud laughter before I could continue . . . But we walked on, and talked of plants and pots and of the wonderful people gathered here under the gentle wings of Dorothy and Leonard Elmhirst, and of my own family, and particularly – since Lucie was a refugee from Vienna and Hans from Dresden – of Dietrich.

It was here that I bought our first of Lucie's pots – two coffee cups, white inside, with saucers like mushrooms with radiating sgraffito lines in dark manganese; a lipped cream jug of the same family; and a boat-like dish scored from end to end under a blue-white glaze. These will always seem our greatest treasures among our collection of her work. Hans promised to make me some of his gourd-like black and white pots with marvellous dry, scratched textures, and these too we prize above all his later, greater work.

On the last hot day of the conference, when I was taking a farewell stroll through the cool camellia walk, I came upon Dorothy Elmhirst: a tall wavering figure in a vast hat and a dress of heavy silk printed by Barron and Larcher. She had come with basket and scissors to 'dead-head' her favourite rhododendron. As I helped her we talked as though we had always known each other, and when her husband – the magnificently vital Leonard – joined us she called me 'Rahrbin', in that sad American voice I was to know and love so well in the years that came after. They took me into their own part of the house to show me Christopher Wood's paintings and to let me hold their precious pots from Korea, China and Japan. They let me out through the door leading into the Great Hall, where I exclaimed at the beauty of the plants of *Sparmannia africana* – the German 'house lime' – in the tall windows; and when I came to pack my belongings that evening I found a beautifully grown specimen with a loving message attached to it placed beside my bed. I knew with a firm certainty that one day I should return.

[146]

With the completion of the garden-house and the maturing of the beech and lime and hornbeam and horse chestnut trees we had planted in 1930 our garden was beginning to have something of the settled, timeless feeling we had always desired. Its anatomy was now shapely and well-defined; the hazel copse had become a good shelter against northwesterly gales, and the boundary walks were nicely established. There were surprises, vistas, and unexpected prospects, but it was not yet well furnished in all its parts. We were customers of the Royal Nurseries at Merriott in Somerset, and we struck a bargain or, rather, made an arrangement for barter with the nurseries: I was to draw plants to illustrate the catalogue, for which I should be paid no money, and I was to continue ordering all the shrubs and other plants I needed, for which I should pay no money. The plan worked. Straightway we introduced many evergreens to give the garden a clothed and comfortable appearance in darkest winter – *Arbutus unedo, Erica arborea alpina, Garrya elliptica, Eucalyptus gunnii, Choisya ternata, Kalmia latifolia,* species rhododendrons and some of the gently-coloured campylocarpum hybrids, Skimmias in plenty, various kinds of *Eleagnus* and *Berberis, Eucryphia Nymansay,* and our first camellias. It had taken us a long time – and our village has not fully recognised it yet – to realise that our acid, sandy soil supports lime-hating plants far better than any others. It was heartening to watch them respond and flourish. In the kindly dappled shade of a white poplar that had appeared from nowhere, for we certainly did not plant it, the strange Wakehurst Pieris and *Zenobia pulverulenta* and the tenderer varieties of rhododendron were safe and happy and those first japonica camellias – the perfect single white *Alba simplex* and *Devoniensis* and the splendid red Adolphe Audusson – never flinched, never browned in severe frosts, and grew fast and strong.

This was the time too for planting drifts of daffodils in grass – our native wild one and as many white and pale-coloured sorts as we could afford. Bullfinches had not yet become the appalling curse they are today, and the cherry and apple and plum trees made a roof of blossom above the bulbs. Now those trees are of use only as hosts for climbing shrubs.

We planted too much for winter and spring, supposing that summer and autumn would look after themselves, and to this day these two last are our dullest seasons. We planted too thickly also. My heroes were William

Robinson and Gertrude Jekyll, and had they not decreed that all bare soil should be hidden by ground cover, that a maquis of low shrubs should rise above this cover, and that taller shrubs and trees should form a third storey, so to speak, with climbers over-reaching the tallest of these? As lusty growths encroach and so-called dwarf shrubs like *Magnolia stellata* reach the roof I take comfort from these two bold Victorians, and hope they would not condemn. The best that can be said perhaps is that the plants look happy; they jostle and compete for space and light, but they seem to enjoy one another's over-close company, and the tougher subjects protect their delicate neighbours.

Making pen drawings for the catalogue was a solace during those years when to embark on the long slow process of etching was out of the question. Unlike the illustrations for our projected book of woodland plants, which showed each one growing in its own setting, these were drawings of cut sprays only — a task so much less exacting that I could take it up at any moment. But whenever I became engrossed in one of the more intricate designs of woodland plants I'longed for the day when I should be able to take up my etching needle again. I brooded over ideas for etchings, some of which took such clear shape in my mind that I almost thought I had actually worked them out on copper. *Easter* loomed large and dramatic; *The Clapper Bridge* teased me constantly; and I made countless studies of the moon at its full for an idealised landscape at haymaking time.

The fifties were a decade of startling change. The only use for horses now was for riding or for hunting; noisy tractors replaced them on farms, and carts and wagons rumbled about the village no more. Electricity reached us, with its muddle of poles and wires. Without any consultation with us, poles were set up in our boundary hedge, and we made the men who put them there remove them to the other side of the lane under the trees, where they can hardly be seen; and for ourselves we spent our savings on underground cables.

The word 'technology' suddenly appeared in the English language: there were radio discussions on the distinction between true science and the mere use of scientific findings, which we were now to call technology. We were constantly reminded that we were now living in 'A Technological Age'. In

COMMON WINTERGREEN

July 1956 the ATCDE (Association of Teachers in Colleges and Departments of Education) held its annual conference in Oxford, and I was asked to address this formidable assembly on 'Creativeness in a Technological Age'. I rather enjoyed myself. After trying to sound grateful for the material benefits from technology I returned to the unchanging problems of creativeness. I spoke of the essential completeness of any real work, and happened to say in passing, 'Now no artist would have allowed an aeroplane in its present unfinished, imperfect state to be put on the market. An object making an intolerable noise must be wrong somewhere and should never have been allowed to be manufactured. The wretched thing is only half conceived!' In the educational journals that week was the headline 'HMI says aeroplanes are unfinished!'

It was not considered modern and enlightened to decry the greedy, ugly, haphazard, indiscriminate, shortsighted technological advance of the time. Poets proclaimed the nobility of pylons, and painters revealed the wonder of a flimsy plastic world.

The summer of 1956 saw the close of an epoch and the opening of another for me: my work in Bristol and Gloucestershire was now over, and in September my care was to be for Oxfordshire. I little knew that these last eight years of my life as an inspector were to be my happiest and best.

Gradually over the past twenty years I had come to see that my own views were totally opposed to our educational system, and I had often found myself in the enemy's camp. As our society was becoming increasingly competitive, and success was measured materially, I saw how wrong were the generally accepted and lofty aims of education. For clearly the only goal was material gain, fought for in bitter competition with one's fellows. The great unmeasurable qualities of feeling, of personal creativity, of discrimination, of sensitive awareness of others, and of dedicated service seemed more and more to be regarded as lesser by-products, commendable but unimportant. The few children who were academically bright – which, more than anything, meant that they had retentive memories and could regurgitate the factual knowledge poured into them – were fostered at the expense of the majority; and schools still tended to be valued according to what are called 'results', though everyone knows that the true results of

BETONY

education only show with maturity. 'The system' was designed to create an elite – and, moreover, a not truly educated, cultivated, vital elite.

So I was determined in Oxfordshire to be even more outspoken in my beliefs, leaving no school or college in any doubt as to where I stood and what I considered should be our priorities. I would wage a private war against 'the system', condemning its false assumptions and values. I would strive only that ordinary children and ordinary teachers should realise their gifts and powers. For the less favourably endowed make up the great majority of our people, and only by broadening their attitudes and raising their standards can ours become a more enlightened country. Small wonder that William Morris declared that reforms were of little use, that nothing short of revolution was needed. While each Education Act has brought some necessary reforms the central flaw in 'the system' remains. A capitalist country believes above all in privilege – that is, privilege for the few at the expense of the many. Education is seen as a long competition. And the rewards of the winners are conceived entirely in material terms: they will 'get on', 'do well', and become 'top' people – expressions as vulgar and ruthless as the competition itself – while the great multitude of losers must somehow find their way in a heartless and uncaring world.

9

It is not laid upon thee to finish thy work –
thou shalt not therefore cease from it.
THE TALMUD

I set out very early on the first Monday morning in September in 1956 to spy out the land, to beat the bounds of my new territory from Kelmscott in the South-West to Cropredy in the North and as far East as the boundaries of Oxford itself. The Cotswold area, watered by the Windrush and the Evenlode, seemed like an extension of Gloucestershire that I already knew so well, but the ironstone country from Chipping Norton northwards and the valley of the Cherwell to the East were new and strange to me. Before entering a school I always visited the church, which was usually close by, and that day I enjoyed six churches and greeted the teachers in six schools – Shipton-under-Wychwood, Charlbury, Spelsbury, Great Rollright, Adderbury and Ducklington, and spent the night in that kindly hostelry, the Lamb Inn at Burford, which was to become virtually my headquarters.

That first week was a wonderful, surprising, and tiring experience. It was wonderful visually, for I had never seen the great spire of Bloxham church, nor the incredible wall paintings at Hornton and South Newington, nor that remote upland border country of Hook Norton, Sibford Gower, and Shenington; and to feel that I now really belonged to Morris's Kelmscott and the villages nearby – Kencott and Filkins, Alvescott and Langford – gave me a peculiar satisfaction.

It was surprising, because it was such a sharp contrast to my first experience in neighbouring Gloucestershire some twenty years earlier. For here, although many schools fell far short in their visual standards, each one felt cared for and well nourished: it was clear that no-one was neglected or allowed to struggle in isolation. I, a stranger, was at once welcomed and used: I was questioned, listened to, and brought right into the centre of whatever activity the school was concentrating upon. It was hard to get away

[153]

at the end of the day. Where was I staying the night? someone would ask: and whether it was The White Lion in Banbury, The White Hart in Chipping Norton, The Shaven Crown in Shipton-under-Wynchwood, or The Lamb in Burford, teachers would drift in to talk with me over a drink. Most were young men who were finding their feet as recently appointed headmasters, and they were ready to talk about children, churches, poetry, the affairs of the world, or their own families and homes and gardens.

And all this, though extremely heartening, was also very tiring. By the end of the week I was glad to escape to my own home, and there quietly to share and unravel the week's adventures.

Some time later I sent the playful lines that follow to the Inspectors' Bulletin – a sort of private magazine written by inspectors for their own interest and pleasure:

DRIVING HOME ON A FRIDAY AFTERNOON IN NOVEMBER

Driving home from Shipton-under-Wychwood C. of E., J.M. and I,
I think of my colleagues all over triangular England –
We, the fortunate ones who work in country places,
Who spend wonderfully unpredictable days in schools of twenty children and
   one teacher,
Or those a little larger, with a young headmaster and his one assistant,
(Where we take a bunch of rose cuttings along with our notebooks,
Listen to news of the expected baby, or a village drama out of Mrs. Dale's Diary,
Give advice about a climber for the school house,
Offer a possible derivation of the place name,
Or help to choose a carpet for the sitting room.)

I think of a colleague in Cornwall now, driving against an Atlantic gale
On roads with the trees bent double;
One coming home through the gentle New Forest, to find laundry and milk on
   the doorstep,
No fire in the grate of her immaculate room;
A countryman travelling down from a Lakeland fell, the sounds of water and
   sheep in his ears;
Another returning by chalky lanes from a downland school on the top of
   Wiltshire,
To a family waiting to hear his adventures;

[154]

A woman forging across the flats of Essex, with spindle berries and bracken
    filling the back of her car –
All of us threading our ways at this hour to what are called our Headquarters.

I pursue mine through this winding Windrush valley,
Remembering men and women who were country inspectors before me –
Names like Walsh and Wright, Large and Light,
One of them carrying prehistoric flints in his wallet,
And she with seed of epipactis in her pocket;
Remembering colleagues now boarding trains and buses, bound for
    suburban houses,
And those exiled in the indigo dirt I knew in Leeds;
Remembering my lunch hour today in the church at Swinbrook –
The Fettiplaces propped on their alabaster elbows,
The faultless grace of eighteenth century lettering,
The domed gravestones in the steep churchyard.

I drive home through auburn aisles of beeches,
Through lanes where elms stand tranced in ochre –
A little picture of the distance hung between the branches;
Grey walls of loose stone wriggle over the uplands,
And shapely woods of umber stand upon the sky line.

My milk has been collected, the laundry laundered;
Logs burn as for a festival to greet this spoilt inspector –
And a voice within reminds him: 'And you are paid for all this!'

But this told of only a part of my work in this live county. Everywhere there
were signs of growth. In nearly every school I was put through a searching
examination, and whatever I said was pursued. I myself was pursued, even
to my own home forty miles or so away, where soon groups of teachers
would come – sometimes for a special reason, as on one occasion to read and
discuss an anthology Heather had devised just for that day, called *Committed
Poetry*, and sometimes only to enjoy talk and a meal together.

Clearly, we had entered a golden age for primary education, and we knew
we had. At the Ministry of Education, Christian Schiller continued to give a
powerful and inspired lead. Indeed it was this man's rare combination of
vision, singlemindedness, and tenacity that, more than anything else,
brought about the greatest revolutionary advance in primary education of
this century. Oxfordshire was not only singularly ripe for this advance: it

was unusually fortunate. Its shy, elusive Director of Education was a man of vision who cared about every individual school and each teacher in it. His deputy – with a head that I always thought matched his classical mind – had a gift of quarrelling with no-one and of seeing every situation in the round. The Chairman of the Education Committee – a robust, shrewd, large-hearted man – was a positive ally. Edith Moorhouse, the senior adviser, had given her whole life unstintingly to the cause of young children's education, and it was she and her group of advisory teachers who more than anyone had brought about this searching, questioning, forward-looking, electric attitude in the schools. There was a sense of harmonious well-being, for everyone in every sphere was working towards a common end. There was no hierarchy. Every teacher was known and valued. Everyone counted: no-one was in danger of falling by the wayside. The schools stood on tiptoe.

I was in no hurry to offer direct help: it seemed enough for a while to make myself a part of this great family. I had met Edith Moorhouse a year or two before at a national course, and looked forward to working with her. Our first meeting in her office in Oxford was only polite and formal, and I saw that I must get to know her away from her desk piled high with papers. So I invited her to lunch at The Lamb in Burford, and there we hatched up all manner of plots together. This was the start of a long, continuous, productive, always accelerating partnership in which each unquestioningly made tremendous demands on the other, and both made exacting demands on the schools, but where she and her colleagues and the schools and I were all carried along by the beliefs we shared, and we would not have had life otherwise.

For the last of my first round of visits I had saved St. Christopher's C. of E. Aided School at Langford; it was the nearest school to Old Chapel Field, and I chose a Friday afternoon. I had spent the morning in what must have been the dreariest school in all Oxfordshire – at Kelmscott, opposite the church. Small wonder, I thought, that William Morris had a low opinion of state education if this lifeless place was as negative in his day. True, a few children had heard of him: one told me he thought he was a farmer, and another a preacher, and yet another a mayor!, and that was all. I took the fifteen children into the homely little church – which few had ever entered, and showed them Morris's wool damask hanging behind the altar – its indigo and madder still looking fresh – and we enjoyed the faint fourteenth century figures painted under their trefoiled canopies in the North transept that he had saved. Then I drove on across the flat, open cornlands to see the astounding church at Langford. I possessed photographs of its Saxon sculpture on the South porch, but to come face to face at last with this masterly headless Christ figure with long outstretched arms and this moving low relief of the crucifixion was a thrilling experience. When I reached the school – a traditional Cotswold building standing in isolation among tall elms on the edge of the village – I was feeling positively uplifted and inspired by what I had seen.

The headmaster, a young Welshman called David Evans, greeted me in the dismal corridor in a cordial, hearty, jocular way that perhaps disguised a certain nervousness; then he introduced me to his two colleagues and to the surprisingly tall and large bucolic-looking children in his own class. They sat in rows, silently working at some sort of academic exercise. We left them to it and went for a stroll outside. 'And how does this place strike you, then?', asked the headmaster. 'Well: it's rather like coming into a public lavatory', I said, laughing. 'And your top class might be in a very traditional secondary school.' He enjoyed this: we immediately liked each other, and he talked freely. He told me that he had previously taught mathematics in a secondary school. 'I only took a headship for money', he said, with a knowing guffaw, for he must have seen that it was already clear to me that he had a wonderful way with young children, and that he knew he was in his proper sphere. When we returned to his classroom we found that these calm, businesslike boys and girls had collected and put away their books and pens and had left everything neat and shipshape for the weekend. They said 'Goodbye, Sir', but as I moved to go too he opened further conversation and led me upstairs to his little study that overlooked the level fields stretching away to Kelmscott Manor, and started to make tea. We settled down to serious talk. I happened to mention Morris, but I got no more response than I had had on my morning visit – save that he gave me a curious, quickened glance, and I saw that he had registered the name. We talked long, and he asked countless questions, many of them personal – yet I saw that he asked not out of mere curiosity: he wanted to know all he could. 'I always make hay while the sun shines', he laughed, giving me what was almost a punch as he said it.

I spared him nothing; he listened eagerly to my impressions of his school, both good and bad, and to the vivid description I gave him of the sort of school it could be, if . . . 'Oh, come again soon', he urged. 'Come often!' I did not realise then how often I should come, nor that this man who hid his deepest feelings behind a bluff, bantering exterior would become one of my staunchest allies in the growth that was to take place in the schools in the years that followed.

My next visit was to Shipton-under-Wychwood primary school, where a very different Welshman was head. David Evans grew up among the coal fields of South Wales; Tom John's home was Haverfordwest. David hid none of his feelings, and his open personality came out to meet one. Tom, while warm and easy, kept some part of himself in reserve. I had made rubbings in Shipton church of some of the handsome eighteenth century incised inscriptions on the memorial slabs on the floor of the aisles and chancel – using white wax crayons. I washed over the rubbings with black ink afterwards so that the lettering shone out black and clear; and I met Tom John as I was putting them in my car. He saw that a copy of Dylan Thomas's *Deaths and Entrances* lay on one of the seats, and at once with unmistakable Welsh intonation and uninhibited enthusiasm he talked with me about his poetry, and at intervals throughout the day he returned to it. I spoke of those other Thomases – Edward and R.S., the latter being new to him; and I promised that we would have a reading called 'The Three Thomases' in his school one evening. That happened some months later, and was a great occasion, several of us sharing the reading. I let everyone handle Edward Thomas's remarkable *Nature Notebook* which he had compiled during holidays in Wiltshire when he was eighteen, and which Helen, his wife, had given me in the mid-twenties. Later I gave it to the University of Wales to add to their precious Thomas archive.

In those days I used to buy most of the books of verse by poets I admired as they were published. I would select poems from these and from a number of journals, and make small anthologies centred on particular themes, which were then typed and distributed among the schools of the neighbourhood. Then a group of us would meet in one of the hospitable schoolhouses to share the reading of the collection. This was always followed by dinner at one of my favourite hostelries.

We frequently celebrated the poetry of A.S.J. Tessimond and Louis Macneice; and often I gathered a collection round a theme. Some of these small anthologies which I remember had such titles as *Art without Epoch*, *The Thrones of Earth and Heaven*, *Centuries of Love*, *Unpublished Verse*, *The Well is Deep*, *Colophon*, *We need to dream*, *Towards a Truth*, and *Children and Today's Poetry*.

One of my early visits was to Alvescott school, calling on the way to enjoy the crudely carved Sagittarius in the church porch at Kencott, and then to see the little secluded cruciform church near Alvescott school.

Winifred Pope and her twenty children occupied a large, cold, lofty, barn-like room built of the local stone. The sight I met was a supremely happy one, for every child, from the five-year-olds to the ten-year-olds, was deep in some absorbing job, and although most of them greeted me very civilly they were soon engrossed again. Winifred Pope, a tall, robust, open-air young woman with a loud, hearty laugh and a cheerful, generous disposition and enormous common sense, seemed the ideal teacher for this isolated group of children from unusually mixed backgrounds. Two or three were obviously under-privileged, while most were well cared for, and a few were the children of wealthy farmers or officers from Brize Norton airfield. I found it astonishing that this calm, matter-of-fact teacher could somehow contrive to teach these boys and girls as twenty individuals, learning at their own best pace. She fostered the strengths of each one, and allowed no-one to fail. Here, I felt, was surely the ideal one-teacher village school.

At first she was reticent and even a little guarded with me, though I think that by the end of my visit she saw that I was as simple as I appeared. Would I have a meal with her one evening, she asked? 'Then we could really talk things over'. So on a mellow autumn evening I arrived at the handsome old Cotswold schoolhouse and carved a pheasant she had prepared. We talked of many things: her girls and boys, her colleagues sparsely scattered in the outlying countryside, local buildings, local parsons, her family and mine, and the poor visual standards in most schools.

When later this stalwart, balanced, questioning woman became head of a town school, which she led with distinction, I doubt whether this could have given her greater satisfaction than her days at Alvescott.

Not so perhaps with Tom John. Later he was to open a large, exciting

[159]

school at Witney, called Tower Hill, where he spread his wings and soared high, and greatly enjoyed the experience. When at the zenith of his powers he left to join the Welsh branch of HM Inspectorate, returning to his homeland, he was able to spread enlightenment in primary education; and when he retired in 1982 he left behind a trail of deep influence: what began in Shipton-under-Wychwood in the fifties yielded great riches.

Brize Norton primary school when I first visited it had Madge Welton as head – a calm, quiet, diffident woman with a keen intellect and balanced judgement. She pretended to shun what she called 'these modern methods', but in reality she gave her pupils a full and expanding life. Praise for herself she refused to accept, and she liked to tease me about 'this breakthrough that is beginning in Oxfordshire'. Clearly she herself had long ago broken through the early bondage of the elementary school, though she would never admit that she was 'a progressive'.

When she retired her place was taken by George Baines. I had met this young ex-bank clerk at a national course at Woolley Hall in Yorkshire, where I had tried to help him to draw. I have a vivid recollection of my first meeting with him at Brize Norton; he looked out of his element and caged. But I was wrong. In an astonishingly short time he became the centre of that small rural community.

He quickly made radical changes in the physical arrangements in the school, removing a partition wall to create a more inviting space where children could work more expansively. Every area, within or without, was put to vital use. The space was zoned: Here was a carpeted corner with chairs and shelves of books to which anyone could retreat for quiet reading. Here was a place where problems of number, volume and weight could be pursued. And in another area a wide range of materials for painting and constructing things in wood and card and for making books was stored. There was no arbitrary division of the school into classes: older and young children often worked together; even play – for example, water play – was shared by all. Gradually the children's learning embraced the history and the natural history of the village, and the school hummed with urgent and enjoyable engagements. An attitude of exploration, with quite extraordinarily careful recording, developed. No time was wasted. Every day was varied, rich, and full. For these boys and girls work and play were almost synonymous, and George Baines and his colleague, Wendy Thompson, were constantly surprised at their immense thoroughness and care. In the little village hall near by the children enjoyed Movement as an art. It was wonderful to watch and listen to these sessions and to see with what natural grace and feeling the children responded to this fresh experience. How well prepared and singularly well equipped through his time at Brize Norton George Baines was when ultimately he opened the new school at Eynsham, which pioneered the idea of shared teaching and working in a building designed specifically for fluid methods and a full use of its amenities!

Edith Moorhouse and her colleagues arranged occasional courses or conferences in pleasant places for groups of thirty to forty teachers. The first which she asked me to attend was at Brighton, where a hospitable college of education was happy to house us. My part was only to bring a small display 'of something good to look at', and to make myself known to the group by talking about it. So, with a background of white corrugated card, six feet high, arranged to make columns and deep bays and flat areas, I showed pots, block-printed and woven textiles, books, calligraphy, and a collection of natural objects such as pebbles, stones and shells, seed-heads and lichened bark. The colour was subtle and muted. Nothing was costly or rare, but each piece of craftsmanship had been made by my friends or by me.

The response was immediate. People stood, rapt and silent and almost prayerful before it. One said, 'What a beautiful new world you've made!' And another, 'I like this quiet display, but don't you like bright colours also?' And I of course remembered the similar reaction of the Wiltshire teachers in my Saturday class many years ago. But I also contrasted the attitude of this kindly, sensitive group with that of the teachers I had addressed at that chaotic NUT meeting at Sheffield University in 1935!

My address was brief. All I claimed was that children are uncannily perceptive, and catch standards from us; that what we surround them with is of vital importance – in short, that a shipshape, wholesome, handsome, stimulating environment is a prime need. No classroom need be ugly, I insisted. And of course I quoted William Morris! He seemed hardly known by most of the group. Only David Evans of Langford was beginning to realise the magnitude of this man, and how pertinent his philosophy of purposeful work in a good environment was for us today.

[161]

However, soon now there was a change in the attitude of the schools to the background they provided for their pupils' learning. The clutter of obsolete materials was destroyed, and the worth of everything that was left was questioned. Ways of displaying children's work effectively were considered, and many schools established the custom of setting up changing exhibitions of well made things for common enjoyment and interest. Classroom slums became rare, and there were very few so lacking in order and plan that the children showed no affection or respect for them. For there seemed to be a general quickening of awareness. As, more and more, the children themselves took part in creating their own background for learning, the more deeply rooted these good standards became. At this time many old and unpromising buildings were most ingeniously transformed at no very great cost but with much creative thought, making possible a life undreamed of before. Very few were left in a primitive, depressing condition. The effect upon the life and work of the schools was startling.

The work done by the Langford boys and girls has never been exceeded anywhere. At this time Kelmscott Manor had hardly changed since Morris's day, and the children paid frequent visits and were allowed the freedom of the house. Also they studied every available book about Morris and his work, his family and his friends. (They were quick to discover that Rossetti fell in love with his wife, and their sympathy was all on Morris's side.) I was able to give the school a few of the original printed cottons by Morris – *Brother Rabbit* and *Strawberry Thief* among them, and later I gave David the remarkable American facsimile of the great Kelmscott Chaucer, which the children positively devoured. Using local plants as their source, they designed and cut beautiful, ambitious linoleum blocks with which they printed papers and cloths with amazing skill. They even engraved delicate patterns on wood. The younger children gathered, spun, and dyed wool (using vegetable dyes of their own making), weaving skilfully with it, and the infants enjoyed making discharge patterns on cloth. The entire school rose to undreamed-of heights. The once dreary building was now an arresting sight. There were changing displays of the work in progress, and always a Morris exhibition! The children talked of him almost as though they knew him personally. They even referred to him by his friends' nickname for him – Topsy. Edward Burne-Jones and Dante Gabriel Rossetti were very real people to them too, and they greatly revered their work. When the William Morris Society paid a visit to the school one Saturday its members were astonished, and found it difficult to believe that these ordinary country children from Kencott, Kelmscott and Langford had shown such creative imagination and acquired such exquisite skill. In 1965 Eileen Molony produced a BBC television film of the life of the school, which she called *Learning By Design*, the perfect title to describe the miracle that happened in that school. It is significant that David Evans, though not himself a skilled craftsman, had complete faith in his children's powers. They never had accidents with the sharp adult knives and burins they used, handling their tools with uncanny understanding and respect for their natures. It is comforting to know that a collection of their work is now preserved by the Wiltshire Libraries and Museum Service.

I was fortunate still to have many opportunities for teaching. A responsibility I particularly enjoyed was designing, organising and directing national Ministry of Education courses on the place of art and craft in education, mostly in primary rather than secondary schools. Each course lasted about ten days. Through taking part in the first full inspection of Dartington Hall School I came to know Dorothy and Leonard Elmhirst well, and soon we were very good friends. When they invited me to make the Hall the home of these annual gatherings my colleagues and I seized this unique chance most eagerly.

We occupied the bedrooms round the Courtyard and beyond; we dined at The White Hart, and we used the beautiful Solar above it for some of our meetings. The Round Room, a few hundred yards away, which was once the home of the Joos Ballet, was the centre of each course. There we arranged exhibitions, gathered for talks, and pursued a variety of activities. We were given the freedom of the Great Hall, the grounds and gardens and greenhouses, and we became temporary members of The White Hart Club. Truly we lived in paradise. It was extraordinary to watch the transformation in some members of the conference from tired, jaded, dispirited people to smiling and relaxed personalities, producing work moreover of which they had never dreamed they were capable.

I was constantly reminded of Tessimond's lines:

And work will be simple and swift as a seagull flying,
And play will be casual and quiet as a seagull settling,
And the clocks will stop, and no-one will wonder or care or notice,
And people will smile without reason, even in the winter, even in the rain.

And because these courses were usually in April it often rained at Dartington! But how the camellias, rhododendrons and magnolias and the great handkerchief tree and the spreading *Cornus capitata* loved it! Henry Moore's great reclining stone figure on the top terrace, under the sweet chestnut trees, was rarely dry, and small birds bathed in its water-filled hollows.

I started to plan each course several months before it was due. Each member was sent a detailed introduction, together with an invitation to choose one of 26 ideas to pursue as a major piece of personal work. The booklet came to be known as *A to Z*, and never I think did anyone fail to find a subject of consuming interest.

Each day, except Saturday and Sunday, followed a simple pattern. The morning and early evening were devoted to individual work – drawing, painting, book production, modelling, block-cutting and printing, photography, etc. Every afternoon was free. After dinner, usually in the Solar, we met for some special talk or celebration. From after lunch on Saturday till dinner on Sunday there was no fixed programme. Always the course assembled for its opening in the Solar, where we poured a glass of red wine for every member. Leonard and Dorothy Elmhirst joined us. First he told the story of finding derelict Dartington in the early twenties and its extraordinary development over the years. Leonard's alert, sprightly, enthusiastic, optimistic personality won everyone at once. He was followed by Dorothy, who told the story of the making of the Hall gardens and grounds. I see her now, a tall wavering figure, wearing exquisite clothes and a hat with a vast brim, telling in her soft musical New York voice the story of this unique imaginative venture. What a pure artist she was! And what power there was behind her gentle, loving presence!

The part which my marvellous colleague Christine Smale played from start to finish was truly great. She was a good painter, a rare designer, a master of the art of display and of drama, a collector of costumes, textiles, and all manner of objects both natural and man-made, a compelling teacher who never countenanced failure, a warm, caring human being who respected the essential dignity and latent powers of everyone she met. Her enthusiasm and buoyancy were infectious. She loved life, and found each day an adventure. Her masterly exhibitions in the Round Room, usually celebrating her beloved late Victorian period, will never be forgotten. Nor will her magnificent improvised costumes and settings – made by the simplest means and from the simplest materials; and the way in which she unerringly chose the right men and women to wear and use them was extraordinary.

Phyl Maurice and Ruth Wertheimer were perfect joint hostesses, who coped so lightheartedly with any crisis that few ever knew there had been one: their work was never-ending. Grant Uden, a historian whose fertile mind was filled with extraordinary knowledge he had found not in books but in life, made a very rare and unforgettable contribution. He always held his audience spellbound. Once when he was speaking about shepherds and sheep bells and he shook a fine old bell, all the sheep in South Devon responded with a prolonged baa-baa-ing! It was as though Grant had planned it with them!

Besides these members of the Inspectorate I invited some friends to help. Ewart Uncles was such a good teacher and so versatile that he was indispensable. David Medd spoke about the design of school buildings with a knowledge that was deep and sensitive. Susan Bosence displayed her printed stuffs with rare skill, and described how Barron had inspired her to continue the tradition. Beautiful Paula Morel called her memorable talk, 'Scrubbing and Sewing', and invited us to visit her at her spotless cottage at Rattery. At first Barron almost rejected my invitation to talk about her life as a block printer, declaring that she was no speaker and that she knew nothing about education. But I persuaded her to come, and she was greeted in the Round Room by such a powerful display of her printed cottons, linens, silks and velvets that she felt at ease and at home immediately. And she told her story so vividly and with so much wit that at the end of the session she was positively besieged, and instead of returning home to Painswick next day as planned, she became part of the course and stayed till the end. She was now an integral part of these annual conferences until my retirement and her death in 1964. Her personal influence and the influence of her own and her partner Dorothy Larcher's beautiful printed stuffs (as they liked to call them) has been and continues to be tremendous and profound.

Bernard Leach was always delighted to return to Dartington – his spiritual home. He loved reminiscing to us about his early years in Japan, and he brought ancient treasures and his own and his friend Hamada's pots for the group to handle.

When Lucie Rie and Hans Coper agreed to talk in conversation with me about their pots, Dorothy Elmhirst suggested that we should display a collection on the very long oak table in the Great Hall. I think they have never looked so supremely pure and perfect. Behind them in the deep window embrasures rose tall plants of *Sparmannia Africana*: the soaring, pale stonework and weathered timbers and the diffused light made an enchanting setting, and the entire session was a miracle.

Whenever I think about the succession of Dartington courses I always see their engrossed members at work in the sunny gardens, in the ancient Courtyard, or in the pleasant workrooms, so deep in the pursuit of the themes of their choice that it would have been folly to disturb them; and I remember vividly those joyful gatherings at the end of the day, up in the Solar, to listen to talks. Sunday evening was particularly notable, for then the course was reunited after the free weekend. Heather always gave the Sunday talks, and I was her reader. The readings chosen to illustrate the talks were taken from the commonplace books we had both compiled over many years. Dorothy and Leonard joined us, and Dorothy insisted on having copies of both talk and readings made in the Dartington Hall office, one for every member. Heather put her whole self into these sessions. The titles of some of them were *Why?*, *Only Connect*, *Heavenly Alchemy*, and *Towards a Philosophy for 1964*. Twenty years after, Dartingtonians – as members of those courses came to be called – still seem to cherish those scripts, and often refer to them. Dartington, which had so much to give, also somehow exacted the highest standards from us all.

Towards the end of our stay each year every member contributed to what was an astonishingly beautiful exhibition –a revelation of what became possible under such privileged conditions. There was quite remarkable diversity – paintings and drawings, records of textures and colours of natural materials, lettering and calligraphy, books, embroidery, patterned papers, and block-printing. The collection was exhibited for all to enjoy: the cunning art of display flattered the least accomplished work, and even served to emphasise the qualities of the most distinguished. It was a memorable climax to the fortnight.

In this golden age of primary education as I knew it was, and as all – schools and colleges and my inspector colleagues – knew it was, I took part in many courses – at Woolley Hall and Bingley in Yorkshire, at Roehampton, Whitelands, Avery Hill, and Goldsmiths' in London, at Bristol and Exeter and elsewhere; and all were exacting, stimulating, and forward-looking. But Dartington Hall – the very place, and the saintly Elmhirsts – was of itself a strangely compelling influence. Every one of us belonged: we were not visitors; for two weeks this sheltered and enclosed paradise was ours. That I think is why these courses had such powerful and lasting results.

It was positively exhilarating to be a part of the remarkable advance in primary education in Oxfordshire in the late fifties and early sixties. The Ministry of Education was warmly encouraging and appreciative, and the Local Education Authority was enlightened and wise. Teachers felt cared for. They worked extremely hard, and they shared their triumphs and their few disappointments with one another. They also shared a full social life: no-one could have felt lonely or neglected. And surely their children's achievement was higher than ever before.

For me there was little rest. Apart from Oxfordshire, I presumed to advise my colleagues on junior schools throughout the South West, and I also inspected Art over a wide area. It was a time too when many visitors from overseas came to spend time in the schools – and small wonder! For undoubtedly primary education was England's very best export. Some of these visitors, notably Ken Larson and Marilyn Hapgood from America, are still our close friends today.

Mine was a nomadic life, but it was full and satisfying. Often though I longed to return to my abandoned craft of etching. However, no day passed but I spent some time drawing: in boring or irritating official meetings I drew to keep my temper! In hotels I seldom dined alone, but invited one or other of those I had 'inspected' during the day as my guest. I seemed constantly to be making new friends. I sometimes wondered why I was paid for the fascinating life I led!

But when I reached sixty, in April 1964, I determined to retire. I had sacrificed much – and Heather had sacrificed more – for nearly thirty years in the Inspectorate, and now I felt justified in taking up the threads of my earlier years and beginning again as an etcher. So I resisted the invitation to continue working, but agreed not to retire until the end of the year.

My official farewell to the Inspectorate was at a conference at the hospitable R.C. college of education at Newbold Revell, where I was asked to mount a double exhibition – a display of children's work, and one of natural objects and fine craftsmanship from my own personal collection, just for the pleasure of my colleagues. John Parr, I remember, took remarkable photographs of both displays. Particularly fine were those of Barron's block-printed textiles.

In 1962 she and I had begun to make a detailed record of her and Dorothy Larcher's work. There were to be two very large books of mounted and fully documented examples, one for her and one for me. We had completed about twelve of these great pages when Barron died, just before I retired. In her will were the words, 'I leave all my work to Robin. He will know what to do with it.'

I certainly did not! Her death was a terrible blow, and here was a new and heavy responsibility. Without delay, Dietrich took a number of photographs inside Barron's house, and we collected most of the printed stuffs, but not the covers and curtains, which later, alas, were sold for a song, and so a valuable record was lost. Heather valiantly sorted and catalogued the vast collection, establishing the name of each design, and I began to plan further work on the great record.

In December I paid a long round of farewell visits to the schools; and on a cold dark night we had a final meeting at Tower Hill School in Witney, where – after quiet Philip Best had presented a lovely gift to me – I addressed the assembly, choosing as my title, 'Where do we go from here?' A kind secretary had made 200 typed copies of my fat commonplace book, *Memorable Speech*, which I had begun in 1940 and which had become well known to many teachers; and I gave them to all who asked for them. Next evening a few friends from the schools joined me for dinner at The Lamb in Burford; and on the following morning – the last of the term – I paid my final official visit. This was to Filkins school, near Lechlade. Then, by way of

Langford and Kelmscott, with a very full heart, I took a circuitous route home.

10

Tomorrow to fresh woods and pastures new.
MILTON, *Lycidas*

I shall never forget the sense of freedom I felt in those early weeks of 1965 on casting off the yoke of day to day responsibility. There were many days of sunshine after frost. The first crocus opened on New Year's Day, and our wych hazel began to uncurl its brassy petals and to fill the air with its warm cinnamon fragrance. We planted six young camellias from Dartington. I wore old clothes. I took time to read *The Guardian*, and for the first time for many years I pottered. It was good just to be at home without a rigid time-table, and to watch daily the slow coming of spring, and in early May I wrote these lines:

> The innocent turtle dove says all there is to say;
> Cuckoo and bare-faced jay,
> Indolent blackbird in his rich articulate way,
> Chiffchaff and great tit ticking monotonously all day –
> Every bird in the wood, the harsh and sweet,
> Has his poetry complete:
> There is no more to say.

Because I had loved my work, particularly in those last eight extraordinary years in Oxfordshire, I knew I should always look back on it with happiness and thankfulness – yet I wanted no more of it. I knew too that my countless friends, scattered all over England and far beyond, would remain my friends for ever. But now my thoughts were invaded by a fresh and compelling challenge, so strong that it often woke me in the small hours. During the whole of my life I had etched only fourteen plates, the last of which was finished eighteen years ago. Now I must begin again. All my stored vision must be called upon at last. I must gather together the neglected materials of my craft and establish working conditions again.

This was difficult, for materials which were once in easy supply were now

[170]

hard to find. The long, slow deterioration in the standards of ordinary English life, which later became chronic and disastrous, had already begun. Only with the help of my friend Denis Welchman – an electrical engineer of Bath – was I ultimately able to make a fresh start. He electrified my steel printing table which I had previously heated with paraffin; he procured enticing sheets of excellent copper for me; he replenished my Dutch and nitric baths, and even went to the length of making me a hard ball of whiting from powder. It was fortunate that I should not need more paper for printing, since very little good handmade paper was available now.

Two vast, growing pressures began to steal much of our time and energy – the desperate need, in the face of the lunatic and immoral arms race, to strengthen the anti-nuclear movement, and – at a time of greedy and ruthless raping of the land, and the awful 'monoculture' that was stifling and killing traditional agriculture – the need for conservation measures. Renewing contacts with long-neglected friends and regenerating the garden also occupied our attention. I had been warned, in a silly document prepared for retiring 'First Division' civil servants, that adjustment to retirement would be painful. Rather than pain I felt total pleasure! The pamphlet urged retiring men to take up 'some useful hobby'! – a suggestion I found laughable.

Throughout my first three or four years of retirement I concentrated on completing the two great volumes of the record of Barron's work, and also on drawing. I continued to make studies of woodland plants – a practice I had begun in 1940 and had continued even in my most crowded years as an inspector, and I sought out lingering examples of country craftsmanship to record before they perished. I had no desire however to represent the accidental, photographic, surface appearance of things, but rather to probe beyond the material likeness into their inner life. The meadow stile at Kilvert's 'Poet's Gate', a stone's throw away from my workroom, and the unchanged pastoral landscape fading away to the Marlborough Downs, filled me with a longing to make an etching that would portray not just that particular stile but would speak for all the 'squeeze-belly' stiles that had ever been made by Wiltshire carpenters and joiners. The gate itself had been made from a measured drawing of an older one, by Alan Duckett, a distinguished woodworker employed by our local firm of builders, and Walter

Cowen, a Yorkshire friend, had made the incised inscription on it to Francis Kilvert's memory.

The words of Richard St. Victor, uttered in the 12th century, haunted me: 'For the outer sense perceives visible things, and the eye of the heart alone sees the invisible.' And did not Jesus say, 'Then ye shall know the truth, and the truth shall make you free'? I had long learnt by heart that unassailable assertion by the 14th century Paduan painter, Cennino Cennini, in his *Book of the Art*, and I repeated it again and again: 'An art dependent on the operations of the hand . . . for which we must be endowed with both imagination and skill in the hand, to discover unseen things beneath the obscurity of natural objects, and to arrest them with the hand, presenting to the sight that which did not before appear to exist.'

Maybe it was presumptuous to suppose that out of a simple oak stile and the fields beyond I could convey something timeless and universal rather than something merely pleasant and fugitive. Yet that was what held me captive and goaded me on.

It was not until 1969 that I was ready to etch the first plate of what I did not know then would be a far longer series than all I had done in all my life before.

But first I had to re-learn to etch. As soon as I had grounded the copper and begun to use again the needle, still sharp and sympathetic, I had bought as a student in the twenties, I felt at ease. I was back in my lost world. It was like returning home after a long and hazardous voyage, and finding familiar things unchanged and welcoming. Slowly, as I etched, I felt the great gap of more than 20 years closing over, and I saw the path that had seemed to end with my *June* etching in 1946 opening into a wide and lustrous vista – a landscape inviting, illimitable, magical, compelling.

Sometimes as I worked the once familiar voices of old colleagues and other friends came to me and arrested me for a while. None of them perhaps would feel concern for a meadow stile, nor think it worthwhile to try to immortalise it. Yet I felt I owed it to them and everyone to put my all into this second generation plate. And more than to them I owed it to this old besieged countryside, whose very existence was now being challenged, and in some parts of England was being callously destroyed.

I did not bite the plate until late October 1970, and the result was disappointingly thin and bald and empty. I laid a second ground and added more needling, and I chose to bite it in the greenhouse in December, having been assured by scientist friends that acid fumes would not harm plants. Alas! they were wrong: flourishing plants of cyclamen and pelargonium were killed.

I made my return to the Royal Society of Painter-Etchers with this etching in the spring of 1971, but no edition was printed until seven years later, when Loraine Smith pulled 100 superb impressions on rare old paper for the specially bound copies of Robin Garton's reprint of *Wiltshire Village*.

I now felt ready to attack a much larger and more ambitious plate. For nearly two years a design for Easter had teased me, and from time to time while working at *The Meadow Stile* I had turned to it and enjoyed its slow maturing. Dietrich greatly helped me by photographing what I had not time to draw – the broken Romanesque figure in its niche at Stanton St. Quintin church, and tombs at Kington St. Michael and Asthall in Oxfordshire – and he reduced my final design to a manageable size photographically, though even then, at $15\frac{1}{2}'' \times 10\frac{1}{2}''$, it was the biggest I had ever attempted.

Nothing in the design was invented. Early morning sunlight streamed through Kington Langley elms, and silhouetted the oil-lit signpost on its stone steps at Upper Castle Combe that I had drawn with immense care forty years ago. The clotted primroses and fingered ivy I drew in our garden. Etching the vast surface was pure pleasure. As I worked in the spring of 1970 I watched the unusual sight of goldcrests building their hanging nest in an ivied hazel – rather than a conifer – just outside my window.

A superstitious person would have called this a well-omened etching, for the biting was easy, and by the end of the year I brought it to its final state; and although the printing was something of a physical feat it was entirely straightforward and pleasant.

However, few people liked *Easter*. Some found it 'rather disturbing'; others thought it 'too eerie' or 'a bit mysterious'. This moved Heather to write about it, and her words express exactly what I set out to do:

> To take the most obvious aspects first, this design celebrates the English countryside in spring – the countryside as happily it still is, here and there, and where it is lost could be again, did man want it enough; with winding rutty lanes and hedgerows, tall elms thickening up into red flower and loud with rooks, and

Norman churches, their graveyards of richly carved tombs starred with primroses. For each one who sees this etching it should evoke all the country springs he himself has seen, his own familiar churchyards, his birds and trees and muddy ways, his childhood primroses.

To me at least though it evokes more. I feel the chill damp of dawn yielding to the first rays of sunrise – warmth after cold, hope after darkness: I see the continuity of the centuries in the figure that has seen face after face come running down the lanes, stroll down the lanes, and be carried down the lanes to its last rest, while birds and buds prepare for a new generation. Then there is the pitiful propitiation of Death in those ostentatious monuments, whose encomiums, meant to enshrine to all eternity both the remembered and the remembering, are already indecipherable. Yet though they could not defeat the grave their very faith has won them immortality, and the passing of time has only ripened the beauty of their memorials, that proclaim: 'Fear not, I am the first and the last: I am he that liveth and was dead. I am alive for evermore, Amen; and have the keys of hell and of death.'

With the warm acceptance of his wife, Nina, I dedicated *Easter* to the memory of Frederick Landseer Maur Griggs, who I am sure would have agreed with Heather.

I soon felt spurred on to further work. Early in 1972 came *Flowers of May*. It had begun as a glass jar full of the wild flowers I associate with that month – chequered snakeshead fritillaries, the rare snowflake of the damp meadows of North Wiltshire, lily of the valley, the very local oxlip, the white burnet rose, germander speedwell, and the common daisy, with hartstongue ferns curling like violins behind them – standing on the sill of a round-headed window with a landscape beyond. But somehow I couldn't feel happy about this formal arrangement, reminiscent of Dutch flower paintings. Dietrich said teasingly, 'But why don't you place the flowers on one of your beloved ivied tombstones?' Which I straightway did! and at once the design sprang to life, and all was well.

Then, later that year, *The Clapper Bridge* saw the light. I had long wanted to commemorate the curious old bridge in the Weavern valley which Heather and I had crossed so often in our school days. I enjoyed setting it among willows, with mounds of marsh marigolds and a bed of dog's mercury on the banks of the stream so aptly called the Wavering. But for the first time ever I had to cope with a ground that was so brittle that I came near

[174]

to abandoning the plate: it was quite impossible to needle freely or closely. The first trial proof was sadly under-bitten and anaemic, and much work on second and third grounds was necessary before I could feel at all happy about it.

Next year, 1973, I turned with relief and excitement to a design that had asked to be made so long ago that I could now 'see' it in every detail. This was *Full Moon*.

The passing of the old ways of haymaking had been sad to watch. The great hoop-raved wagons drawn by horses, the old splayed wooden rakes, the scented haycocks, all had gone. In my design I 'saw' soft, receding haycocks under a huge full moon. In 1961 I wrote a lament (which was published that summer in *The Countryman*), in which I was able to admit that even the machine-squared hayblocks grouped about the fields today cannot entirely rob the scene of beauty; but nevertheless those who are too young to have known what we knew have missed something essentially English and immemorial.

HAYMAKING

Where once the haycocks lay
Soft-mounded and sweet,
Compounded was that hay
Of sorrel and cow-wheat,
Trefoil and tormentil,
Potentilla, meadowsweet,
Melilot and storksbill
Pungent in June heat;
Lady's bedstraw, woodruff,
Lady's mantle, marguerite,
With marjoram flowers enough
To make the air sweet;
Wagwants and nameless grasses,
Goosegrass, cocksfeet,
Feverfew and creeping Jenny,
Eyebright neat.

Where once the wagon rolled
Hoop-raved and proud

[175]

Across the shorn wold
Under the June cloud,
With slow sound of horse and wheel
Through aisles of grass and vetch,
Meadow vetchling, selfheal,
The scented load to fetch –
Knapweed, silverweed,
Hawkweed and clover,
Meadow sage, meadow rue
The pasture over:
Meadow fescue, millet grass,
Timothy and rye,
Salad burnet, creeping cinquefoil
Under the June sky –

Now the stinking engine roars
Down streamlined fields.
Oblong hayblocks
Its vomit yields.
Of sterile and purest ley,
Parcelled and hard,
Compounded is that hay,
By no flower marred;
Tested and scentless,
Weedless and clean,
Clinical bales
Litter the June scene.

Yet when the summer moon
Rises over the wood,
They are like standing stones
That have always stood;
Primeval and high,
Ageless, stark,
Their long shadows lie
In the June dark.
Older than haycocks
These cromlechs stand:
Immemorial
They rise from the land.

WOODRUFF

Man's strange ways,
Newfangled and odd,
Are all one
To the June god.

The setting that chose itself for the etching was that untouched country, the valley of Woodford Brake, a few miles away, near the old cobbled ford across Broadmead Brook which winds between Nettleton and Castle Combe – where even the field gates are still fine old wooden ones, with chamfered rails fixed with oak pins, and with gouge patterns on the handsome posts.

I needled the plate throughout a week in July 1973 when the moon happened to be full, and therefore taught me much. And I bit it in hot August weather, and printed the first impression at once. Little extra work seemed called for, and I was soon able to print the final state. Printing raised interesting and subtle questions. I pulled an absolutely clean impression, then one with slight retroussage, and one that was rag-wiped only. This was the first time I had ever printed without hand-wiping, yet there was no doubt that it was right for this particular plate; wiping as clean as possible with gauze only did not obscure the drawing, and at the same time gave a rich moonlight atmosphere.

There was a nice diversion at the end of 1972 when Paul Drury, who was then President of the Royal Society of Painter-Etchers, asked me to etch the 1973 Presentation Plate for the Print Collectors' Club. 'A small plant set in a landscape, please', he suggested. So, having made more than fifty drawings of wild white violets, I used these studies and began the etching at once, needling direct on to the twenty square inches of copper. It was a satisfying job, and in late January 1973 Heather and I together printed the 150 proofs required, and 10 for ourselves. Then I yielded up the plate to the Society. I was elected a Senior Fellow in July.

At this time I could not give shape fast enough to the ideas that acutely occupied my mind. The next to emerge was *The Plough*, at which I worked throughout 1973.

Ever since our early days at Old Chapel Field I had longed to celebrate the carved and gilded gypsy caravan that used to 'pitch' at the head of Morrell

Lane. I remembered how bright and pale it used to look against the dark hollies; and I shall never forget seeing it once in late November, its lamp-lit windows aglow, and a drift of wood smoke streaming across it before a fallen elm, with the seven stars of the Plough in a clear, dark sky. That is how I etched it. After three days' biting in early autumn I printed a first quite promising impression, but I did not reach the final state until late November.

I continued to work at the vast record of Barron's and Larcher's work, which Ewart Uncles and I bound into two huge volumes. In 1965 I had set up a small, memorial exhibition at Painswick, in association with the Guild of Gloucestershire Craftsmen, followed by a larger one in Cheltenham Art Gallery. And in spring next year we mounted a full scale exhibition, to include as many of Dorothy Larcher's paintings as could be gathered together, at the Royal West of England Academy in Bristol. In another part of those handsome galleries there was shown at the same time a collection of the work of Duncan Grant and Vanessa Bell. John Betjeman opened both exhibitions with characteristic generosity. He knew only what we told him about Barron and Larcher half an hour before the opening, but his innocent delight in every item on display carried him through.

Now there was a cry on all sides that this important and beautiful work should not be dispersed, and that examples by other great artist-craftsmen of this century should be rescued and gathered together before it was too late. So a group of friends – craftsmen and educationists – met from time to time under Ewart Uncles' chairmanship to discuss the possibility of founding not a museum of objects untouchable behind glass but a living, expanding Study Centre where work could be held in the hand and enjoyed, and a whole archive consulted. And ultimately we established ourselves as a Charitable Trust – the Crafts Study Centre Trust. Our friend Bernard Leach said he would readily lodge a collection of his pots with us if we could find a home. Katherine Pleydell-Bouverie offered the same. Rita Beales – surely the greatest of linen weavers – announced that I was one of her executors, and that the fine collection of her incomparable hand-spun, vegetable-dyed, hand-woven linens was ours as soon as we could house it. Other friends were ready to give calligraphy by Edward Johnston, Grailey Hewitt, and Irene Wellington, furniture by Gimson and the Barnsleys, and the residue of weaving done by Ethel Mairet and those associated with her. But the struggle to raise funds to establish a Centre was long and frustrating, and sometimes it seemed that we should never succeed.

Meanwhile a new ally had come into our ken – Joe Graffy, of Penn Print Room, who arrived unexpectedly at Old Chapel Field one day to ask if he could publish a portfolio of twelve of my etchings to celebrate my 70th birthday year. The editions of some of the larger ones would be printed by the renowned old firm of Thomas Ross & Son at East Putney, and the rest Heather and I would print at home. The very reasonable price of the collection, which included *Christmas*, *Harvest Festival*, and *Easter*, was £195, including a handsome handmade portfolio. They sold readily and increased in value rapidly.

In conjunction with this publication Joe Graffy arranged an exhibition of English Pastoral Etching called *After Many a Summer*, which he showed first at Abbot Hall Art Gallery at Kendal in September and October 1974, and then at the Holburne of Menstrie Museum at Bath in November and December, and finally at the National Book League in London in January 1975.

By now, through the imaginative insight and vision of Dr. Rotherham, Vice Chancellor of the University of Bath, and Professor Deryck Chesterman there was real hope that a Crafts Study Centre might be housed in the Holburne Museum, which was now to be administered by the University. When the resident caretaker retired his ground floor flat was offered to us. For £40,000 it could be transformed into a small but handsome Centre.

We set up a display in the museum to show the range and quality of our collection and to make clear our aims. For this a rather sumptuous catalogue was produced. There was a large attendance, but there were no offers of help. This was when the payment from Joe Graffy, all of which we gave to the cause, came as a godsend.

For the transformation a superb architect was engaged, for whose ingenuity and skill we shall always be grateful; and after many crises and disappointments the Crafts Study Centre was opened in June 1977 on a beautiful evening when the cuckoo was still calling, clear, loud and long.

Ever since 1946, when I etched *June*, it had been in my mind to celebrate each month in turn. As soon as *Flowers of May* was finished I began to design

February. For this I gathered together some of the firstlings of spring – primrose, celandine, coltsfoot, winter aconite, violet, and stinking hellebore – and placed them in a favourite old fluted cup, standing in an open window, perilously exposed to bitter weather. In front I laid a dead, lichened branch, a skeletonised holly leaf, and two empty beech nut husks. Over the years I had made countless studies, with which I now surrounded myself, leaving much to be composed and needled direct on to the plate. It was not possible to bite it until December 1974, and I printed the first impression of the final state in the New Year.

By now too I had designed *November*. It really began fourteen years before as a large drawing, in brown ink with washes of bistre, of the thatched cottage we see from our bathroom window. This was shown at the Royal Academy in 1932 under the title *Gough's Cottage*, because Joe Gough and his wife, Tilly Bubb, lived there then. In my etching, I placed the Biddestone well-house in front of it and introduced three groups of figures. Beyond the wooded distance a typical November sunset lit up the entire wide sky. What I longed to convey was the sad, homesick, nostalgic feeling of early evening that settles on a village in late November. After a long struggle, with further needling and much burnishing and scraping, I printed a few proofs of the final state in February 1975.

I found it increasingly satisfying to have designs for several etchings developing simultaneously, their different moods asking for particular handling. *The Old Thorn*, a memory of a stile in Kington Langley, where in the 1890s my parents were betrothed, was a great contrast to *August in Wiltshire*, the only downland etching I have ever made. The small plate, *The Old Thorn*, showed a land flowing with milk and honey: the large plate was half filled with flowers of the chalk uplands, and half with a sweep of stormy downland and a field of ripe corn. I enjoyed turning from one to the other. Both were finished in time for the Royal Society of Painter-Etchers exhibition in the spring of 1976.

When we came to live in Kington Langley this was a village of majestic elms: the lanes and hedgerows were lined with them. Our milkman used to say that he was always frightened when calling on us because of the dark ranks of lofty, brooding elms he had to pass through on the way. In the hedge of Kilvert's Field that borders the lane there stood twelve mighty giants. On windy nights their moaning noise was tremendous, and we came to accept and love what Edward Thomas called 'this roaring peace'. But by 1973 a slow, inexorable, disastrous change was beginning to come over the landscape. Warm, dry winters, and spring and summer drought, with generally far higher than average temperatures, produced ideal conditions for the merciless, death-dealing fungus to spread the dreaded Dutch Elm disease. At great expense we had our twelve giants injected with a fungicide in 1974, but after coming into full and healthy leaf next spring they suddenly succumbed in June. They were felled, and we planted twelve small-leaved limes in their place.

To picture England without elms is a nightmare. The sudden empty nakedness, the absence of shade and shelter, and the sadly altered scale of everything were hard to bear. (Had we known then that within ten years fresh elms, quite 12 feet high, would have appeared by natural regeneration – an amazing sight – we should have felt less miserable.)

Hastily, throughout 1974–5 I made drawings of healthy but doomed trees, in preparation for an etched elegy for them. I made a design in which elms fill an ideal summer landscape of sun and shadow, lanes and fields, hills and valleys, where 'Everything was at rest, free and immortal'. I repeated Traherne's words over and over as I composed the design, and I listened enthralled to Wilfrid Brown singing them in Gerald Finzi's *Dies Natalis*. That was the feeling I longed to express. For the closed gateway, overgrown with dog roses, which I placed across the foreground, I used a drawing I had made at Upper Castle Combe in the twenties. The old milestone I drew on the roadside at Sutton Benger. I called the design *The Old Road*, as this seemed its inevitable title.

By January 1977, the etching was finished, and I straightway began to think of a second *Elegy for the English Elm*, set in bare December. I had not etched elms in winter since my *Christmas* plate of 1929. Now I surrounded myself with drawings of elms I had made and photographs Dietrich had taken in what proved to be the last year of their lives; I used elements from the tiny North Wiltshire church of Inglesham, which William Morris saved from restoration. The old wooden plough in the foreground I drew from one rescued by Lackham College of Agriculture.

But before starting this plate, which I called *December*, two other designs

THE OLD THORN

forced themselves upon me in 1977 and 78 and occupied my working hours throughout the year – *The Wicket Gate* and *The Cheese Room*.

Only one wicket gate of the 19th century was still in use in Kington Langley. This may well have been used by Francis Kilvert, for it swung at the entrance to Sydney's Wood, where he often walked. The splendid wrought iron latch and hinges – obviously a local smith's work – remained, and there was provision for locking the gate. There were still traces of the original pretty chamfer-work on the palings. Wild honeysuckle, bugle and spotted orchids, with buttercups, moon daisies and fine grasses grew around it – a setting so ideal that it called for no idealising. A path led into a glade of ancient oaks.

I needled the design in late October 1977, and bit it in early November in extraordinarily mild weather. Our bold pet robin would come through the big open studio window – a little embarrassed at first by his unwonted surroundings but soon at home. Each time I left the room I had to cover my plate for fear he might hop on it. By 4 p.m. each day he would depart: he would first perch on the wheel of the press, then face me, and sing a sweet sub-song in a minor mode, and then blow away like an autumn leaf into the hazel copse.

I finished the etching in the New Year, and showed it at the Royal Society of Painter-Etchers in March. In September Robin Garton published an edition of 50 impressions printed on fine old paper by Loraine Smith.

At the same time, on the same fine old paper, Loraine printed an edition of *The Cheese Room*, which I had worked at alongside *The Wicket Gate*, and which I had also shown at the annual exhibition of the RPE.

Ever since the early thirties when Heather and I spent a memorable day at a farm at East Coulsdon, near Bratton under the Downs, making exhaustive drawings of the dairy and cheese room and all their accoutrements for our book, *Wiltshire Village*, I had vowed I would make an etching in memory of that idyllic day.

The two busy sisters who kept the farm left us entirely alone, and we drew obsessively till evening. The great press with its leaden pans to take the liquid pressed from the cheeses, the fragrant cheeses themselves – some of them wrapped in sprigged and striped cottons – ranged upon low benches, the flight of stone stairs leading to a further room full of maturing cheeses, the great oak pillars and finely constructed roof – and even the huge green family umbrella hanging near the stairs, were all wonderful to draw. The atmosphere was extraordinarily peaceful, mellow, and as rich as Talbothays farm in *Tess of the D'Urbervilles*.

It was not just a record of a beautiful pastoral scene that I wanted to etch, but rather a protest against the fast-growing insidious destruction of traditional agriculture in favour of a wrong-headed, greedy monoculture. I had started composing my design in the late sixties, but had put it aside. Now I worked at it again, changed it considerably, and at last finalised it. I needled it as soon as *The Wicket Gate* was finished. Alarming gales raged throughout the four days of biting, but the plate gave little trouble, and I printed the first proof of the final state in January 1978.

Often at this time my thoughts turned to problems in education. The reactionary and retrogressive official attitude was becoming increasingly wrong-headed. The very craft of teaching was being challenged: many colleges of education – all with honourable histories – were about to be closed as though they had never been; the training of primary school teachers particularly took an alarmingly wrong turning. In March 1976 Jonathan Crowall of *The Times Educational Supplement* invited me to write a full page article giving my views. He assured me that if I would do so he would not change a single word. So I agreed.

The greatest disaster at this time was the appointment of Mrs. Thatcher as Minister of Education. I wrote, 'When an ambitious politician rather than a dedicated educationist is made Minister, disasters must be expected; and one who would be glad to see the return of capital punishment and who in the name of economy deprives young children of free milk is hardly likely to show sensitive understanding. The vast accumulation of patiently acquired knowledge about the ways in which young children are best helped to reach their full educational and social stature is now discarded. Smart new academic jargon supplants straightforward language; time is wasted on fruitless testing and marking; day-to-day guidance for a student from a concerned tutor is no longer feasible. All is docketed, prescribed, and 'validated'. Everything that can – or cannot – be examined must be examined, and 'accountability' is the great word of the day!' I ended thus: 'Yet, though

I regret the present changes, and the loss of HM Inspectors' pastoral and advisory work in schools and colleges that was their best influence, I remain an optimist. Meddling and ignorant politicians will never prevent good teachers from following their ideals. Colleges will find ways of circumventing the worst academic obstructions. But they are powerless to halt the lunatic arms race. The government squanders our billions on so-called 'defence' (one useless Polaris submarine costs a hundred million pounds to make and ten million pounds a year to maintain) and impoverishes education in order to do so. This is appalling robbery. I cannot respect such a government. I believe in the unshakable dedication of that great body of teachers in both schools and colleges to whom we owe the finest achievement in primary education there has ever been.'

When I wrote the article I little dreamed that within three years – largely because of our obsolete and monstrously unfair electoral system – that abrasive, domineering Minister of Education would become Prime Minister. It was a terrible tragedy, not only for education but for the whole of English life. She started at once to strip the country of all that had made it great – the arts, the National Health Service, the Social Services, and even the landscape. She supported the stupid lust for nuclear power (with its attendant poisoning of land and sea). Money and power were her gods. Hard-won human rights and democratic ways were ruthlessly cast aside. In fact this dictatorial woman turned her back on all our progressive traditions and the values embodied in them, and preached the need for 'a return to Victorian values'. Shamefully, she spurned the trade unions and promoted unemployment. She and those ministers who would submit to her ill-fated monetarist policy deliberately legitimised and encouraged selfishness and privilege; they trampled on the time-honoured ways of altruism and public service; they split the country in two. They deliberately widened those gulfs of class, colour, and economic circumstances which inevitably divide society against itself. They callously eroded all the fundamental liberal values – tolerance and fair play, readiness to negotiate and to respect the rights and freedom of others. Our country was daily becoming a crueller, meaner, duller, uglier place in which to live.

It was sad and depressing to have to watch this sinister erosion in every department of life. There was a heartless attempt to erase from history

[186]

those two great landmarks of human progress in our time – the Welfare State and the Education Act of 1944. This was not from any lack of resources but from a return to blind capitalism. 'Privatisation' was its watchword. The rich were made richer and the poor poorer. Exaggerated official secrecy bred 'leaking', and the government dealt brazenly in lies. The evils of a police state were coming ever nearer: George Orwell's *1984* was all too prophetic.

It was refreshing therefore to meet at this time someone who seemed oblivious of everything beyond the small specialised world of etchings and engravings and books dealing with the fine arts. My first meeting with Robin Garton was on a day when I was engrossed in helping two Oxfordshire friends, Leslie Bennett and Jack Simmons, with a book they were writing called *Children Making Books*. He told me he was a Fine Art dealer interested in publishing. He greatly admired *Wiltshire Village*, and felt strongly that it should be republished. Heather and I advised against it as we felt it would no longer have much appeal. He was sure we were wrong, and when we questioned whether, since the original blocks were no more, the drawings could be reproduced satisfactorily he assured us that they could. So we agreed that he should experiment with a few pages. He was right. In a few months he published his new edition, together with 100 copies quarter-bound in leather, with an impression of the etching, *The Meadow Stile*, as frontispiece.

A much more ambitious project of Robin Garton's at this time was the publication of the monumental, encyclopedic work called *British Etchers: 1850–1940*, compiled with immense care and understanding over the years by Kenneth Guichard. On its title page *Wren and Primroses* was excellently printed by 'Editions Alecto', and for the first edition only they printed impressions of *Full Moon* and *The Old Road*, which were tipped in after the books were bound. Small wonder that this compendious book with its three signed prints sold at a moderate price was an instant success. A second edition, without the etchings, was published in 1981. We were now able to give a substantial sum from royalties to the Crafts Study Centre. *British Etchers*, for all its quirky prejudices and, perhaps, misjudgements, established itself at once as an invaluable source of information.

In 1979 a remarkable exhibition, *A Vision Recaptured*, was shown at the V.

and A. This embraced the complete etchings of Samuel Palmer and his paintings for Milton and for Virgil. I vividly recalled that memorable exhibition in this museum in 1926, when Palmer's genius was first revealed to us. Since then Geoffrey Grigson and others had asserted that after his brief, inspired period at Shoreham the light went out of Samuel Palmer's vision and never shone again. This collection showed how misleading that judgement was. The exhibition was both a vindication and an inspiration. At last here was a just estimate of his great work seen as a whole.

A modest etching which I called *The Drinking Trough* gave me much interest throughout 1979 and the first months of 1980. Heather and I had known the stone-framed trough, set in the steep bank in the hill running down to the Roman Bridge in Castle Combe, for seventy years, but we had not visited it for a long while, and we feared it might by now have perished. In spring, when we knew the wild garlic would be in flower and streaming down through the wood into the lane, we returned to the site. The trough was quite unharmed, though half concealed by ferns and ivy and the lustrous, quilted leaves of young sycamore; and the wood was starred with garlic. There is actually no inscription over the trough, but there is at Derry Hill an incised verse by the poet Bowles, who was the parson at Bremhill from 1804 to 1850. The words 'Drink Thy Fill' seemed appropriate, for as children we often drank from the ice-cold stream issuing from the limestone rock; but when I returned in 1979 I was disappointed to find only a steady trickle. Work on three successive grounds was necessary before I finished the plate at the end of January 1980, when I printed a few impressions for friends, using exquisite old papers.

In the spring of 1980 Francis Greenacre and Kate Eustace of the City of Bristol Museum and Art Gallery visited us with the proposal that they should mount a retrospective exhibition of my work. This would include all my etchings, my few water-colours and egg tempera paintings, a large number of plant drawings, our books, and some of the work of my Ivy Lane pupils. It was pure pleasure to co-operate with them; the loving care and immense thoroughness and intuitive understanding which they showed over several months of preparation were an inspiration; and the selection and framing and the shaping of the exhibition were masterly. At the Private

THE DRINKING TROUGH

View at the museum on 14th November a vast crowd assembled, which I addressed from an upper gallery, and afterwards we enjoyed a celebration supper at Francis's home at Clifton.

Francis and Kate were interested to see the detailed catalogue of my etched work that I had kept since 1927, and I agreed to make a written copy of it, in my usual everyday hand-writing, which the Friends of Bristol Art Gallery said they would like to publish. This was a quite delightful task. *The Etcher's Craft* was produced and bound at the Scolar Press. Unfortunately the edition of a thousand copies at only £10 soon disappeared, and the book was not reprinted.

In mid-January 1981 Kate and Francis transferred the exhibition to the Ashmolean where, because it had been designed specifically to fit the Bristol gallery, it somehow looked less of a whole. But how grateful and heartened I was for the generous and understanding review in *The Times* by John Russell Taylor! And how delighted I was to hear how the Oxfordshire schools flocked to the museum, and astonished the apprehensive attendants by their quiet poring over their Mr. Tanner's work!

1981 was indeed a prolific year, for it saw the publication by Robin Garton of *Woodland Plants* and *Gray's Elegy*. The chequered history of *Woodland Plants* goes back to 1940, when Collins had asked us to follow *Wiltshire Village* with another book. In those dark days of war I had found it solacing to draw every wild plant as it came into flower – or at least as many as I could find time for. Our original plan to draw and write about every one was soon abandoned, and we decided to concentrate upon those that grow in woods – many of them strange, witchy, secret plants that have therefore escaped popular notice. A few paragraphs which Heather submitted to Collins met with disapproval because she had used such terms as 'stamens' and 'sepals': a cosier, less botanical style was desired! So we happily gave up the notion of writing a book but continued to pursue our interest. Heather, with her love of names and of plants would write about them, and I would continue to draw them. Over the years I must have made quite a thousand studies, each one the exact size of the plant. I had made many of these in the woods. My aim was to draw not picked specimens but entire plants growing in their woodscape in association with others. While attending carefully to the detailed construction of each – making sure that I was botanically accurate –

I tried above all to convey the peculiar personality of each one, drawing it full size.

Having roughed out the design in pencil on Bristol Board I drew direct with Indian ink, usually starting from the bottom right hand corner (for I am left handed), and let the design grow outwards and upwards from the foreground. Like an insect I would find my way through the interlacing undergrowth, climbing up stalks and over and under leaves to reach the flowers and sometimes the distant country beyond the wood. In some ways this work was little different from etching. If I made an error in the drawing or if I confused the tones I used Process White paint and a fine brush to put it right.

I have never found a perfect pen – one that would give me lines as fine and as flexible as I would like. The best of Gillot's and Mitchell's I found reasonably responsive but temperamental. The German Pelikan ink seemed as dense and reliable as any, though from time to time I had to add a drop or two of distilled water when it tended to thicken, and I found it necessary frequently to chip away flakes of dried ink from the nib.

Sometimes, having declared a drawing finished, I would return to it to work at the subtle problem of tone relationships, which I fear I never solved to my satisfaction.

The full life I had led as an inspector, while it ruled out etching, had nevertheless allowed me to draw. One weekend when after many months I had at last found some free time to continue with my plant drawings, they were not in their usual place. I searched everywhere, but at last had to face the hard fact that they were lost.

Nearly seventeen years later, when I needed an outsize sheet of card, from a pile which I had stored under our double bed, as no other place was large enough, I found inside it a package labelled, I guessed, in Philip Best's neat italic hand, *Robin's drawings of Woodland Plants*. Then I remembered.

At a course for Oxfordshire teachers in July 1962 – held, I remember, at a small Fröebel College called Offley Place, near Hitchin – I had displayed some twenty finished pen drawings of plants, each one growing in its woodland setting. This was at the special request of the teachers, who had chided me because I had put up many displays for them but never of my own work. Those kind friends who had insisted on dismantling my display at the end of the course had packed them securely, naturally assuming that I should find them when I unloaded my car at home. They were unharmed, and looked so fresh that we both determined to continue our self-appointed task – though we had no thought of publishing.

Then, when I had done nearly fifty drawings, Robin Garton, happening to visit us, saw them and read some of Heather's writing; and he immediately begged us to let him publish a book. Again we tried to dissuade him; such a specialised subject would have little general appeal, we thought, but he would not listen. His assistant, Gordon Cooke, who soon became his partner, undertook the difficult business of seeing the book through the press. Gordon's quiet determination, careful timing, and discretion were astonishing, and the book was published in 1981 on exactly the date he had planned. The BBC *Nationwide* television team descended on us, and the short film they made in our garden spread the news so far and wide that within twelve days the first edition was sold out. Next year Schocken Books of New York published a handsomely boxed edition, and Robin Garton brought out a second edition.

The story of the publication of a small edition of Gray's *Elegy written in a Country Churchyard* by Robin is an entirely happy one. We had become friends of Nicolas and Frances McDowall of Blackheath through their interest in my etchings. The Old Stile Press which they had established in their home had already won our admiration. As a student and as a young teacher I had lived but a few hundred yards away, so it was specially interesting to see Nicolas's great Albion Press of 1858 standing in his garage, and his Columbian in the centre of the main room of his house. I enjoyed designing his printer's mark, based on an old Wiltshire 'squeeze belly' stile, and his bookplate too, which I drew exactly to his description. So when Robin Garton suggested making a fresh, limited edition of Gray's *Elegy* which Nicolas would print and I would illustrate with an etched frontispiece and ten pen drawings, I immediately agreed.

I chose to relate the etching to this verse –

> Beneath those rugged elms, that yew-tree's shade,
>   Where heaves the turf in many a mould'ring heap,
> Each in his narrow cell for ever laid,
>   The rude forefathers of the hamlet sleep.

[192]

ILLUSTRATION FOR GRAY'S ELEGY

Robin had kindly taken me to his favourite downland church in Berkshire, Compton Beauchamp, which he felt would make a perfect setting. It certainly would have done. Griggs's marvellous etching of the South porch at Stoke Poges had made me long to visit that church. This was a disillusioning experience, and I found myself returning to my old source, the scenes near home. I put the *Elegy* into Wiltshire. I stood at snowdrop time in Langley Burrell churchyard, where Kilvert's parents lie, and drew the rugged elms and the yew-tree there. I finished the plate at the end of January 1980. Loraine Smith undertook the difficult task of printing the hundred and fifty impressions, which she did perfectly. They consorted well with the Garamond type of the title page opposite. Living closely with Gray's familiar lines was to discover fresh depths of thought and fresh beauty, so that making the drawings seemed a rare privilege. In the best tradition of the English private press the book was entirely home-made. Even the binding was done by the monks of St. Michael's Abbey at Farnborough, in their own home, and the book was published in 1981.

This was a year of phenomenal weather. January was the mildest we had ever known, and by mid-February all the flowers of spring were in bloom. We celebrated our golden wedding on April the fourth on a perfect day, with camellias, rhododendrons, magnolias and viburnums at their best, and drifts of pale daffodils in the glade, while blackcaps, willow warblers and chiffchaffs called all day. Moschatel and woodruff starred the floor of the copse. We tried to picture the scene of half a century ago, before there was a copse, before we had begun to make a garden, and before so many wild birds had found sanctuary here.

From 19th May till 11th June we spent a perfect holiday in South-West France, where I drew lizard orchid, wild gladiolus, blue gromwell, pheasant's eye, and Nottingham catchfly, and where golden orioles, nightingales, and hoopoes were everywhere.

But summer and autumn were disappointing, and in mid-October came the first frost, with tremendous gales and lashing rain.

After a succession of harmless mild winters, with little snow or frost, we experienced from 11th December 1981 more than a month of disastrous weather. While fieldfares were feasting on the 'strawberries' of the arbutus tree four or five inches of snow fell, the heaviest for thirty years. Trying to

THE WOODLAND FLOOR IN AUTUMN

free the evergreens was a hopeless task. Next night the temperature sank to 2°F., the lowest we had ever known, and not until New Year's Eve was the world green again. Just four snowdrops appeared, with a few flowers of winter heliotrope and wych hazel, but many evergreen plants were browned, and some looked dead. On the 8th and 9th of January heavier snow than ever obliterated everything. Nothing looked alive, and the solemn, hollow silence and the paralysing cold were deathly.

Fortunately all our birds save the wrens and goldcrests and tree-creepers were still in evidence, and they fed ravenously at the half coconut shells stuffed with Dietrich's 'pudding' made of suet and bird seed. Appalling frost gripped the garden till the 16th of January, when at last there was a blessed thaw — only to reveal alarming damage to our splendid mature arbutus, to the group of eucalyptus trees which were as tall as the house, to many camellias, both bay trees, *Choisya ternata*, and the tree heaths. Quite surprisingly, no rhododendron was harmed. Not until mid-May could we be certain of the extent of the damage. The eucalyptus trees had to be felled. Several camellias and even a pyracanthus were almost defoliated. Yet a few months later all these put out fresh young growths, and the only total death was the large single white camellia, devoniensis, which we had always considered the hardiest of all. By the end of the year the recovery was quite striking. Only the arbutus was slow; though there were tender young shoots from the base, and I planted a Félicité et Perpetué rose to clamber up the framework of dead branches.

Early in 1981 Margaret Benton, a BBC Television producer in Bristol who had seen my retrospective exhibition there, telephoned to ask to visit us to discuss the making of a film. I wasn't very welcoming, explaining that we were people who shunned publicity and had no wish to be well known. However, of course I agreed that she should come. As usually happens, we immediately liked one another, and we saw that she had envisaged a serious piece of work with which we could co-operate happily. This was the first of many visits, since the film, which she called *A Vision of Wiltshire*, was designed to show us three at work in all seasons. The plan was entirely her own. It embraced our everyday lives — our many interests and concerns, writing, etching, and gardening, and our love of the North-West Wiltshire countryside.

WOOD CRANESBILL

Each expensive day's filming was a carefully planned event. The team, who were in the main working free-lance and had travelled far, assembled early, and our day was a long one, with a pleasant break for lunch at the pub in Kington St. Michael. The quiet efficiency and skill and understanding of each member amazed us. Margaret had secured the services of her favourite photographer, Clive North, whose clear record of me designing, needling, biting, and ultimately printing the *March* etching must, I think, be unique. It was composed of a mass of wind-blown wild daffodils in a budding hazel copse, with a dark path and the first primroses and wood anemones. I gave Clive the impression Heather and I had printed under his camera. Clive was a perfectionist. On a cold day when he was photographing me kneeling in wet grass drawing snowdrops he stopped because an aeroplane droned above us, and we started again. Then a car drove by, so once more we began again. But now Clive discovered a hair on his lens! So we made a fourth attempt, and all was well.

On a sullen sunless day in May when sunshine was essential for me to draw plants in the bluebell woods above Castle Combe, a member of the team was despatched to Bristol to bring back 'Instant Sunshine'! Heavy batteries were lugged up those steep heights, and I drew in blissful artificial sunlight!

Margaret asked us to choose music to accompany certain passages in the film. Vaughan Williams's *The Lark Ascending* was perfect. James Hogg spoke the commentary with rare understanding and skill.

It was not the first film about our work; Alan Duckett had made one several years before, which he called *The Dying Craft*. Alan was a member of a local film-making group. He had often seen me working at my large studio window, and became so interested that he begged to make a film of the entire etching process. I explained that this would necessarily entail a number of visits over several months, but he accepted that cheerfully. His 20 minute film was singularly sensitive and true. The BBC saw the film and praised it highly.

At the same time I was working at *September*, which was shown at the opening of the *Vision of Wiltshire* film with the title. I had long wanted to celebrate the corn harvest as we used to know it, with the long rows of stooks like tents, and at the same time to etch the hoop-raved Wiltshire wagon that was a part of it. I pondered over the design for many months – and then suddenly on the 23rd of August 1981 it became startlingly clear, and I drew it quickly. I laid a nice ground in September, and needled steadily for a fortnight. It was specially enjoyable because of the gradual recession from the strong foreground to the far-off hazy distance. Drawing hundreds of separate ears of corn was never tedious; in fact each shock of wheat presented its own peculiar problem.

I bit the plate on the 9th, 10th and 11th of October. A raging gale, with incessant rain, continued throughout those three days spent at the open window, and I was glad when they were over.

I encountered many difficulties before reaching the final state in August 1982, but this will always be a plate of happy memory; I feel less dissatisfied with it than with many others.

Every year now saw a further decline in the quality of life. Old-time shops closed down, and supermarkets took their place, or they became offices, largely for building societies. Countless materials in common use were no longer available. Well-established firms went bankrupt, and thousands of people highly experienced in their work were made redundant. 'Redundancy' was now a word in common currency. Every department of life was impoverished – and many were sacrificed. The Prime Minister was a willing vassal of America, and we became an occupied country, with well over a hundred U.S. nuclear bases, all poised to attack the 'enemy', hatched up by lying propaganda. This was our late ally, Russia, a country that had suffered far more in the last war than any other. Soon there were more than four million unemployed, unwanted people in Britain, and most boys and girls leaving school faced a dark future. Even highly qualified graduates failed to find work.

What was heartening however, at this worrying time, was the growth of the Peace Movement. Bruce Kent and Joan Ruddock were as calm, composed, reasonable, and unassailable when they addressed the vast demonstrations and spoke on television as Margaret Thatcher was strident, shifty, arrogant, and drunk with nationalism.

Encouraging too was the growing realisation that our country was fast squandering our natural resources. Problems of ecology and conservation were at last brought to the fore; and the growth of the 'Green Movement'

[199]

so concerned Thatcher that in April 1984 she 'instructed the Minister of Agriculture, Mr. Michael Jopling, to draw up specific proposals to counter the rapid increase in popular support for the conservationist movement.' (*The Guardian*, 12th April 1984). This never happened, which would seem to show that she was made to realise it would now be impossible. For once she had failed. But that any Prime Minister of England should seek to leave the country to the fate of money-worshipping 'developers' was shameful. 'The enemy within' about whom she often spoke was herself.

All this had a direct effect upon my work as an etcher. My prints were becoming well known, and I was usually described as one of the last of that school of pastoral etchers whose source was the English countryside. But for me that was not enough. I wanted to make it clear that my work was a protest against the ruination of this source through exploitation, greed, and deplorable thoughtlessness. I wanted to show what could still be ours if we had a passionate desire for it. Almost every week there were reports of ancient woodlands and hedges being destroyed, and of important habitats such as the Somerset Levels being drained.

It was with these feelings in mind that in 1982 I began designing *The Fritillary Fields*. The meadows in North Wiltshire where snake's-head fritillaries grow in glorious profusion are probably the richest site for them in all England. Time was when I saw bunches of them being sold in the streets of Cirencester, but now fortunately the best fields are in the care of the Wiltshire Trust for Nature Conservation. Hay is never made until the flowers have faded. One meadow has more albino than purple-chequered flowers. I drew the bridge in my design in a wet meadow at Kemble. I wanted to convey the opulent profusion and variety, and of course the puckered and chequered forms were an enthralling study. It proved a straightforward etching, and I showed it at the RPE and the RWA in 1983.

When the copper was cut for *The Fritillary Fields* I found myself left with a small piece that seemed just the right size for the design for *January* which had been in my mind for many months, so I straightway laid a ground for it. I have always wanted to etch snow, though I am no lover of it. Since the elms perished ashes have become more prominent in the landscape, so I let the ash tree have pride of place in this design. I used no studies of trees or snow, but composed the design from memory. I remembered the blown wings of snow in the lanes some ten years ago, and hoar frost spangling the branches. I drew steadily without artificial light, on days of cold, bright sunlight, and finished the design in mid-February 1983. Although I needled the plate at once it wasn't possible to bite it until midsummer, and not until late December was I sufficiently satisfied to print a few final impressions.

I have always thought of April as my own special month, and I considered many ideas before deciding how to celebrate it. Above all, I wanted to etch plants in a landscape. I had made many studies of flowering blackthorn from Kington Langley hedgerows, and I chose to etch sprays, full size and stark white, against an ideal landscape without a single building, spanned by a double rainbow, with dark clouds and much rain falling. I let elms recede downhill into a Weavern-like valley with a silvery winding stream running through it. By January 1984 I had finished the preliminary drawing, but I abandoned it for a while because two other designs pressed to see the light – *October* and *Aldhelmsburgh*. Coming across a forgotten piece of copper, I set myself the task of making an October design to fit it exactly without any further cutting. In those forty square inches I wanted to create a feeling of 'mists and mellow fruitfulness', with outsize hops and white 'autumn crocuses' (colchicums) in the near foreground; a laden plum-tree behind a roofed well in the garden of a thatched cottage; and slanting across the entire design I let there be wide misty rays of sunshine – not as in *Martin's Hovel* or *Easter*, but as a more significant and essential element in it. By late February it was complete, and I straightway started yet another!

I had longed to celebrate the ancient town of Malmesbury, especially the Abbey on the skyline seen from the bridge over the stream at the foot of the hill on which it stands. But I had no desire to be topographically true; rather, it was the feeling of the place that I wanted to convey – the town whose first Abbot was St. Aldhelm. It had suffered much mutilation over the centuries, and was now being set upon by developers. My Malmesbury was to be un-mauled and Griggsianly perfect! So I let the Avon be crossed by the Fosseway Bridge near Long Newton; and I brought into my foreground the medieval chapel from Cowage farmyard at Foxley, and behind it I placed a great barn, an amalgam of several not far away. Behind that rose the gables of Easton Piercy farm; and beyond, among bosky trees, I placed humble cottages. I tampered so little with the Abbey itself that it is probably recognisable. Strangely, all these elements fell into place easily, and I think I have never enjoyed composing a design more than this, though it was the largest I have ever attempted.

To be in the throes of working at three very dissimilar etchings simultaneously was both challenging and exciting. I enjoyed turning from one to the other, finding it fascinating to lend myself to their different moods – 'the uncertain glory of an April day', the mellow ripeness of *October*, and the lean architectural severity of *Aldhelmsburgh*. When biting this last I found that my nitric acid was spent. Last year I had had to renew my Dutch bath, which was only possible after considerable difficulty and delay. Now Messrs Boots said they could not supply nitric acid – but after being pressed they said they could obtain $1\frac{1}{2}$ litres at a cost of fifty pounds! A kindly science teacher came to my rescue; he obtained $1\frac{1}{2}$ litres for me for £3.50. I learnt later that nitric acid is in short supply because it is used to treat high-level nuclear waste at Windscale!

Because I was now an octogenarian Robin Garton arranged with Wiltshire's Library and Museum Service for a collection of my complete etched work and our books to tour thirteen public libraries, beginning at Salisbury in January 1984 and ending a year later at Marlborough. We drove to Mere to see it, and to our joy found that William Barnes's little town had been bypassed, and was now as quiet and undisturbed as in his and Thomas Hardy's day. At Malmesbury I was asked to speak at the Private View. I so horrified an august county councillor when I told the assembly to which peace and conservation causes Heather and I give all our earnings that she would not buy an etching she greatly coveted. I did not in the least mind, for there were as many purchasers as I could cope with – and perhaps I should confess that I was glad for once to have some power!

While the exhibition was at Devizes I was asked to give an address as part of its Festival of the Arts. I told my audience how in my Edwardian childhood I had loved even more than coloured pictures the engravings that illustrated many books, and that all through my teens, while of course I painted a great deal, my chief delight was working in black and white. Books like Moxon's *Poems of Tennyson*, with marvellous work by Rossetti, Millais, Holman Hunt and others, enthralled me. But it was not until 1922 that, in the Print Room at the V. and A. Museum, I held in my hands the incomparable etchings of Rembrandt. They had shattered me. For me they seemed to hold even more colour than his paintings – through that vast range of tones from dazzling whites and tender silvery greys, to deep, rich, velvety, luminous blacks. It astonished and almost frightened me that with a sheet of copper and a needle he could convey his deepest feelings – for human tragedy and ecstasy, for the poignant beauty of the natural world and of the human head, for light and darkness, sunlight, moonlight, lamplight; and the depth of tones in clouds and rain, drapery and architecture and the earth itself. Clearly, I thought, in the hands of a great master, and within its chosen limits, an etching can say all. And at this time, because I was ignorant of the work of the English etchers, Palmer and Griggs, I associated etching entirely with Holland.

I told my audience that I had always wanted to live two lives – as a teacher and as an etcher. So it had been a great event for me when, having trained to be a teacher, I was at last able to learn the craft of etching.

I explained that all I have ever wanted to say on copper is contained in a small corner of North-West Wiltshire – a land of Cotswold stone, but a countryside that is Cotswold with a Wiltshire difference: warmer and more lush than Gloucestershire: pastoral dairy country, with small meadows and high hedges, and an ancient church every three miles or so in all directions. Small wonder that it is designated an Area of Outstanding Natural Beauty.

I said I never sought a subject, but rather, subjects sought me out and craved to be born! Indeed they seemed to queue up for my attention. I rarely needed to go beyond our own untamed woodland garden or the lanes and fields and woods about the village. I struggle for many weeks to visualise an etching, finished and perfect; but in the cold light of day I realise that I cannot command enough skill or poetic vision to bring it to birth. So every plate I etch is a disappointment and a partial failure. Yet I am never totally discouraged for, however inadequately, each one celebrates a vital experience I have had.

I defended my etched world as my own world of ideal pastoral beauty, where the clutter of poles and wires, corrugated iron and barbed wire and all the dirty devices of the modern world are unknown – the 'real and eternal world' of William Blake and of Traherne where 'the corn is orient and immortal wheat, which never should be reaped nor was ever sown.' I

Robin Tanner, 1981

spoke of the anguish of facing the final print after the long travail – that chastening moment of pulling the first proof; how it always made me realise with a deep sense of responsibility that it was I who had brought this child into the world, I who had invented this design for all to see. Ought I to have done so? Was I justified in using precious copper in this way? Was it worth spending a thousand, perhaps two thousand hours over? With each etching I set out in pursuit of excellence which I never reached, yet I knew I should be driven to do so again. Louis Macneice called this urge 'a birthright and a burden', and I knew I could not possibly live without the birthright or the burden.

But why etch? one might ask. Why not paint instead? The craft of etching plays into my hands as a William Morris socialist who wants art for the many, not for the few; a steel-faced plate can yield countless impressions, and one of my greatest joys is sharing my work with many people. A painting can be the possession of one person only.

If I had my way I would never sell any of my prints, but would give them to anyone who really wanted to possess them for pleasure. The limited edition has never appealed to me. Nor am I impressed by the rarity value of an impression of a particular state of an etching because of its uniqueness. I never cancel a plate; as long as it is capable of producing a perfect impression I like it to be used.

I shall bequeath my plates to an English museum, hoping that if we have not, by our own wanton wickedness, reduced this planet to the ashes of a dead nuclear winter before the dawn of the 21st century, a few people might still care to print from them and see what pleasure I took in trying to record the world I knew.

The pursuit of excellence is necessarily a solitary but compulsive struggle. The artist must never waver. He must for ever question his own awareness, his own sensitivity, for that is at the centre of his art.

In November 1982 I had written these lines, with which I now ended my talk:

If the day ever comes
When I take a robin's close companionship for granted
And hardly note his cocked head as he looks up to me and sings,

If the day ever comes
When I am no longer moved to find a hartstongue fern has planted
Itself perfectly among the primroses that bitter March brings,

If I ever fail
To be stunned and shattered by Schubert's heart-breaking slow movement
In that vast quintet he probably never heard,

If I ever fail
To relish that sacramental moment
When we gather for a family meal, and the vermilion-breasted bird
Trustingly hops at our feet and adds his tuneful word,

If twilight ever passes
Into the country dark and I feel no more its deep and ancient peace,
If I ever wish
That the noisy calls of the late-roosting blackbirds would cease,

Then I am old and lost: my end has come:
I have met my decease.

In 1983 I gave a large collection of my Ivy Lane School pupils' paintings, block-printed textiles, and book production that I had used throughout nearly thirty years as an HMI to the Wiltshire Library and Museum Service. Already the Barclay Russell Collection of Children's Art had come into its care, so this local work was gladly received.

A selection was framed, and in December 1984 was beautifully exhibited in Ivy Lane School, and the National Association for Primary Education arranged a meeting at which I was asked to speak. I had not seen the school since I left it in 1935, and it had been improved and enlarged out of all recognition. A great crowd filled the hall some time before the meeting was due to begin, and many people had to be turned away. I found it extra-ordinarily moving suddenly to be surrounded by 'girls' and 'boys' I had not seen since I taught them half a century ago. Fortunately, to their surprise and obvious pleasure, I remembered all their names; and what they remembered about me and what we did together in those fruitful years from 1929 to 1935 was astonishing. We laughed over old photographs, and everyone had stories to tell. Some had brought lovely pieces of their work which they had cherished over the years. Sadly, I learnt that that remarkable boy-artist, Denis Noyes, had died; and Edwin Pearce had become a recluse.

To address such a mixed gathering of teachers, educational officials, interested members of the public, and these elderly men and women who had produced this wonderful work when they were children was not easy. It seemed best to relate the Ivy Lane story from 1921, when I was a student teacher there. The kindly head of the school welcomed the public to see the exhibition on three subsequent days, so those who had failed to gain entry to the meeting were now happy.

Now it was good at last to start work on the long abandoned *April* design. I began needling in the spring of 1984. The ground had stood up well to the very close needling the design demanded, and by mid-June the plate was ready for biting. But I could not clear a sequence of days for this until November. A first proof showed some promise, though it was necessary to lay a second ground and add more fine needling, especially to the distance. Much burnishing of the rainy sky was needed, and I was forced to employ the scraper on a few over-bitten passages. By the end of the year I felt I had done all I could for the plate, and in January 1985 I sent both *April* and *January* to the annual spring exhibition of the RPE.

An inevitable sadness of old age is the death not only of members of the family circle but of friends. Hans Coper was only 61 when, after a long and humiliating illness, he died in 1981, and a light went out of our world. I shall never forget the stupendous retrospective exhibition of his work in the Serpentine Gallery. The foliage of the catalpa trees brushed against the great windows, and the pots stood in magnificent splendour like monuments in those airy spaces. My great helper, Dennis Welchman, who had provided me with etching materials over many years, was stricken with a tumour on the brain, and mercifully died quickly. When Philip Noel Baker died at a great age England lost one who had fought against wars and preparation for wars throughout the century, and had spent his life trying to educate governments and people towards a sane international outlook. That great and lovable journalist, James Cameron, whom we never met but who for many years had been a constant prop and solace to us, died early in 1985. The tonic of his Tuesday articles in *The Guardian* was always immediate, pungent and lasting. Our old friend, 'Beano' (Katharine Pleydell Bouverie) was spared a lingering illness. She had added much to the pleasure of our daily living. Over the years we had filled our greenhouse with her handsome plant pots. Their perfect shapes and porous nature made them the best of all for that purpose. On our last visit to her at her home at Kilmington in South Wiltshire she had insisted on climbing up an almost perpendicular ladder and handing down from her loft the two largest plant pots of hers we had ever seen, which she had made in her heyday, and these she pressed upon me. The swift calligraphic pattern incised round each was as sure and perfect as the form it decorated. These masterpieces will of course join the collection at the Crafts Study Centre.

In 1983 our friends at The Old Stile Press, eager to produce a substantial book, asked us to make *A Country Alphabet*. I would design an alphabet of capitals two inches high and decorate them with country things within an area of about five by four inches. Each would fill a page, and on the opposite page Heather would write approximately two hundred words about it. This proved a light-hearted and enjoyable job. Many were the long and often hilarious discussions before deciding what to draw and write about, Dietrich often offering wild suggestions! Only the letter X brought us almost to a standstill: the text of our discussion was printed opposite my drawing of the two varieties of that weed of cornfields – Xanthium. Heather would scribble her witty and illuminating paragraphs on old envelopes and scraps of paper as she cooked, and then would read them to us. Throughout that long hot summer I was glad to retire to my cool studio to draw. There were twenty-seven designs in all, the final one being the ampersand. Sometimes Heather would take a few to her sister's home at Asthall Leigh where, with no visitors to disturb her, she could work in peace, and she would read her writing to us on her return. Strangely, there was never any sense of pressure or haste: the work from start to finish was pure pleasure.

When all was ready we made a pilgrimage to Blackheath and saw the press room recently built in our friends' garden where the book would be produced. We also discussed details of paper, type, and binding. On a wet day in early December 1984 two stalwart Yorkshiremen brought the entire edition of two hundred copies down to us from the bindery in Otley for us to autograph, and two days later Nicolas and Frances came for a celebratory lunch and took the books home for distribution. We marvelled at the exquisite paper, the perfect association of the Poliphilus and Blado type with the excellently reproduced drawings, the way in which one of my patterned paper designs was used on the boards, the careful quarter-leather binding, and the neat, well-made case. William Morris himself, I think, would have been pleased!

Because the book was well received Nicolas asked us to follow it with another. It was Dietrich who arrived at a suitable title – *A Country Book of Days*. We had many breakfast-time discussions, often amusing, about its contents, before we started to write and draw. Throughout the cool, wet summer of 1984 I worked at the 26 designs to illustrate the book, and I also finished the etchings, *October* and *Aldhelmsburgh*.

Francis Bacon wrote, 'It is a great happiness when men's professions and their inclinations accord.' I realise how fortunate I have been to live those two lives side by side, neither cramping the other, that I had longed from boyhood to live – as a teacher and as an artist. Through them I hoped to give back to life something of my own from my enjoyment of teaching and of the natural world and of those things that 'men have made with wakened hands and put soft life into.' But how little would have been possible without first Heather's love, and then later, Dietrich's also. True, Heather wrote the texts of our four books and I illustrated them, yet they were essentially the production of two minds working in such close unison that it would be impossible to separate them. What is remarkable is that our very different gifts and our deepest interests have complemented each other, and that throughout our lives we have pursued the same path and striven for the same goal; and when Dietrich joined us three minds worked in harmony on every problem before us. It is this state of happiness over long years that has made possible anything we have achieved.

While my love of etching has driven me on, it has brought to birth only forty plates. Were I to live to a hundred though, I should not have exhausted the subjects I feel passionately about. Nor should I ever cease to express through them my sense of outrage at the destruction of Britain. My etchings are not just pleasant pastorals: they are my protest.

Robin and Heather Tanner, 1981

As an etcher I have been lord of my own creation. I have ordered my landscapes according to my wishes: I have placed this tree here and that one there, and nothing has interfered. I have selected and rejected just as I have desired: I have been master of my own world. It matters little to me whether what I leave behind is called good or bad: I have enjoyed the experiences it celebrates. It would be presumptuous to claim kinship with John Clare, Edward Thomas, A.E. Housman, and Andrew Young, or with men like Vaughan Williams, Gerald Finzi, and George Butterworth, though they as much as Samuel Palmer and Frederick Griggs have been my inspiration and anchorage. Without them my work would have been much poorer.

I am far less happy about my struggle as a teacher to encourage people to think independently, to be caring, sensitive, discriminating and questioning. In this I, with countless others, have utterly failed. The jingoistic reaction of most people to the shameful farce of the Falklands War, their acquiescence in the irreparable damage to education and the arts, their apathetic acceptance of the drastic curtailment of democratic rights, their silence in the face of official, public vandalism, and above all their supine willingness to absorb government lies and military propaganda must leave all dedicated teachers with a sense of failure. I had thought we had advanced much further. But courage to proclaim a minority view or to state an uncomfortable truth is almost as rare now as it was in my youth. Much that was won after a long struggle has been trodden upon: we seem no more advanced than when William Morris was striving to enlighten the masses nearly a century ago! Even materially our advance has been faltering. Few of the discoveries of science and technology have made life happier or more secure: indeed most have done the reverse, and have brought the world to the edge of the abyss.

In the sleepy England of my childhood it was an event to see a motor car, or watch a biplane for the first time until it became a speck in the distance and vanished. Nothing ever changed. Sugar was twopence a pound, and a letter required a penny stamp. Yet the ugly and stupid technological revolution was imminent. Over the years I have watched the change from age-old agriculture to a mechanised 'agro-business'. Horses and men have gone, and traditional farming craftsmanship such as rick-building and thatching, coppicing and hedge-laying has been extinguished in the process. A hedge has become an obstacle to be removed, and wild flowers troublesome weeds to be exterminated.

William Morris declared, 'Man has gained mechanical victory over Nature, which perhaps in time to come he may be able to *enjoy* – instead of *starving* in the midst of it! It may well be that the human race will never cease striving to solve the problem of the reason for its own existence; yet it seems to me that it may do this in a calmer mood when it has not to ask the question, "Why were we born to be so *miserable*?" but rather, "Why were we born to be so *happy*?"'

If we could but come to our senses and rise above petty materialism how joyful and splendid life could be! If we had the courage to disarm totally, to use our resources humanely and sensibly, and to see Britain as but 'a part of the main' we should win the admiration and be the envy of the world. Our safety would be certain. The arts and education would flourish once more. There would be no unemployment, and every person in the land would feel a sense of purpose and be happier.

Yet I cannot say that the alarming deterioration in the quality of life during the past few years has diminished my own inner happiness, for I am determined never to be defeated by what I know to be wrong – though the time spent in fighting opposition should properly of course be spent in creative action.

Ann Lea, the founder of the American sect, the Shakers, said, 'Do your work as though you had a thousand years to live, and as if you were to die tomorrow'. That is sound advice for an octogenarian. Equally I try to heed the words of Hugh Miller: 'The air is full of sounds, the sky of tokens, the ground of memoranda and signatures; and every object is covered over with hints, which speak to the intelligent.' 'I can look at a knot in a piece of wood', wrote William Blake in a letter to George Richmond 'till I am frightened of it!'

Miller and Blake were saying the same thing. So was Hardy when he declared 'My art is to intensify the expression of things so that the heart and inner meaning are made vividly visible'. That must of course be the aim of every artist. From our brief sojourn on earth we cannot, I suppose, expect to see spectacular results; hard as it may be to accept it we have to put ourselves in the long perspective of time, recognising that our contribution to

[212]

progress is necessarily slight; but this would be easier to take if retrogression in our own day were not so disastrously evident. I turn to *The Dream of John Ball* for comfort: 'Men fight to lose the battle, and the thing they fought for comes about in spite of their defeat, and when it comes it turns out to be not what they meant, and other men have to fight for what they meant under another name.' I count myself among those 'other men', still a minority in an apathetic country, who must continue to fight, for we are still inspired and tantalised by his vision of a world as it might be if we had the will and determination to make it so.

It is said that old men contend always that 'the old days' were better than the present. How I wish I could be the exception and declare that today we are a more honourable, more beautiful, more generous and outgoing, more internationally-minded country than when I was a boy! What has become of the great aspirations of that brave Labour government of forty years ago? Where are our visionary thinkers? What great poets, writers, artists, musicians and dramatists have we? How many fine new buildings have we to our credit? and how many splendid old ones have we destroyed? How many plants and living creatures have our craze for insecticides and our destruction of native habitats made extinct? What do we care about the less fortunate men, women and children here and in the Third World? What has become of our parliamentary standard of scrupulous adherence to truth? Why has vandalism, unheard of in my youth, become almost an accepted hazard? Why has official spying upon law-abiding people become a major profession? And why has the lust for money become a prime aim, propagated and lauded by our government? Why are policemen, for whom we once had great respect and affection, now used as a political tool – and sometimes a viciously violent one?

In this world of high technology and technocratic thinking the life of feeling – where the emotions are regarded as important, to be recognised and nourished – tends to be shunned as being irrational and too difficult to deal with. It is easier to live a half-life. W.R. Lethaby said, 'That country must be the greatest that has the most to love.' Year by year we lose more and more of the things we have loved: ancient woodlands, flowery meadows, handsome old farm buildings, stiles and field gates of oak and ash; things made of wool, linen or silk; cloth-bound books of lissom paper, their sections properly stitched so that they open easily; and a multitude of domestic things that were good to handle – all made before the fatal invasion of synthetic substances and shoddy methods.

Yet the path is not wholly downward. Thirty years ago such movements as the Campaign for Nuclear Disarmament, Friends of the Earth, and Greenpeace had not been born; and the Council for the Preservation (later, Protection) of Rural England was a genteel body quite unlike the positive and outspoken organisation that it is today. What was a tiny minority that the government could ignore is now a formidable minority that even its opponents must admit has a tremendous influence. Where there were hundreds of people dedicated to a sane and peaceful life and a caring attitude to their fellow men and to the earth's resources, there are now countless thousands. And at this time when the arts and crafts are being deliberately impoverished there is an upsurge of endeavour in fertile pockets all over the country. The graph of social progress can never perhaps be a constantly rising one – and there have been some dispiriting reverses in my time – yet I see the ultimate situation full of hope. We have not striven in vain.

My two long lives – in education and in art – have left me greatly strengthened in the beliefs that began to dawn on me as a young man. I believe that each one of us is born with creative power – with the attributes of the artist and the craftsman. I believe that the arts must be at the very centre, the core of our lives. I believe that if the proper dignity of every human being were respected and his or her native gifts were well nourished and cherished we should then reach our full stature and come into our rightful heritage – and help others to theirs. I am certain that our brief sojourn on this amazing planet was meant to be purposeful, active, engrossing, satisfying, fulfilling, and happy. The 'human predicament', about which so much is spoken and written today, is something of our own making; for my part I have never encountered this fiction, and I never intend to.

It is now June 1986. After a brutal winter and a cold late spring we are enveloped in blossom more prodigal and perfect than we have ever known, and the air is full of bird song. But what should have been a season of peace and hope has been marred by two appalling happenings, both the result of human folly.

[214]

The first was Mrs Thatcher's giving in to President Reagan, to satisfy his personal plans. Having assured us that the American military bases here were only for 'defence', she allowed US war planes to set off from an Oxfordshire village to raid Libya, killing innocent civilians. This monstrous act did not, however, bring her the Falklands glory she expected; meeting terrorism with terrorism can never succeed.

The second was the terrible disaster at the Chernobyl nuclear plant in Russia. Maybe it has taught the hitherto unbelieving masses of our people that the anti-nuclear movement has been right. A radio-active cloud respects no frontiers: we are all in this together. This small, fragile planet is easily damaged, and moreover, that damage does not conveniently die away, but persists – deadly and invasive – into eternity. We are assured that 'it couldn't happen here; we are perfectly safe.' But the cause of the Russian catastrophe was human error. Are we British above making human error? We are of course very unsafe. The inescapable logic is to reject the entire nuclear concept, to destroy the stockpiles, close down the nuclear installations, and pursue clean, harmless ways of producing renewable energy from wind, water and the sun, and so raise the level of life for the whole world.

I have laid grounds on three new copper plates, and have needled designs on them, ready for biting. The smallest is a celebration of what are normally called 'noxious weeds' – shepherd's purse, bindweed, speedwell and others. The second was inspired by A.E. Houseman's haunting poem, *The farms of home lie lost in even*, for which Heather's sister has composed a perfectly fitting musical setting; and the third will be called *The Hazel Copse*, drawn from our own copse in the fullness of spring.

I stand there now, listening to blackcaps and blackbirds, wrens, willow warblers, chiffchaffs and chaffinches, the purring of a newly returned turtle dove, and a distant cuckoo calling. At my feet are woodruff and moschatel, spreading among wild garlic and Solomon's seal, with fronds of Lady fern and hartstongue freshly unfurled. I am more filled with happiness and reverence for this innocent natural world than I have ever been. If these three projected etchings are to be my last I must therefore make them my very best.